HOUSING IN EUROPE

Housing in Europe

Edited by Martin Wynn

CROOM HELM
London & Canberra
ST. MARTIN'S PRESS
New York

©1984 M. Wynn
Croom Helm Ltd, Provident House, Burrell Row,
Beckenham, Kent BR3 1AT
Croom Helm Australia Pty Ltd, 28 Kembla St.,
Fyshwick, ACT 2609, Australia

British Library Cataloguing in Publication Data

Wynn, Martin
    Housing in Europe.
    1. Housing policy — Europe — History — 20th century
    I. Title
    363.5'56'094   HD7332.A3
    ISBN 0-7099-2708-8

Library of Congress Cataloging in Publication Data
Main entry under title:

Housing in Europe.

    Includes bibliographical references and index.
    Contents: Introduction/by Martin Wynn — France/by
Jon Pearsall — West Germany/by Declan Kennedy — [etc.]
    1. Housing — Europe — History — 20th century — Case studies.
I. Wynn, Martin.
HD7332.A3H68   1984   363.5'0947   83-40129
ISBN 0-312-39351-2

Printed and bound in Great Britain

CONTENTS

List of Figures
List of Tables
Biographic Details

CONTENTS

CONTENTS

LIST OF FIGURES

LIST OF FIGURES

LIST OF FIGURES

LIST OF TABLES

LIST OF TABLES

LIST OF TABLES

EDITORS' ACKNOWLEDGEMENT

Grateful acknowledgement is given to all those who
in different ways have made this book possible.
These include Dr. John L. Taylor, Dr. 'Dick' (P.G.)
d'Ayala, Dr. Roger Smith and John Overall. Special
thanks also to Pat Dellow.

BIOGRAPHIC DETAILS

Dr. Martin Wynn, BA MA PhD, gained his BA and MA
degrees in Geography from Durham University and his
PhD at Trent Polytechnic. He has undertaken
research into housing and development in several
European cities and is also a specialist trainer.
He was formerly Research Fellow in the Department of
Estate Management, North East London Polytechnic and
now works in the Management Services Department of
GLAXO OPERATIONS, UK. His other publications include
Planning & Urban Growth in Southern Europe (Mansells)
and Planning Games (E. & F.N. Spon).

Peter Bassin is a divisional head in the Ljubljana
Planning Institute, Ljubljana, Yugoslavia.

Ian Haywood is Professor of Physical Planning in the
Department of Architecture, University of Khartoum,
Sudan.

Declan Kennedy is Professor at the Institute of
Housing and Urban District Planning, Technical
University of West Berlin.

Jim Lewis is on the staff of the Department of
Geography, University of Durham.

Liliana Padovani works in the Centre for Economic and
Sociological Research into the Building Market
(CRESME), Rome.

Jon Pearsall is Senior Lecturer in the Department of
Planning, Chelmer Institute of Higher Education.

Roger Smith is Reader in the Department of Town and
Country Planning, Trent Polytechnic, Nottingham.

BIOGRAPHIC DETAILS

<u>Gerlind Staemmler</u> works for Planerkollektiv, Hamburg.

<u>Allan Williams</u> is on the staff of the Department of Geography, University of Exeter.

INTRODUCTION

by Martin Wynn

This book sets out to examine housing problems,
policies and products in selected European countries
in the post-war era.[1] The nine countries studied in
detail provide a fair cross-section of Europe's
varying socio-political systems, two thirds of which
may be described as market economies, and the remainder as centrally planned economies. Housing
policy and production is, of course, closely linked
to a number of socio-political-economic factors and
relationships. As one author has recently comment-
ed, "housing manifests the political and economic
climate found in a society as well as does any other
facet of national experience."[2]
    Despite cultural, political and economic
differences, the tools adopted by European governments for intervening in the housing sector are not
that diverse, although how they have been used in
shaping housing production has varied considerably.
Most of Europe faced acute housing deficits in the
post-war, and the overall goal of meeting these
shortages was common to most European governments
until recently. Now, however, with the quantitative
deficits gone or much diminished, qualitative
deficiencies are emerging as a major focus for
revised or new policies, involving more sophisticat-
ed instruments, often more difficult to administer.
    At the end of the Second World War, as much as
22%[3] of the housing stock was destroyed or damaged
to such an extent as to be uninhabitable. National
deficits were exacerbated by the return of troops
and the unpreparedness of the building industry -
run down after several years of relative inactivity
- to cope with production requirements. The search
for new housing and employment opportunities resulted in massive country-city migrations, above all in
Southern and Eastern Europe, where urban growth

1

rates were three times comparable national figures over the period 1950-70. The need to invest in industry and infrastructure meant that housing deficits remained or worsened in the forties and fifties in many countries, and only by the late fifties were shortages beginning to be substantially reduced by increased production.

During this post-war era, housing policy in Western Europe tended to focus at first on the use of rent freezes as a means of protecting the consumer from rapid rent increases. Later, subsidies to house constructors were introduced to stimulate production, and the promotion of public and non-profit housing agencies was encouraged in some countries. Meanwhile in Eastern Europe, the foundations of large scale production machinery in the construction industry were laid. In all Europe, land-use planning and environmental considerations were often overlooked in an era when the emphasis was on housing production figures rather than qualitative aspects.

By the 1960s, the construction industry was expanding rapidly and the 'boom' growth of major urban centres followed. Annual housing production figures attained new peaks, averaging eight dwellings per 1000 inhabitants in Europe in 1970. Many countries in both East and West markedly changed their housing policies in the sixties and seventies to bring about a more efficient and equitable use of resources. In Western Europe, a variety of new forms of subsidy were introduced. In France, new forms of cheap loans for aspiring house purchasers came into effect in conjunction with a radically reformed savings scheme for home purchase - the Compte d'Epargne Logement - to encourage individual savings. Similar developments occurred in other countries: in West Germany, Netherlands and Denmark, new systems were introduced in the sixties which resulted in a far higher initial subsidy of rents in state aided construction.

Many other variations were introduced as regards the size and nature of state subsidies and inhabitants alike, benefitting from such schemes. Rent controls which had originated in the immediate post war or before were phased out in many western countries in the sixties, and incremental rent increases authorized. Direct financial aid to low-income groups also came into prominence in the West. The private sector (aided and non-aided) accounted for the bulk of new construction in these years, although public managed bodies (including co-operatives and associations) constructed over a third of the new stock in Belgium, Holland and the United Kingdom (Table 1.1). In the East European

Table 1.1 Private Sector-Public Sector House Construction in Some Western European Countries, 1960-75 (annual average).

Country	Public authorities and publicly cont- rolled associations and co-operatives	Private sector
Belgium (1964-74)	34.4	65.6
Denmark	31.1	68.9
France	32.1	67.9
Netherlands	47.2	52.8
Spain	10.1	89.9
United Kingdom	45.5	54.5
West Germany	24.5	75.5

Source: Annual Bulletin of Housing and Building Statistics for Europe 1975 (ECE/UN, New York, 1976)

Socialist States, although there were considerable differences between individual countries, the rise in house production figures was somewhat less marked than in much of the West. Housing, viewed as a social right, was paid for by small percentage contributions (usually less than 10%) from personal incomes, often supplemented by extra funds from the national budgets. Compared with the West, this produced somewhat less overall investment in hous- ing, with the respective figures for housing produc- tion and usable floorspace per dwelling being lower in the East than the West in the seventies. (Table 1.2).

The economic recession which started with the oil crisis of 1973-4 hit the construction sector particularly hard, and above all the house-building sub-sector. The drying-up of demand, the increase in the material costs of production and higher interest rates contributed to significant drops in annual house construction in Western European nations in the seventies (Table 1.3), with its consequent implications for employment and overall housing provision. Government responses have in- cluded a reduction of subsidies to house construct- ors and increases in direct aid to families for house purchase. In West Germany and Spain, there

Table 1.2 Selected Comparative Figures on Housing Investment
and Construction for all Europe, 1976.

Country	Investment in Housing as % of Total Fixed Capital Investment, 1976	Existing Dwellings per 1000 Inhabitants 1976	Average Usable Floorspace of Dwellings in Existence 1976 (m^2)
Austria	15.4	388	86
Belgium	29.9	395	97
Denmark	23.1	397	122
Finland	23.3	318	71
France	31.0	399	82
Ireland	25.9	259	88
Luxemburg	26.2	349	107
Norway	15.5	365	89
Netherlands	24.4	322	71
United Kingdom	20.0	368	70
Sweden	20.3	394	109
Switzerland	26.3	390	98
Greece	21.5	301	80
Italy	29.2	329	−
Spain	27.2	344	82
Portugal	20.7	−	104
West Germany	21.4	383	95
USSR	14.2	230	49
East Germany	11.4	390	60
Bulgaria	9.5	281	63
Hungary	18.0	341	65
Poland	12.8	276	58
Rumania	5.1	−	54
Czechoslovakia	15.5	298	69
Yugoslavia	15.2	268	65
Canada	21.9	323	89
United States	20.0	333	120

Source: CIDHEC (Paris), based on Statistics from the World
Bank and Economic Commission for Europe (UN).

has been much debate over how direct aid can best
function and whether it should complement or replace
subsidies to constructors. Similar developments
have taken place in France, Holland and Denmark.
Nevertheless, with net housing deficits minim-
ised or even reversed, attention has increasingly
focused on the more qualitative aspects of housing,
highlighted by the often poor standard living

environment created in the massive housing estates
which were built in and outside most European cities
in the fifties and sixties. Rehabilitation and renewal have taken on new significance, particularly
in the old housing areas, and planning controls on
new development have been tightened up as attempts
are made to improve the co-ordination in the planning and implementation of housing and infrastructure
programmes.

Table 1.3 Annual House Construction Figures in some
           Western European Countries in the 1970s.

Country	Dwellings Constructed per 1000 Inhabitants	
Italy	7.0 (1970)	2.6 (1977)
Holland	11.6 (1973)	7.7 (1978)
Great Britain	6.7 (1971)	5.4 (1978)
West Germany	11.5 (1973)	6.0 (1978)
Spain	10.5 (1975)	7.2 (1979)
France	10.9 (1972)	8.4 (1978)

Source: Annual Bulletins of Housing and Building
         Statistics for Europe (ECE, Geneva/UN, New
         York).

     In Eastern Europe, the seventies has seen
increased state encouragement of co-operative and
private ownership. Co-operatives receive extensive
aid in East Germany, Poland and Czechoslovakia in
the form of long-term, low or no interest loans.
Governments have begun to tacitly admit that individuals may, if they have the means, gain access to
housing that goes beyond what the state can provide.
Co-operatives also tend to provide a wider range of
housing types, distinct from the multi-storey apartment blocks that characterize state housing. Home
ownership, on the other hand, always has been predominant (outside the USSR), as most private
residences were excluded from nationalization in the
immediate post war. Today, many eastern bloc
countries have home ownership rates in excess of
those in the West.
     In summary, then, Europe contains a mix of
market-orientated and centrally planned economies,
with most countries lying between the two extremes,
and elements of both systems co-existing in several
countries. In the United Kingdom, for example, over
30% of both existing stock and new construction in
1981 was promoted by the local authorities, whilst

in Yugoslavia, where the production and management of housing is very much devolved to the local 'commune' level, over 60% of new construction was private in 1979 (Table 1.4), and 71% of dwellings were in private ownership.

Table 1.4   Dwellings Constructed, by Type of Investor, in the 70s and 80s.

	1970	1975	1979	1980	1981
DENMARK					
State & Municipalities	2.2				3.0
Housing Associations	27.3				31.4
Private	70.5				65.6
- Aided	7.6				4.9
- Unaided	62.9				60.7
FRANCE					
State & Local Authorities	0.7				1.0
HLM Organs	32.2				19.0
Corporations (private, including nationalised)	32.1				27.6
Private persons	35.0				52.4
WEST GERMANY (FRG)					
Public Authorities	2.3		1.2		
Housing Associations and Co-operatives	18.4		8.3		
Private (including Housing Corporations; partly aided)	79.3		90.5		
GREECE					
Private, unaided	100.0				100.0
PORTUGAL					
State & Local Authorities	6.0			13.7	
Semi-public bodies	4.4			0.1	
Housing Co-operatives	0.2			1.2	
Private bodies & persons	89.4			84.6	
Nationalized Enterprises				0.4	
SPAIN					
State & Local Authority	2.9	2.6			
Other public bodies	3.9	5.0			
Private (aided & non- aided)	93.2	92.4			
UNITED KINGDOM					
Local Authorities & New Towns	48.6				32.3
Housing Associations & other public sector	3.3				10.8

Table 1.4 continued

	1970	1975	1979	1980	1981
UNITED KINGDOM					
Private					
- unaided	46.4				)
- aided	1.7				) 56.9
YUGOSLAVIA					
State	34.5		38.1		
Private	65.5		61.9		
EAST GERMANY (GDR)					
State	75.8				50.0
Co-operatives	20.9				32.9
Private, aided	3.3				17.1
POLAND					
State	23.5				17.3
Co-operatives	48.9				58.1
Private persons	27.6				24.6

Source: Annual Bulletin of Housing and Building Statistics for Europe 1981 (Economic Commission for Europe, Geneva/UN, New York, 1982)

With population growth rates now declining and the world recession keeping house construction figures well below 1970 levels (Table 1.5), the future now requires new governmental initiatives in the housing field, aimed at longer term, more equitable and cost-effective solutions to existing problems. Despite the large number of houses built in Europe since the war, design and building standards, infrastructure provision and general environmental quality leave much to be desired. It is hoped that this book, by providing an in-depth examination of different countries' experiences in the past, will aid those with responsibilites for resolving housing problems and shaping policies in the future, as well as providing a useful reference work for others working in related fields.

NOTES AND REFERENCES

1. For a thematic discussion and analysis of housing in post-war Europe, see the United Nations Report, Human Settlements in Europe: Post-War Trends and Policies, (ECE/HBP/18, United Nations, New York, 1976).
2. C. McGuire, International Housing Policies (Lexington Books, Massachusetts/Toronto, 1981), p.3.
3. Ibid, p.5.

Table 1.5 Population, Housing Stock and House Construction for Some European Countries, 1981

Country	Population		Dwelling Stock 1981		Dwellings Built 1981	
	Total (millions)	Annual average change per 1000 inhabitants 1970-1981	Total (millions)	Per 1000 inhabitants	Total (thousands)	Per 1000 inhabitants
Belgium	9.86	+ 1.9	3.8^d	386^d	48.6^d	4.8^d
Denmark	5.12	+ 3.4	2.2	424	21.6	4.2
France	53.96	+ 5.6	21.1^a	399^a	390.1	7.2
East Germany	16.74	− 1.7	6.5^a	390^a	185.4	7.5^d
West Germany	61.67	+ 1.4	25.0^c	407^c	389.0^d	6.3^d
Italy	57.20	+ 5.8	18.5^a	329^a	154.1^b	2.8^b
Netherlands	14.24	+ 8.1	5.0	348	88.8	6.3^c
Poland	35.90	+ 9.0	10.0	277	186.4	5.2^d
Portugal	9.93	+ 8.6			40.9^d	4.1^d
Spain	37.65	+10.0	12.4^a	344^a	233.0	6.2
Switzerland	6.37	+ 2.6	2.7	424	45.7	7.2
United Kingdom	55.83	+ 0.7	21.7	388	214.8	3.8
Yugoslavia	22.52	+ 9.2	6.2^c	278^c	145.7^c	6.6^c

a = 1976, b = 1978, c = 1979, d = 1980.

Source: ECE Commission for Europe, Annual Bulletin of Housing and Building Statistics 1981 (United Nations, New York, 1982); except for 1976 figures which are from World Bank data.

2. FRANCE

by Jon Pearsall

Introduction

The development of post-war French housing policy
must be seen in the context of a period of historically remarkable economic, demographic and urban
growth, followed more recently by the shock of a
reduction in the economic growth rate, and a slowing
down in population increase.[1] Policy and means of
implementation developed incrementally[2] but if any
continuous threads of policy can be distinguished
over the last three decades or so, then they are
firstly, the gradual withdrawal of the state from
its role as the principal provider of dwellings and
secondly, the equally gradual increase in demands
made upon householders (whether renting or
purchasing) to increase their share of housing
costs. Governmental activity was paramount during
the 1950s and 60s, but in the latter decade the role
of the private sector developed fast, leading to its
domination of the 1970s. Yet it was not until the
1977 Housing Act that the paramouncy of private
finance and initiative was confirmed as being both
desirable, and to be pursued as a principal element
of future policy.

In the immediate post-war years resources for
housing construction were strictly limited as
investment was devoted to economic reconstruction,
and it was not until the IInd Plan of 1954[3] that a
national housing programme was fully outlined and
targets established. A holding operation was put
into effect at first, with rent control as its key
element, whilst financial and other institutions
were re-organised in preparation for their major
roles in future housing programmes. Economic growth
of the 1950s and 60s enabled the state to put these
programmes into effect with impressive results and
the numbers of new dwellings built increased

9

annually throughout the decades, a peak being
reached in 1972. Crude output was emphasised however, at the expense of quality, and many dwellings
were constructed at standards and in locations
unacceptable today.

Urban growth associated with the transformation
of France from a rural to a modern industrial society was ineffectively controlled by the State.
Plans and planning procedures introduced in the
1950s largely failed to prevent anarchic peripheral
growth of the cities, whilst often huge, speculative
town centre redevelopment schemes destroyed viable
communities and areas of modest housing. Popular
reaction led to new planning policies and legislation and perhaps more importantly to a political
commitment on the part of government to better
planning, and to environmental conservation and
improvement.

The poor economic situation of the past few
years has further encouraged the state to pay
attention to rehabilitation of the existing stock,
accompanied by a positive response to political
pressure and social arguments, for the conservation
and improvement of individual dwellings and of whole
areas of towns. The private and public sectors
increasingly sought to meet consumer preferences by
providing a greater variety of dwelling types and by
improving their quality. In particular one can note
in the 1970s a marked demand for two storey detached
houses, la maîson individuelle, rather than flats,
and dwellings to purchase rather than to rent. It
is these phenomena which have had considerable significance for the financing of housing programmes,
and considerable influence on the form, and the
problems of contemporary urban growth.

The 1977 Housing Act rationalised the complex
pattern of housing finance that had developed over
the years, and laid down the general directions of
policy for the future. Principally, it enabled the
state to reduce its overall financial contributions
to construction, whilst directing its remaining aid
to households (rather than dwellings) according to
need. Private initiative, both individual and
corporate, was expected to be paramount in new
building and in rehabilitation, undoubtedly
reflecting the political and economic philosophy of
the government of the day. The present Mauroy
government of President Mitterand is tilting back
towards the public sector, but the exact balance it
seeks to hold remains to be seen.

The rate of population growth had already begun
to slow in the late 1960s and continued to do so in
the following decade, yet the rate of household
formation has not shown a similar decline, and
this, combined with falls in housing output has led
to talk of a housing crisis in the 1980s. The new
Socialist administration has however, adopted an
expansionist economic policy, and increasing output
of housing is seen as a key element in the stimulation of the construction industry and thence the
economy. To this end then, it is planned to increase construction of new housing to approximately
500,000 units per annum reaching levels last seen in
the early 1970s. It would be premature of course,
to make a judgement on what is an ambitious programme, designed to meet the needs of the 1980s,
particularly as its success or failure depends on a
number of factors, some of which are outside the
control of the government.

The Post-War Years 1945-1953
In 1945 at the end of the Second World War, France
had a severe housing shortage. Half a million
dwellings had been destroyed during hostilities and
some 1.4 million badly damaged, together accounting
for about 20% of the total housing existing in 1939.
Much of the stock that was untouched was often in a
poor state of repair and lacking in modern amenities.
In the inter-war period (1919-1939) only some 1.6
million new dwellings had been constructed, whilst
existing housing had been badly neglected. Rent
controls, first introduced in 1914, had acted as
disincentives to landlords to spend on property
maintenance. The immediate problem of housing the
existing population was exacerbated by a sharp and
unexpected increase in births, and by the influx of
many thousands of displaced persons and others
looking for work.[4] Immigrant labour from Southern
Europe (notably Portugal) and more recently from
North Africa has contributed greatly to France's
economic success, but housing the immigrants and
their families in satisfactory conditions has proved
to be an intractable problem.[5]
Increased demand upon a reduced housing stock
threatened spectacular increases in rent, and as
only limited resources were to be allocated to
housing construction, (priority being given to
industrial reconstruction) inflationary pressures
had to be controlled by legislative means. In 1948
a new Rent Act[6] was introduced to codify existing

rent control legislation and to make it more extensive and effective. Initially, some 6 million pre-
1948 dwellings were incorporated into what has come
to be called the secteur taxé,[7] (fixed rent sector),
but over the years the numbers both absolutely and
as a proportion of the total stock has fallen. The
legislation is only of importance in fairly
localised areas such as Paris, and the inner areas of
other large towns and cities where inflationary
pressures are greatest; and where a high proportion
of tenants are old and with low incomes and who still
require the protection afforded by the Act.

The Act allows for decontrol to take place with
change of tenant and by ministerial decree, in the
latter case according to category of dwelling and
taking into account a number of elements including
geographical location. Theoretically, rents were to
be reviewed every six months with the long term aim
of increasing them to market levels, but as Duclaud-
Williams has shown,[8] successive governments have not
implemented this part of the legislation in a consistent manner. Even the Giscardian regime,
ostensibly committed to a liberal economic philosophy, made extensive use of rent freezes and
restricted rent increases in this (and other) sectors
of rented housing.

Despite rent control and the traditionally low
proportion of income devoted by householders to
renting (or purchasing) accommodation not all tenants
could pay their rents and charges[9] without
difficulty. To assist such tenants, a system of
personalised subsidy was introduced called Allocation Familiale de Logement or AL. Still in
operation, the scheme allows for payments to be made
by the Caisses d'Allocations Familiales[10] to certain
categories of householder, defined by income and
family circumstances, to help meet their housing
costs. In 1971, the scheme was extended to certain
categories of retired people, handicapped persons and
young workers (the Allocation Sociale de Logement)
These were the only forms of personalised housing
aid until the introduction of Aide Personalisée au
Logement (APL) in 1977, for the greater proportion
of state aid to housing has, since the war, been
directed towards the construction of dwellings - the
so-called aide à la pierre policy, with little discrimination in allocation of funds between income
groups.

Housing construction in this immediate post-war
period was limited, only some 200,000 dwellings
being built between 1945 and 1950 (Table 2.1) over

half constructed using private funds alone, the rest being publicly financed. Of the latter, most were built as part of the special reconstruction programme (La Réconstruction) directed towards towns and cities of the war zones. Special grants were made available for rebuilding or repair of war damaged property in these zones, and in some instances, large areas had to be completely rebuilt, enabling the state to engage in experiments in town planning.

The Dominant State 1953 - 1963

Housing construction could not be delayed indefinitely, particularly as it became clear that the post-war increase in births was not a passing phenomenon. The 1948 Rent Act was not a measure to stimulate new housing investment from the private sector, and La Réconstruction had only limited goals. Decisive action was required, and the policy was adopted of developing housing programmes relying principally on public finance and initiative. Private sector finance, for the time being at least, was to play only a secondary role in housing construction, its principal efforts being directed towards industrial and commercial investment. The state was able to do this because of the very considerable degree of control it exercised over banks and other financial institutions. Traditional tutelage over the banks was considerably tightened up in 1945 and legislation expanding the role and status of State banks, and restricting further that of private banks, was passed. Company law remained restrictive, allowing only limited involvement of financial institutions in construction, and initially preventing the establishment of modern company structures. One must not exaggerate the role of the state in housing construction in this period, but the figures (Table 2.1) indicate that dwellings built using private funds alone (categorised as 'other') made up only a small proportion of the total. The majority were constructed under state direction and control either as Habitations à Loyer Modéré - HLM (dwellings at moderate rents) or as secteur aidé (subsidized private dwellings) units. The characteristics of both these sectors of housing are described in the following sections.

13

Table 2.1 Number of Dwellings completed by Sector.
Selected Years 1945-63 and all years
1963-81

	HLM			State Aides (Secteur Aidé)[1] [2]	[2] [3] Other	Total
	Récon- struction	Rent	Sale			
1945-48	19,000	400	1,000	–	47,800	68,200
1953	36,000	15,800	8,400	44,400	15,400	120,000
1958	24,200	68,700	18,900	154,400	25,500	291,700
1963	3,800	78,900	22,500	191,900	38,900	336,000
1964	2,400	92,300	24,900	207,300	41,900	368,800
1965	1,300	95,800	28,600	227,000	58,800	411,500
1966	700	96,900	30,100	201,800	84,700	414,200
1967	300	105,300	31,500	193,100	92,700	422,900
1968	100	116,600	31,800	176,800	85,800	411,100
1969	–	116,800	31,300	181,900	97,000	427,000
1970	–	121,300	34,100	199,600	101,300	456,300
1971	–	127,800	34,400	205,500	104,000	471,700
1972	–	126,900	49,400	233,800	136,200	546,300
1973	–	109,000	55,000	173,700	162,800	500,500
1974	–	121,700	60,000	122,700	196,000	500,400
1975	–	111,500	58,000	124,300	220,500	514,300
1976	–	98,100	42,300	113,200	195,300	448,900

	State aided Rent[5]	State aided Sale[6]	Other[3]	Total
1977[4]	90,600	167,200	193,100	450,900
1978	75,300	166,500	203,200	445,000
1979	63,000	148,300	192,300	403,600
1980	55,000	118,000	204,400	377,400
1981	53,400	134,300	203,200	390,900

Source: Statistiques de la Construction,
Ministère de l'Urbanisme et du Logement

1 Depending upon period includes PSI, PSD, PIC.
2 For rental and for purchase.
3 Private including mortgages, savings, bank loans.
4 Housing reform, change in definitions and of
   presentation of house construction statistics.
5 PLA replaces all HLM rented.
6 PAP replaces PSI and HLM sale.

The HLM Sector. The HLM movement as it has come to
be known, was and remains today, the principal
source of publicly financed or 'social' housing to
rent for the lower income groups of France. The
movement originated as independent philanthropic
groups in the late 19th century seeking to provide
good basic accommodation at reasonable rents, for
working class people. Because of legal, financial
and operational weaknesses, the local authorities,
(the communes) were in no position to provide
housing, and so the State adopted the founder HLM
groups in the early 20th century, and has since expanded the scope and scale of their operations. In
1948 in particular, the movement was reorganised in
preparation for the major role it was to play in the
following decade.

Today the movement consists of over 1200 autonomous organisations controlling 2¼ million rented
dwellings, and having built over one million for
sale. The organisations can be divided into two
principal groups: the Offices Publics d'HLM (OPHLM)
and the Sociétés d'HLM (SA),[11] the difference between
the two groups being essentially a juridical one, the
former subject to public law, the latter to private.
The Offices Publics are non-profit making and have
concentrated on providing rented accommodation whilst
the Sociétés are allowed to make limited profits and
have been chiefly responsible for the construction
of dwellings for sale. The organisations vary
greatly in scale of financial activity, number of
dwellings controlled and geographical area of operation, but they are grouped together on a Départmental[12] and regional basis for the purposes of co-
ordination of activities, and come together at the
national level in the Union Nationale des
Fédérations d'Organismes d'HLM (UNOFHLM). The Union,
an umbrella organisation, is a powerful body and
continues to have a very influential voice in determining state housing policy.

Tutelage of the movement is exercised by the
state through the Départmental Prefects, who have
the task of ensuring the legal and financial
propriety of the organisations, and that their operations are conducted in such a way as to meet the
housing needs of the areas they serve. The state
has passed extensive legislation over the years
determining the activities of the movement, but more
particularly, through its control of finance it has
determined output in light of its own wider economic
and social objectives. It is important to remember
that the HLM organisations, because of the make-up

of their governing bodies, are well placed in the
governmental power structure of France. They are
thus able to maintain their autonomy to a significant
degree, a fact which has made difficult at times the
successful implementation of reforms instituted by
the state.

The movement is charged in general terms with
improving the condition of the housing stock and
more particularly with making accommodation available for personnes peu fortunées - that is, those of
the lower income groups. In selecting tenants a
ceiling of resources or income (plâfond de résources)
is applied to all applicants, the ceiling being
determined by the size and circumstances of the
household, the category of dwelling and its geographical location. Rents are determined by the OPHLMs
within ranges related to surface area and other
factors, the limits set by ministerial decree. Rent
control legislation relating to this sector (secteur
reglémenté) in practice, if not in theory, gives
considerable autonomy to the movement in establishing
rents, a fact which has not been popular with
successive governments. Though non-profit making an
OPHLM must not incur losses, and the organisations
conduct means tests to exclude those whom they judge
to be unable to pay, on a regular basis, the rents
and charges for their dwellings. Means testing has
meant that some significant groups of the population
have been excluded from social housing and have been
forced into the worst housing in the private sector.
These include the very poor, the old, and the handicapped, single parent households and those with
large families.

Also taken into account, though not overtly, is
whether the applicant will make a "bad tenant" or
not. The definition of "bad tenant" includes the
social but more particularly, the racial origin of
applicants, and racial discrimination in lettings is
notorious. The Départmental Prefect in theory has
some say in lettings policy and is able to nominate
persons for HLM property in his Départment, but in
practice this can be circumvented by the organisation. Such discrimination goes hand in hand with the
situation of affluent tenants occupying higher category HLM properties (ILN, ILM)[13] which if in the free
market sector (secteur libre) would command considerably higher rents than they, the tenants, currently
pay. Governments over the years have sought to
resolve these abuses with only limited success,
though provisions of the 1977 Housing Act are now
making some impact.

Finance for HLM construction is provided by the state in the form of loans and grants. In the early 1950s in order to stimulate output, these loans were very cheap, being made available at a fixed rate of 2% per annum to be paid back over 65 years. Ninety per cent of the costs of construction were covered by the loan, the balance to be made up by supplementary loans from a variety of sources, most notably the Crédit Foncier de France (CFF),[14] the Caisses d'Epargne (savings banks), the state itself or from the Comités Interprofessionnels du logement (CIL).[15] The state established a cost ceiling for each dwelling and ensured that certain minimum standards in layout and materials were met. Initially, the ceiling was adjusted to take account of inflation but in the late 1950s it failed to keep up with increased construction costs, and the movement was forced to make greater use of supplementary finance which resulted in higher rents for new property, and a slowing down of output. Despite this the HLM movement retained its privileged financial position and continued to dominate construction into the 1960s.

The Secteur Aidé. The HLM movement builds for sale as well as for rent but the principal agency for stimulating home ownership in the 1950s was the Crédit Foncier itself, operating the secteur aidé. The CFF was empowered to make loans of up to 70% of approved construction costs of new dwellings at a fixed rate of interest extending over 25 years, with an additional grant of 600 F (old Francs) per square metre of habitable floor area. Standards of construction were controlled, and in the case where loans were used to build dwellings for letting, rents were, and still are, controlled and constitute a significant element of the secteur plafonné (sector with a rent ceiling) of the rented housing stock. The loans were made either directly to an individual (with no income restrictions imposed) having a dwelling built for himself, or to builders who would then sell (or rent) to the public. It was intended that the individual applicant or purchaser would find the balance of the cost of the dwelling, though the CFF could make supplementary loans available. Dwellings built under the scheme (introduced in 1950) became known as '600s' after the 600 F per square metre grant. Clearly successful, the scheme was extended by the introduction of Logements économiques et familieux (cheap family houses) or

17

Logecoes in 1953, which were cheaper versions of the
'600s' built to a plan type with space standards
similar to those found in HLM dwellings. Financial
arrangements were similar to those for the '600s'
though a higher grant of 1000 F per square metre was
paid, the Logecoes thus earning an alternative title
of '1000s'. This dual system was very successful,
some 1.6 million dwellings being constructed before
its abolition in 1963. The very favourable financial
terms opened up home ownership to the growing and
increasingly affluent middle classes of France.

Housing Finance and the "1%". Since 1953, all firms
employing ten or more people have been required to
contribute approximately 1% (at present 0.9%) of
their wages and salary bill towards housing construction.[16] In return they get rights to nominate a
proportion of their workers for priority access to
accommodation for rent or for sale. The contributions are either retained by the firms themselves for
direct use (only the very largest do this, and only
exceptionally) or are made over to organismes
collecteurs (collecting organisations), the most
important of which are the Comités Interprofessionnels du Logement or CILs. These are non-state
organisations, made up of nominees or representatives
of contributing firms, which developed out of co-
operative ventures of textile manufacturers in the
North-east of France in the 1930s, who wanted to
provide housing for their workers. Most firms take
little practical interest in how the CILs distribute
their contributions, regarding the '1%' as merely an
unwelcome tax, and it is only the larger firms that
use their nomination rights for dwellings as part of
their personnel policies.
    The '1%', which can only be used as supplemen-
tary finance to other sources, both public and
private, is of very great importance today. From
humble beginnings in 1953, the sums collected now
are huge and even by 1975 outstripped the state's
budgetary allocation for housing construction in
that year. As the state has sought to reduce its
proportion of housing costs, the role of supplementary finance in public and secteur aidé construction
has increased, and it has always been expected that
the '1%' should play a major role in financing this
type of housing. Unfortunately, because of the lack
of employer involvement, and public control, the
Comités have become largely autonomous and many have
developed investment policies akin to those of

property development and insurance companies, concentrating on speculative housing adventures at
prices, and in local and regional locations, which
make them inaccessible to many of the employees of
the contributing firms. This is a situation that
the present government is seeking to rectify.

The Construction Industry and the State. Provision
for finance for construction is one essential of a
housing programme, but there has to be the capacity
available to actually build the dwellings in that
programme. The building industry in the 1950s was
typical of so much of French industry in general. It
was dominated by small firms, traditional in management and financial practices and resistant to the
use of new building techniques and materials. As it
stood it could not meet alone the demands which were
placed upon it and the state was compelled to take
action. The Ministère de la Construction et du
Logement,[17] responsible for the housing programme
undertook to play an active role in stimulating
modernisation of the industry. It carried out (and
still does) research into new materials and construction techniques, and encouraged firms to merge
into larger units and adopt modern financial and
management practices.

In addition the state established two companies
of its own. The Société Centrale d'Equipment du
Territoire (SCET) in 1953 and the Société Civile
Immobilière de la Caisse des Dépôts (SCIC) in 1954.
The SCIC is the state development and construction
company still active today and which built most of
the HLM dwellings of the 1950s and 1960s, whilst
SCET can take on the responsibility for the initial
stages of urban management schemes, particularly
those involving clearance and redevelopment and
where there are problems of land acquisition and
service provision.

In 1963 legislation was passed allowing for the
establishment of a new type of company: the Société
d'Economie Mixte (SEM). The SEMs (which can be used
for widely different purposes) are joint private and
public companies which in the case of development,
combine some of the prerogatives of the state, such
as compulsory land acquisition, with the flexibility,
skills and finance of the private sector. They have
come to be a widely used form of organisation particularly in urban development projects. From the
point of view of the state, SEMs had the advantage
of encouraging private investment and involvement at

a time when it was entering more fully on its policy
of gradual disengagement from housing provision.

Housing and Planning. Housing construction was
essentially concerned with quantity of output and
only secondary consideration was given to standards
of building, design and layout. This was particularly the case with the mass housing developments
of the grands ensembles.[18] The use of poorly under-
stood and badly applied prefabrication techniques
resulted in the construction of many dwellings with
unsatisfactory thermal and accoustic insulation
properties, and by today's standards, room sizes
were small, and internal layout poor. In addition
technical and financial pressures and the influence
of the modern movement in architecture encouraged
the widespread construction of high rise blocks of
flats.

The larger grands ensembles offered housing to
several thousands of families. Shops, schools,
social and welfare facilities were supposed to be
provided at the same time as the dwellings, but it
was not uncommon for it to take years before they
appeared. For a number of reasons including the
desire to build as fast as possible, many developments took place on readily available plots of land,
usually on the urban periphery, with little attention being paid to location relative to transport
systems, employment and other centres of population
and retailing. Dealing with the problems of the
grands ensembles is of major concern to government
today, but it is easy to exaggerate how poor the
housing of the period was. The majority of
dwellings, particularly of the secteur aidé and the
private sector were built in smaller developments
with better standards and better locations. And of
course not all grands ensembles were built on a vast
scale in inaccessible locations and nor were all
lacking in amenities and facilities (Figure 2.1).
Speed was considered to be of the essence in the
drive to modernise the economic base of the country
and to meet the unsatisfied housing demand, and it
was not until the end of the 1950s that proper
attention was paid to the spatial organisation of
economic and urban growth and public infrastructure
provision.

After 1958, in an attempt to improve the co-
ordination of house building and the provision of
infrastructure and services in the grands ensembles
in particular, all new developments of 100 dwellings

Figure 2.1   The grand ensemble at Chennevières-sur-Marne.

or more had to be located in Zones à Urbanisé par Priorité (ZUP) (priority urbanisation zones) where public investment would be concentrated. Though the concept was good the results as we have already noted were not universally satisfactory. The ZUPs themselves were to be set in the context of local land use plans, the Plans d'Urbanisme de Détail (PUD) and Plans d'Urbanisme Directeur (structure plans) which were required after 1957 of all urban communes of more than 10,000 in population. The PUDs proved to be as unsatisfactory as their predecessor[19] being slow of preparation, quickly dated and inflexible as tools in controlling urban growth. In many instances ZUPs would be designated before a PUD was completed, and the plan had to be adapted to take this into account.

Attempts to improve matters at metropolitan level were not particularly successful either. The Programmes de Modernisation et d'Equipment (PME) initiated in 1957 were programmes of public infra-structure investment for all agglomerations of more than 50,000 persons. They were to provide the link between the National Economic Plans and the PUDs, but those drawn up could not be operationalised satisfactorily and they were quietly abandoned in the 1970s. It was not until the late 1960s that urban planning began to improve in concept and performance, whilst urbanisation continued apace, and housing construction broke new records. (Table 2.1).

The Rise of the Private Sector 1963-1973

By the early 1960s the French economy had undergone a marked structural change, with a decline in primary including agricultural employment, and an increase in the secondary and, in particular the tertiary sectors.[20] The process of modernisation and change (which continues today) was accompanied by growth at rates very respectable in international terms,[21] the net effect being that the French people entered a period of unparalleled prosperity which affected amongst other things, their expectations in the field of housing.

The population had also grown, from 40 million in 1946 to 46 million in 1962, whilst the proportion of the population living in rural areas had fallen from 43% to 37% (by 1975 it was 27%). The greatest growth occurred in the great cities of Paris, Marseilles, Lyons and others, and in the medium sized towns of 20-100,000 in population, each posing their own sorts of housing and urban planning problems. Urban growth was the result of both natural expansion and immigration from overseas but particularly from rural areas, and of course the exodus from the countryside presented, and still presents considerable difficulties to housing and planning policymakers, especially in those areas, such as the Massif Central, most acutely affected.

Output of housing had increased from 120,000 per annum in 1953 to a new high of 336,000 in 1965, a total of 2¾ million dwellings being constructed in the period as a whole (Table 2.1). Yet despite this, in 1962, 21.6% of principal residences were without running water, almost 60% lacked a W.C. internal to the accommodation, and nearly 40% were overcrowded,[22] 13% acutely so (Tables 2.2 and 2.3). The worst conditions were to be found in older urban areas, notably in Paris and the industrial zones of the north and east, but also in many rural areas particularly the more remote and poorer ones. The most extreme conditions were exhibited by the shanty towns or bidonvilles, populated by immigrants principally from North Africa, which had sprung up on scraps of vacant land in the major towns and cities and on their peripheries. Legislation to

Table 2.2   Amenities: Number and Proportion of
             Principal Residences lacking certain
             amenities.

	No running water in dwelling	No W.C. in dwelling	No bath or shower in dwelling	No central heating	Total principal residences
1962	3.146 m 21.6%	8.666 m 59.5%	10.355 m 71.1%	11.753 m 80.7%	14.565 m 100%
1968	1.450 m 9.2%	7.124 m 45.2%	8.275 m 52.5%	10.261 m 65.1%	15.763 m 100%
1975	0.496 m 2.8%	4.649 m 26.2%	5.288 m 29.8%	8.322 m 46.9%	17.745 m 100%
1978	0.242 m 1.3%	3.895 m 20.9%	4.268 m 22.9%	7.400 m 39.7%	18.640 m 100%

Source: INSEE; l'Enquête Nationale sur le Logement
          de 1978
          INSEE; Annuaire Statistique de La France
          1978

Table 2.3   Distribution of Principal Residences
             according to Occupancy rate*.

	1962	1968	1975	1978
Acute Over-occupation	1.851 m 12.7%	1.398 m 8.9%	0.848 m 4.8%	0.596 m 3.2%
Moderate Over-occupation	3.784 m 26.0%	3.584 m 22.7%	3.167 m 17.8%	2.591 m 13.9%
Normal	4.143 m 28.4%	4.711 m 29.9%	5.404 m 30.5%	5.294 m 28.4%
Under-occupation	4.787 m 32.9%	6.070 m 38.5%	8.326 m 46.9%	10.159 m 54.5%
Total	14.565 m 100%	15.763 m 100%	17.745 m 100%	18.640 m 100%

* Definitions   INSEE

Source: INSEE; l'Enquête National sur le Logement
          de 1978
          INSEE; Annuaire Statistique de La France 1978

deal with the bidonvilles was introduced in 1964 and
1970 giving the communes powers to expropriate the
land and clear the dwellings, whilst the HLM movement
and State made alternative accommodation available.
This normally took the form either of the worst and
most unpopular HLMO dwellings, or of specially constructed cités de transit[23] (now euphemistically
called cités familiales) which in many instances have
been allowed to degenerate so that today, conditions
are arguably little better than in the old bidonvilles. With regard to unfit dwellings in general,
large scale clearance has never been a key element
of housing policy, principally because the complexity
of property rights make the tasks of acquisition of
land and dwellings, especially in the older areas, a
daunting task. In addition, in the period under
discussion, the sheer shortage of accommodation of
any condition meant that efforts were directed towards new construction while keeping as much of the
existing stock as possible. Powers under Public
Health legislation are available to the Prefects to
declare individual dwellings or groups of dwellings
(ilôt insalubre) unfit and be subject to acquisition
and clearance. Those displaced are, according to
their circumstances offered accommodation in the
appropriate HLM category of dwelling, or of course,
in the cités de transit.
     It was against this background of economic and
population growth, (which it was assumed would continue), and of personal prosperity that housing and
planning policies would be adjusted and developed
for the coming decade. The problems of unsatisfied
housing demand and the poor standards of a proportion
of the housing stock were to be dealt with by increasing the output of new dwellings. Rehabilitation
of older dwellings (Table 2.4) was to be a policy of
the 1970s.

The Re-organisation of Finance. The emphasis was
thus to remain upon increased output, but the balance
between public and private finance was to be altered
in this period. The long term aims of increasing the
contribution of households (whether renting or purchasing) to housing costs, and of encouraging private
finance, institutions and mechanisms to play a much
greater role in construction, became very much
clearer. To achieve these, the mechanisms and terms
of finance of both the secteur aidé and the HLM
movement were reformed. In addition the state
relaxed control and introduced reforms into the

Table 2.4   Age of Principal Residences: Number and
            Proportion of Principal Residences by Age

	Pre 1871	1871– 1914	1915– 1948	All Pre 1948	Post 1948	Total
1962	4.653 m	4.295 m	3.127 m	12.075 m	2.490 m	14.565 m
%	31.9	29.5	21.5	82.9	17.1	100
1968	4.109 m	3.963 m	3.087 m	11.159 m	4.618 m	15.763 m
%	26.0	25.1	19.6	70.7	29.3	100
1975	3.441 m	3.448 m	2.883 m	9.774 m	7.971 m	17.745 m
%	19.4	19.4	16.3	55.1	44.9	100
1978	–	–	–	9.557 m	9.083 m	18.640 m
%				51.3	48.7	100

Source: INSEE; l'Enquête Nationale sur le Logement
          de 1978
          INSEE; Annuaire Statistique de La France
          1978

financial system in order to allow banks and other
financial institutions to engage more fully in all
aspects of housing construction and finance.
    The Secteur Aidé - In 1963 the CFF was reorga-
nised and a new and what proved to be a very
successful system of loans for the secteur aidé was
introduced. The Logecoes and 600s were abolished
and replaced by two categories of Prêts Spéciaux
Immédiates (PSI) (special immediate loans), one
designed for construction of dwellings to purchase,
and the other for dwellings to rent. The loans
under this new scheme were not as generous as
previously, it being considered that the rise in
real incomes of those most likely to use the scheme
meant it was no longer justifiable to maintain state
aid at Logecoe and 600 levels. Only 40-45% of the
cost ceiling imposed by the CFF would be met by a
PSI, and it was intended that the borrower should
provide the balance required, either using personal
funds or by borrowing from other sources such as
banks, savings banks, CILs or elsewhere. The cost
to the purchaser or tenant of PSI housing was higher
than before, but this was offset by the fact that
PSI loans were made at favourable rates of interest
and, along with any supplementary finance, attracted
tax relief on interest repayments, whilst rents were
subject to the regime of the secteur plafonné. In
1965 the scheme was extended by the introduction of

FRANCE

Prêts Spéciaux Différés (PSD) (special deferred
loans). The scheme was very similar to PSI but as it
was intended for higher income groups the loans were
more costly and the proportion of the cost ceiling
met by the PSD was lower.[24]
     A crucial part of the PSI and PSD schemes then,
was that a greater proportion of the cost of construction be met by the purchaser, and thus it was
clearly necessary that schemes be introduced on one
hand to encourage prospective buyers to save, and on
the other, to make access to supplementary finance
easier. The existing house savings scheme introduced
in 1953 failed to be sufficiently attractive to
investors, and in 1965 a new scheme was introduced.
The scheme, which is still operational, is called
the Compte d'Epargne Logement (CEL) (house savings
account) and is paralleled by a similar scheme introduced a little later, the Plan d'Epargne Logement
(PEL) (house savings plan). Under either of these
schemes an individual opens a special savings
account with a bank or one of the special savings
banks (caisse d'epargne), and agrees to deposit
certain minimum monthly amounts over a minimum
period. The deposits attract tax-free fixed rate
interest. If the investor has abided by the terms
of the agreement he is eligible for a bank or CFF
loan (Prêt Immobilier) for house purchase. The
state, as a bonus, doubles the interest earned on the
savings if the loan is granted and taken up. The
loan itself is at a fixed rate of interest, and
attracts tax relief on interest repayments. PELs
are very similar to CELs but savings have to be for
longer periods, though with a higher rate of
interest paid on those savings. The funds drawn in
by these two schemes have to be used in one way or
another for house purchase and construction, thus
becoming part of the wider house mortgage market
operated by the banks. Undoubtedly, the schemes
have been very successful and today represent one of
the largest single sources of finance for house purchase.
     In order to introduce these savings schemes,
the strict control over the banks' operations
mentioned earlier, was relaxed, and in 1967 further
decontrol took place to allow the financial institutions to develop a far more extensive mortgage
market. The opening up of this market was intended
to stimulate the private non-assisted sector of
housing provision. Now it became easier to purchase
not only new dwellings but also older properties
particularly for renovation and/or as second homes,

26

and homes of higher quality, even luxury dwellings.
Previously it had only been a rich minority who had
ease of access to the variety of housing available
but now such access was to be made available to a
greater proportion of the population, the newly
affluent middle classes. Certainly these schemes
and reforms stimulated further involvement of private
finance and the activities of property development
companies.25 The increase in private and secteur
aidé construction shown in Table 2.1 is the physical
manifestation of what was happening.

The HLM Movement - Just as the secteur aidé was
reorganised on less favourable terms, so too was the
HLM Movement. A new organisation, the Caisse des
Prêts aux Organismes d'HLM (CPHLM) was established
in 1966 as an offshoot of the Caisse des Dépôts et
Consignations (CDC) the state bank used for financing
communes, départments and other public bodies. It
was through the CPHLM and the CDC that the grants
and loans of the state were to be distributed to HLM
organisations. The state made available grants of
40-50% of approved construction costs through the
CPHLM whilst the rest, up to 95% of these approved
costs could be obtained in the form of loans from
the CDC. The remaining 5% had to be funded either
by the HLM using its own resources or by borrowing
from the usual sources of supplementary finance.
Until 1968 the cost ceiling was adjusted by the
state to keep it in line with construction costs,
but later such adjustments were insufficient and
greater use had to be made of the more expensive
supplementary finance, and the result of this was to
be that by the end of the 1960s there was a faltering
in output and rises in rents. Nevertheless, the
1960s saw the HLM movement at its zenith constructing
some 35% of the new dwellings. After this in the
1970s it was overtaken both by the secteur aidé and
the private sector, as the reforms affecting these
sectors reached fruition.

It was during the 1960s that the HLM movement
sought to improve the quality of dwellings constructed, building to higher standards, and providing a
variety of types to meet different requirements of
households and their ability to pay.

By the end of the decade there were seven categories of dwellings for rent or sale built and
managed by a complex network of organisations that
made up the movement. Arguably the provision and
administration of these dwellings was becoming more
difficult and costly, and it made the apparent flexibility of the secteur aidé and the private sector

very attractive to successive governments.

Urban Planning. The earlier attempts to control and
direct the rapid urban growth at local and metropolitan scales were proving to be unsatisfactory and a
number of changes were made in the 1960s to improve
the effectiveness of urban planning. The establishment of DATAR[26] in 1963, the introduction of growth
pole policy (metropoles d'équilibre) and the establishment of planning and study groups (OREAM)   for
the metropolitan regions outside Paris were part of
a national strategy of urban development. At a
lower level discredited PUDs were replaced in 1967[27]
by the Plan d'Occupation des Sols, POS (local land
use plan) and the Schéma Directeur d'Aménagement et
d'Urbanisme,SDAU (Structure Plan). In addition the
ZUP was replaced by the Zone d'Aménagement Concerté,
ZAC (co-ordinated development zone) which was an
improved version of its predecessor extending its
powers and field of applicability. These changes
and others introduced by the 1967 Act were designed
to make urban planning more flexible and responsive
to changing circumstances.[28]
    The application of these new powers and proce-
dures has not been as successful as intended. The
long-established and powerful attachment of the
French to property rights has often led to fierce
resistance to land use zoning which inherently
restricts those rights, and has resulted in major
delays in completing POS.[29] The capacity of the
Prefect to prevent excessive allocation of land for
housing and other development and to ensure the co-
ordination of POS and SDAU is limited. Unco-
ordinated peripheral growth of not only the major
towns and cities, but also smaller settlements, has
proved difficult to control and though political
pressures to protect the environment acted as a
counter balance particularly in the 1970s, these
pressures have been weakened by the effects of the
economic recession and the calls to reduce control
and hence the costs of development.

Policy Changes and Reform 1973-1982
The early 1970s can be seen as a period of transition
in the post-war history of French housing. The
population growth of the previous two decades
slackened (1954-1962 + 1.1% p.a.; 1962-1968 + 1.2%
p.a.; 1968-1975 + 0.8% p.a.) with the likelihood if
trends continued, of population stabilisation by the

end of the century. The regional patterns of migration and of growth and decline remained much the
same, but urbanisation patterns were changing significantly.

The medium sized towns continued to grow but
the net population growth of the major cities of half
a million or more was much reduced on previous years.
In addition all towns and cities were witnessing
falls in city centre populations and rapid peri-
urban growth on the other, the latter phenomena
being most dramatically illustrated in the Paris
agglomeration but it is not peculiar to it.[30]
Absolute declines in numbers have been accompanied
by change in the social characteristics of the city
centre populations. The original inhabitants, often
the old and the poor, have been displaced not only
by commercial pressures, but also by demands of
sections of the middle class seeking the advantages
of a central location as a place to live.

The high levels of housing output of the previous
years had eliminated the crude shortages of the post-
war years and the overall standards of the housing
stock had much improved by 1975 (Table 2.2), indeed
the housing programmes can be seen as major achievements of the state even if the success must be qualified. Nationally, standards of older housing,
particularly that built before 1914, and which in
1975 constituted 40% of the housing stock, still
left a great deal to be desired; and within this
national picture there were, of course, important
regional and local variations. Places like the City
of Paris, the older industrial areas of the east and
north, and remoter rural areas had a significant
proportion of their stock with particularly low
standards whether measured in terms of facilities,
occupancy rates or conditions of buildings.

Post war urbanisation had been achieved at a
price, and in the late 1960s and early 1970s a
popular reaction against the excesses of the process
set in. Greater concern began to be expressed for
the environment of both the cities and the countryside - much housing and other development had been
ill-planned and destructive of the natural environment. Housing construction without regard to the
availability of means of transport, social and
shopping facilities and easily accessible employment
opportunities, became increasingly unacceptable, and
the types of dwellings provided and the standards
and qualities of much mass housing, typified by the
grands ensembles began to be criticised more widely.
A strong reaction against the modern movement in

architecture (Figures 2.2 and 2.3) as expressed in
the form of high rise, high density housing development (immeuble collectif) set in with a relative
increased demand for two-storey detached or semi-
detached houses (maisons individuelles - Figure 2.4
and Table 2.5).

Figure 2.2   High rise, high density HLM and private
              rented flats at Riquet, Paris.

        The concept and the methods of urban development
and redevelopment were also subject to attack. The
destruction of areas in Paris such as Les Halles,
Main-Montparnasse and Place d'Italie for speculative
commercial and housing development, had its counter-
part in towns and cities throughout France during
the 1960s. Such developments all too often destroyed
neighbourhoods of mixed land use and social groupings.
Small shopkeepers, manufacturers and café-owners lost
their livelihoods, and in many instances the displaced residents had to leave the areas completely,
for the new dwellings that replaced the old were
often beyond their means. Local residents formed

Figure 2.3   Rented flats built with '1% finance'
             "Les Choux", Créteil, Val-de Marne.

Table 2.5   Completions by Dwelling Type: Collectif
            or Individuelle, Selected years 1972-80.
            Numbers and proportions of total.

	Immeuble Collectif		Maison Individuelle		Total	
1972	352,600*	(57%)	270,300*	(43%)	622,900*	(100%)
1974	287,800	(57%)	212,600	(43%)	500,400	(100%)
1976	227,400	(51%)	221,500	(49%)	448,900	(100%)
1978	199,800	(45%)	245,200	(55%)	445,000	(100%)
1980	138,100	(37%)	240,200	(63%)	378,300	(100%)

*   commencement authorised only - not necessarily
     completed

Source: Statistiques de la Construction,
          Ministère de l'Urbanisme et du Logement

Figure 2.4   Owner-occupied, detached house, Evry
New Town, Essonne.

groups and associations to resist such developments
and through the political system exerted pressure
upon government. Undoubtedly, one of the reasons
for the shift of government policy away from major
redevelopment schemes, towards rehabilitation of
older urban areas, was because of local pressure
from what was one of their traditional sources of
electoral support. Part of Giscard d'Estaing's 1974
electoral platform was in fact a commitment to
ensure that greater regard be paid to the built and
natural environment when developing urban policy.
     All these developments must be seen in the
light of changed economic circumstances. The economic growth of the previous decades slackened after
the quadrupling of oil prices in 1973, and the
country entered a period of lower industrial output,
increased inflation and higher levels of unemployment. Doubt was now cast on whether past levels of
housing construction could be maintained and further,
the question was raised as to whether better use
could be made of existing material and financial

resources to meet demand. Attention was now to be
directed towards developing rehabilitation policy
and performance, and towards reform of the existing
system of housing finance.

Rehabilitation. New housing construction remained
a key element of policy during this period but
rehabilitation was soon to be of much greater importance than before. The Nora Report of 1975[31] represented the first official systematic review of the
problems and possibilities in the field of housing
improvement. Its conclusions in conjunction with
those of the Barre[32] Report of the same year, form
the basis of current rehabilitation policy as
expressed in the 1977 Housing Act discussed below.
    Though concerted official attention and action
appeared for the first time in the 1970s, rehabilitation had been carried out over the years as a
result of private, para-public and, very limited
public initiative and expenditure. In 1946 the state
funded Fonds National de'Amélioration de l'Habitat,
FNAH, (National Housing Improvements Body) was
established with the task of encouraging landlords
to improve their property. Its impact was slight as
its funds were limited, its procedures slow and
clumsy and the opposition of landlords and landlord
organisations effective.
    In 1971 the FNAH was replaced by the Agence
Nationale pour l'Amélioration de l'Habitat (ANAH).
Further reorganised in 1975 it has similar goals to
the defunct FNAH but is better funded and organised
than its predecessor. It is an autonomous public
body administered by a council consisting of representatives of landlords, tenants and the state, and
is financed by grant from the state (600 million
francs in 1980-81) and by a levy on all private landlords.[33] The funds are distributed in the form of
grants for the provision of specified facilities and
repairs, and are only available for rented properties
built before 1948, though since 1976 grants for
thermal insulation can be made for dwellings con-
tructed between 1948 and 1975. The level of grants
vary according to a number of factors including
regional location and income of applicant. Unfortunately, the number of dwellings improved using
ANAH grant aid was only 179,000 between 1975 and 1979
out of a total theoretically eligible of 2.5 million.
It was not until the 1977 Housing Act that financial
assistance for owner occupiers was made available on
any scale, and indeed what had been available before

that Act had essentially been restricted to dwellings
of architectural or historical value.

Mention needs to be made of the role and importance of the non-profit making bodies, the
Associations de Restauration Immobilière (ARIM) and
the Centres d'Amélioration du Logement-Protection,
Amélioration, Conservation, Transformation de
l'Habitat (CAL-PACT)34 which have come to play a
very practical and innovatory role in housing rehabilitation. The organisations have only limited
funds of their own but act as intermediaries between
those applying for loans or grants for improvement,
and the sources of finance (including those of the
State) and the construction industry. The Départments and communes habitually make use of their
services as they have built up a wealth of
organisational and technical expertise which the
State itself cannot provide. Between 1954 and 1980
the CAL-PACTS assisted in the rehabilitation of
400,000 dwellings and are currently involved on
another 50,000, mostly for the benefit of the poorer
owner-occupier and small landlord. Despite the
growing involvement of the state itself, the ARIMs
and CAL-PACTs will retain a very important future
role in rehabilitation.

As the economy expanded in the 1950s and 1960s
invididual owners and landlords were better placed
to improve and maintain their property, and
privately financed rehabilitation became more common.
The growth in demand for second homes and for city
centre dwellings gave a particularly important
fillip to rehabilitation, yet not without undesirable side effects. In those rural areas with concentrations of second homes, problems of service
provision, including water and electricity supply,
have been created. Local housing markets have been
upset, the social structure distorted, and compli-
cations introduced into the implementation of rural
regeneration policies. In city centres throughout
the country, but most notably in Paris, whole areas
have been improved by private investment and
initiative, usually resulting in significant social
and functional change. It is of course in the
capital that returns on property renovation are
highest and where market rehabilitation is most
developed. In 1978 the national housing survey[35]
revealed that 23% of dwellings in the City of Paris
were subject to rent control under the 1948 Rent Act,
and as the gap between controlled and market rents
for these properties is so great, eviction of sitting
tenants can be a financially rewarding activity.

Intolerable pressure, not all of it legal, has at times been exerted to secure vacant possession.36 The tenants displaced, usually old, ignorant of their rights and with low incomes cannot afford to pay city centre market rents and are forced out into the suburbs.

Successive governments of the 1970s have been aware of the process of social change and polarisation and the Nora and Barre reports identified it as an important problem that has to be dealt with decisively. In 1973 the scheme Acquisition-Amélioration Locataire d'HLM (HLM purchase and renovation for renting) was introduced by which an OPHLM or SAHLM could, in co-operation with a local commune acquire existing property for renovation to HLM Ordinaire standards.37 It was intended that city centre property in particular would be improved and let at subsidised rents to the existing inhabitants, but because of financial and administrative problems this instrument of social and rehabilitation policy was a failure. It was not until the 1977 Housing Act that the state made clear its practical commitment to rehabilitation through the introduction of financial reforms positively affecting rehabilitation as well as new construction. We shall examine these reforms in detail below.

As indicated previously the problems of poor housing are not restricted to pre-1948 dwellings, and much post-war housing particularly of the grands ensembles of the 1950s and 1960s is in need of improvement and repair. Some of these developments have become social and racial ghettoes, with environments degraded by vandalism and years of HLM landlord neglect.38 In 1973 an interministerial group was established to carry out pilot studies to identify means of dealing with the problems, and in 1977 it was upgraded in status to become the Groupe Interministérial Habitat et Vie Sociale (HVS) (Housing and Social Life). The group has no funds of its own but co-ordinates the individual projects which make up the HVS programme, and the financial and administrative contributions of the various organisations concerned. These include the Ministère de l'Urbanisme et du Logement, Ministère de la Santé, the OPHLM owning the dwellings, usually the local commune and possibly other bodies such as the local branch of a CIL. A typical operation would include improving the dwellings and the environment, providing social and other facilities, stimulating social interaction of the inhabitants and making management of the development more

efficient and sensitive to resident's needs. At
present some fifty grands ensembles are in the HVS
programme comprising over 100,000 dwellings.39 The
HLM movement has its own programmes with some
300,000 dwellings (some inter-war) needing major
modifications and improvements and another million
requiring less substantial works.

The HVS programme is important not only because
it demonstrates the concern of the state to improve
the physical standards and condition of the housing
stock, but also that environmental, locational and
social considerations have been recognised as of
equal importance. Housing programmes whether of
rehabilitation or of new construction are part of a
social policy which aims to reduce social and racial
polarisation and to improve the non-material well-
being of the nation. The approach to housing provision has come a long way since the programmes of construction of the 1950s and 1960s.

Urban Planning and Management. Just as housing
policies were adjusted to become more flexible and
effective, parallel changes were also made in the
field of urban planning and management. By the
early 1970s the policy of developing Poles
d'Equilibre had been downgraded as it was felt that
their growth had been excessive, damaging the lesser
towns and villages of the areas they were supposed
to serve. At the same time, it was decided to adopt
measures to improve the planning and co-ordination
of service and infrastructure provision in towns of
less than 100,000 in population. The system of
Contrats d'Aménagement des Villes Moyennes was thus
introduced, by which an urban commune or group of
communes, signs a contract with the State to co-
ordinate the financial, administrative and technical
aspects of public infrastructure investment and
planning in specified areas. The emphasis is upon
improving co-ordination of the activities of the
different ministries and the communes, lack of which
in the past has led to poor results in many schemes.
Grants additional to those normally available, are
provided by the State for suitable projects, such as
open space provision, car parks, pedestrianisation
of streets and environmental improvement in general.
Inspired by the success of these contracts the
principle has been extended to small towns and
villages in rural areas, in the form of Contrats de
Pays (Contrats Régional in the Ile-de-France) where
similar projects are assisted in much the same way.

The SDAU and POS remain the principal land use plans but their limitations as urban management tools are increasingly recognised. To make the POS more useful, so called Plans de Référence were introduced in 1977.[40] These are statements of various projects scheduled to be started or completed within a stated five year period. The plans are essentially documents designed to improve project co-ordination in a town or parts of a town set within the context of the POS. Much of the initiative in this field will come from the communes themselves but the Fonds d'Aménagement Urbaine (FAU) was set up at the same time to foster State involvement. It is an inter-ministerial grouping (like HVS) without its own funds, but which seeks to co-ordinate expenditure of ministries and other public bodies involved in a Plan de Référence or other similar urban project.

These improvements and innovations are not exclusively concerned with residential areas although these clearly will benefit. Specific measures for the improvement of older and predominantly residential areas (Figure 2.5) have been introduced however, in the form of Opérations Programmées d'Amélioration de l'Habitat (OPAH).[41] The OPAH (introduced in 1977) are conventions or agreements made between the state, ANAH, and the commune or communes concerned, to bring about the improvement of individual dwellings and their environment. The OPAHs cover defined areas which can vary greatly in nature and size, be they densely developed blocks in urban areas or a series of buildings dispersed over a wide area covering several communes. The actual number of dwellings in OPAHs so far established varies from two or three to several hundred. OPAHs then, are essentially management tools to co-ordinate the investment of the state, communes, ANAH and other bodies, and of course the contributions of individual owner occupiers and landlords. The management is carried out by an agreed body which can be the commune itself or an appropriate non-profit making body such as a CIL or CAL-PACT. Similar to a British GIA (General Improvement Area) individual dwellings are brought up to standard and the environment improved by tree planting, pedestrianisation of streets, provision of play areas and the like.

Improvements in the areal approach to urban management have been primarily concerned with older zones of development but attention is now being directed towards inter-war and post-war suburban housing areas. Individually the dwellings may be generally acceptable but in a number of ways the sub-

Figure 2.5   Opération Programmée: Town centre back-
land opened for public access at
Pointoise, Val-d'Oise, 1980.

urbs of the major cities are unsatisfactory. In
1979 the Groupe Intérministérial Permanante pour
l'Aménagement des Banlieus (Interministerial group
for the management of the suburbs) was established.
It has commissioned a number of pilot studies to
investigate the accessibility of shopping, social
and employment opportunities, and availability of
public transport facilities for suburban dwellers.
The group if it continues to function will work like
FAU, co-ordinating investment decisions by all public
bodies concerned in the improvement of the suburbs.

The Housing Act of 1977. Housing policy and the
system of finance had developed incrementally since
1945, and it was increasingly argued from a number
of quarters that an exercise in clarification and

systemisation was required. Most of the arguments
were encapsulated in three major reports, all published in 1975. Two of them, the Nora and Barre
reports, mentioned earlier, were the work of government appointed commissions whilst the third, the so
called Livre Blanc[42] was produced by the UNOFHLM
representing the HLM movement.

The Nora report was principally concerned with
rehabilitation of the housing stock, and recommended
that for economic and social reasons the state should
encourage the improvement of existing dwellings.
Public intervention should be only of a limited kind
and be directed to helping the less well off, whilst
market forces should be allowed to provide the motor
and the bulk of the resources. The report stressed
the importance of considering rehabilitation in the
context of a radical overhaul of housing policy and
finance, if any programmes were to be effective. The
radical critique, proposals for 'the re-definition'
of housing policy and changes in the system of
finance, called for in the Nora report, are to be
found in the Barre report. The report, named after
its chairman and future Prime Minister, found that
the system of housing provision and finance was complex, confusing and difficult to administer. Decision making was over-centralised, inflexible and
insensitive, whilst the distribution of public funds
either to the HLM movement or secteur aidé benefited
the better-off at the expense of the most needy.
Additionally, the report argued, public expenditure
at the levels of previous years was inflationary,
and that it was more satisfactory to let market
forces play the principal role in housing provision.
In contrast the Livre Blanc, though presenting a
similar analysis in many respects, came to rather
different conclusions as to what changes were
required. Principally, it maintained that though
the market had a part to play in the provision of
housing, the state had as before, to play the key
role.

The government of the day, committed to liberal
economic policies readily accepted the analyses and
proposals of the Nora and Barre reports and broadly
rejected those of the Livre Blanc. For the first
time a government explicitly stated that in future
the state would play only a secondary role in
housing provision whilst market forces would, as far
as possible, be given their head. The Housing Act
of 1977 can be seen as a clarification and a conclusion cf thirty years of a gradual if erratic move by
the state to reduce the part it should play in

39

housing finance and construction. The Act is based
upon a number of objectives which are as follows:
(a) Allow market forces to operate more freely and
    increase the contribution of householders to
    housing costs by increasing rents and interest
    rates on home loans to market levels.
(b) Reduce overall state expenditure in housing, and
    direct aid to householders (rather than dwellings)
    according to income.
(c) Increase home ownership levels particularly
    amongst those of modest means and make available
    a wider choice of housing.
(d) Rehabilitate the existing stock.
(e) Simplify the system of finance and improve its
    administration.
The Act made major changes in the system of finance
which are still being phased in as the old arrangements reach their term. The existing forms of aid
for construction have been swept away and much
clearer and simpler arrangements substituted.[43]

Social Housing and the HLM movement - The complex of grants, loans and supplementary finance for
HLM construction (and the different categories of
dwellings) previously available, has been replaced
by Prêts Locatifs Aidé (PLA) (subsidised loans for
rented dwellings). These are loans available not
only to the HLM movement but to other constructors,
including private developers, building non-specula-
tive housing; they can be used for building new
houses but also for rehabilitation[44] - an important
advance on the previous system and in line with
government strategy. The PLA are only made available after a contract has been signed between the
state and the borrower. Originally the contract
would have been given the Départmental Prefect quite
extensive powers over construction standards and
design, but more importantly over lettings policy
and rent levels. It would have given the Prefect
opportunity to reduce discriminatory practices in
letting and to raise rents to levels considered to
be more appropriate for the type of dwellings in
question. In brief it meant that the autonomy of
the HLM movement to manage their properties would
have been severely curtailed. The Mitterand administration, submitting to UNOPHLM pressure, has modified the system of contracts returning to the HLM
much of its autonomy in the field of management.
What has not changed has been the power to increase
rents to more appropriate levels, such increases to
be offset by the availability of the new system of
personalised aid discussed below.

40

Secteur Aidé and home ownership - The secteur
aidé has been reformed in two ways with the particular aim of stimulating home ownership. Firstly, to
assist lower income groups purchase property, a new
type of loan - Prêts à l'Accession à la Propriété
(PAP) (Home ownership loans) have been introduced.
These are cheap loans reaching to a maximum of 70%
of the approved sale price of dwellings but available
only to those within certain income limits. The
loans are made available directly to a purchaser, or
to HLMs, SEMs and similar organisations building for
sale, and are distributed by the principal public
finance agents, the CFF and CPHLM. Supplementary
finance has to be found from the usual sources
including personal savings, the '1%' and bank
savings schemes such as PEL.
    Secondly, and of greater importance to the
strategy of expanding home ownership (Table 2.6), are

Table 2.6   Housing Tenure: Number and proportion of
            Principal residences by tenure 1962 and
            1978

	Owner Occupation	Rented	Other*	Total
1962	6.019 m	6.603	1.943	14.565
%	41.3	45.3	13.4	100
1978	8.694 m	8.190 m	1.756 m	18.640 m
%	46.7	43.9	9.4	100

*   Primarily "tied" dwellings

Source: INSEE; l'Enquête Nationale sur le Logement
          de 1978
          INSEE; Annuaire Statistique de la France
          1978

the Prêts Conventionnés (PC) (contractual loans)
which are directed principally towards middle income
groups seeking to purchase, though they are, in addition, available to landlords building to let. Banks
which conclude a contract with the CFF are enabled
to make loans at rates higher than that prevailing
for PAP, but at less than market levels, whilst the
state makes up, for the banks, the difference. The
loans for property meeting state specified standards
can meet up to 80% of approved costs but, unlike
PAP, are available to all regardless of income.
Supplementary finance comes from the usual sources.

Thus the state in this instance is relying principally on the banks and the individual borrower to
organise and finance construction, and plays itself,
only a regulatory and stimulatory role.

Personalised Housing Assistance - The major
innovation of the reform has been the introduction
of a system of housing aid direct to the householder - Aide Personalisée au Logement (APL) - a
concrete expression of the state's determination to
move away from the pre-existing policy of aide à la
pierre to a far more discriminatory policy based on
ability to pay. APL is intended to help those
renting or purchasing property under the new system
but who cannot afford the consequentially higher
rents and costs of loans. The aid is calculated and
made available on a similar basis to that of the
existing Allocation de Logement which, it is intended,
it will replace in the long run. The funds are
distributed by a new body, the Fonds National de
l'Habitat (FNAH) and is financed by contributions
from all organisations using PLA, and funds which
would have otherwise gone to the AL. The difference
between what is collected and what is distributed to
the beneficiaries is made up by the state. The
levels of APL are determined centrally and are
periodically increased.

Rehabilitation - One advance of the reformed
system has been to extend the availability of the
new loans (PAP, PLA) to the purchase of property
specifically for rehabilitation. To be eligible the
amount of works required has to be substantial and
certain minimum standards have to be met as regards
facilities and state of repair (Normes Minimales
d' abitabilité (NMH)[45] and certain floor space norms.

The role of ANAH, its operations and the financial assistance it can offer remain unchanged by the
1977 Act, but in addition new forms of grant aid
have been created specifically for rehabilitation.
They are the Aides à la Resorption de l'Habitat
Insalubre (Grants for improving slum housing); the
Primes à l'Amélioration de l'Habitat (PAH) (House
improvement grants), and PAHL, Primes à l'Amélioration de l'Habitat Locatif (Improvement grants for
rented dwellings).

In the case of PAHs and the slum housing grants
works have to meet the NMH standards and be carried
out within certain cost limits. In addition
applicants' incomes must be within certain ceilings,
as it is intended that the grants be directed towards
the lower income groups alone. This is, of course,
consistent with the restrictions on the availability

of PAP and PLA and the objectives of the 1977 Act.
The PAHL are available to landlords carrying out
similar work to the same NMH standards, and usually
in conjunction with ANAH operations and financial
aid. Income limits are placed upon tenants of
properties improved using the grants.

Conclusions and the Future

In May 1981 the French people voted decisively for
change and elected a Socialist President and
Government, and yet one of the paradoxes of the
present situation is that so much of pre-existing
housing policy remains unaltered. The underlying
liberal economic philosophy of the 1977 Housing Act
has been abandoned, and with it the intention of
greatly reducing the role of public expenditure and
social housing and yet the financial and administrative changes remain and indeed most of the principal
objectives of the Act: for instance raising rents
and interest charges on loans to market or near market levels, directing public finance towards householders according to income (APL), increasing home
ownership amongst the lower income groups and
rehabilitation of the existing housing stock.
          This picture of continuity is reinforced with
the passing of a new Rent Act in June 1982[46] and
which is progressively being brought into effect.
The purpose of this Act is to simplify the existing
and complex system of rent regulation (see Note 7)
and introduce something which gives adequate protection to tenants and yet is not as inflexible and as
unsatisfactory as the regime of the 1948 Rent Act.
The terms of the Act will apply to all new property,
or existing property subject to major renovation, in
all sectors, including HLM and the secteur libre. In
brief, contractual relationships will be established
between tenants and tenants organisations, and landlords and their organisations, which will determine
the conditions of tenancies - duration of tenancy,
rents, charges and obligations of both parties.
Rents will be at market levels based upon the annual
index of construction costs, and will be subject to
annual review by a new national consultative body
made up of representatives of landlords, tenants and
the state. Those tenants who cannot afford the
agreed rents will benefit either from APL or from a
new fund which is being established for the purpose.
          Great pains are taken in the introduction to
the legislation to state that the private sector has
a vital role to play in providing and managing rented

accommodation, and that investors will get a fair
return. A major aim of the Act is to try and ensure
that any increase in rents that is necessary is
carried out progressively and in orderly fashion.
The idea is to avoid the periodic and erratic
freezes and liberalisation of rents in the secteur
libre which successive governments have introduced,
using powers of decree, but which are very disruptive
to private plans of investment and construction. The
emphasis is upon co-operation and conciliation between the landlord and tenant, though one should note
that the legislation reserves powers to the state
itself to fix rent levels in times of economic
urgency or when the two sides cannot agree.

So in 1982 there exists a streamlined system of
finance, administration and control based upon clear
principles as to the allocation of housing costs between the private and public sectors and the individual. It is early yet to pass judgement on it and
how useful it will be in dealing with the current
and future housing problems. Certainly the history
of French housing over the last thirty years has
been in many respects a story of success but much
remains to be done, as we shall now see.

In 1978 (Tables 2.2 and 2.3) over 17% of the
principal residences were overcrowded and 1 in 5
dwellings had no internal bath or shower. In addition a significant number (2 million) of 1950s and
1960s dwellings principally in the grands ensembles
needed improvement. Certain groups suffer these
conditions more than others. For instance only 32%
of the old enjoy all the basic amenities as compared
to the national average of 56% whilst two out of
every three of the nation's large families (five or
more children) live in overcrowded conditions.
Immigrants either living in family units or singly,
live in the worst conditions by all criteria. Over
the years the housing constructed in successive
building programmes has been primarily designed for
the average family and there is a shortage of suitable dwellings for the handicapped and the aged
(particularly the latter as the proportion of the old
in the population is increasing) for single parent
families and other single person households, notably
for young mobile workers.[47]

The distribution of housing problems is spatial
as well as social. Three types of area can be identified where there are particular concentrations of
housing problems - the more remote rural areas, city
centres and the older housing areas of the cities,
and finally some of the suburban developments dating

from between the wars and the 1950s and 1960s. Of
the quarter of a million dwellings without running
water 170,000 are to be found in rural areas, and it
is in the remoter rural areas that one finds the
compounding problems of providing basic educational,
medical and transport services. City centre redevelopment caused considerable social dislocation,
but the abandonment of that policy in favour of
rehabilitation has brought its own problems. The
older inner areas have become very popular with
young affluent middle class, who move in and displace
the existing inhabitants. It is a development which
is most acutely displayed in Paris, but it is not
peculiar to it. Social polarisation is occurring in
most cities and towns.

The rate of population increase has fallen, but
household formation has not yet followed the down-
ward trend, and those born in the boom period of the
1960s are now entering the housing market. According
to the VIII Plan Study reports[48] an annual construction rate of 420-460,000 new dwellings per annum is
required throughout the VIII Plan period (1981-1985)
to meet demographic needs, replacement of lost stock,
the demand for second homes and the maintenance of
a pool of vacant stock. In addition, some 200,000
dwellings per annum need to be rehabilitated and
brought up to standard. If such a programme is to
be carried out then proper regard needs to be paid
to correct planning. The locational mistakes of the
1950s and 1960s must be avoided, and proper attention
paid both to the design of the dwellings, and to the
environment.

The Barre government operated the 1977 Housing
Act in the context of a programme of reductions in
public expenditure, but it was expected that such
cuts in housing would be more than offset by
increased private investment, both private and
institutional. An expansion in demand for PCs was
seen as the key to the success of government strategy, but in the event the anticipated growth did not
materialise. As inflation, interest rates and
unemployment increased, prospective purchasers saw
the burdens of house purchase as too daunting and
thus did not step forward. In addition, banks and
financial institutions looked not towards housing
but elsewhere for lucrative investment. The net
result of all this was a continuation in the decline
in output, a further decline in the construction
industry and increased unemployment amongst its
workforce.

In contrast to the previous government's approach, the Mauroy government of President Mitterrand is pursuing a policy of increased public expenditure in a number of fields including that of housing. Housing investment is seen as having a dual function of meeting demand and of acting as a stimulus for the economy as a whole, and has thus become a key element in the government's expansionist economic policy. The 1982 Housing budget will finance some 240,000 new dwellings (75,000 PLA, mainly for the HLM movement, the balance PAP) and provides for the improvement of 150,000 housing units, two thirds of them HLM. It is expected that an equivalent number of starts on new dwellings will be made in the same period by the private sector, and if all that is programmed is completed, then the annual output reckoned to be required by the VIII Plan report, would be reached. It is hoped that similar output can be kept up over the next few years, but clearly the success of the housing strategy will depend upon the overall success of the government's economic policy. The political will to pursue the course is there, but external economic forces will play an important part in determining how far it is maintained.

In the introduction it was suggested that two continuous threads in housing policy over the last thirty years or so can be distinguished. Namely to reduce the role of the state as the principal provider of dwellings and to increase the contribution of householders to housing costs. The new Socialist administration has certainly not broken the latter thread - householders will continue to pay more but with those in need receiving special means tested aid - whilst as for the former the present increase in state expenditure and activity may only be temporary. The state has been forced to adopt a more interventionist role, for arguably the economy and more particularly the housing market are unable to rise unaided from the present situation. Just as the state sought to rebuild a shattered economy after the Second World War (and succeeded), so the state, in the form of the Mitterrand administration, is trying to play a similar role today.

NOTES AND REFERENCES

1. J.W. House, France an Applied Geography, (Methuen, London, 1978). Includes a useful overview of the demographic, economic and urban development of France since 1945; C. Dyer, Population and

Society in Twentieth Century France, (Hodder and
Stoughton, London, 1978), pp.132-234; J. Beaujeu-
Garnier (ed), La France des Villes, (6 vols., La
Documentation Francaise, Paris, 1978-), vol.1,
Le Bassin Parisien, 1978. A series on post-war
urban growth and management since 1945.
    2. R.H. Duclaud-Williams, The Politics of
Housing in Britain and France, (Heinemann, London,
1978). Excellent study of the politics of housing
policy up until the mid-1970s; R. Butler and P.
Noisette, De la Cité Ouvrière au Grand Ensemble: La
Politique Capitaliste du Logement Social 1815-1975,
(Maspero, Paris, 1977). A Marxist analysis of
housing policy including most of the post-war period.
    3. National plans are drawn up by the
Commissariat Général du Plan at five yearly intervals
stating national priorities and investment programmes
in industry, commerce, housing and other areas. The
annual budget of the Ministry responsible for
housing makes financial allocations to the programme.
The present plan period for the VIIIth Plan is 1981-
1985.
    4. Dyer, Population and Society, pp.208-212;
House, France, pp.155-158.
    5. Duclaud-Williams, Politics of Housing, pp.
134-135; Le Logement des étrangers, Fiche No.10,
Ministère du Travail et de la Participation, 1979;
D. Weiller, "Le Logement des Travailleurs Immigrés",
Dossiers GRECOH, No.3, March 1974; Les Migrants,
Dossier 3, SONACOTRA, Paris, 1979; Le Logement des
Familles, Dossier 5, SONACOTRA, Paris, 1979; Annual
Reports of SONACOTRA 1975-1981. SONACOTRA - Société
Nationale de Construction de Logements pour les
Travailleurs. A public body constructing dwellings
for immigrants financed by French, Algerian and
other governments.
    6. 1948 Rent Act. Loi No.48-1360 of 1
September 1948.
    7. Secteur taxé. Fixed rent sector of the
rented housing market applying only to dwellings
covered by the 1948 Act. There are four other
rented sectors referred to later in the text.
Secteur reglémenté. Regulated rent sector - HLM
rented dwellings only. Secteur plafonné. Sector
with a rent ceiling and the tenants income does not
exceed a certain level. (Includes secteur aidé
dwellings (see later) where income limits imposed.)
Secteur conventionné. Introduced by 1977 Housing
Act and applies when landlord and state sign a contract determining rent levels. Secteur libre. Free
market sector uncontrolled except for rent freezes

and limitations applied from time to time. All these sectors are to be eventually phased out by provisions of the 1982 Rent Act.

8. Duclaud-Williams, Politics of Housing in Britain and France, pp.56-59.

9. Charges. Charges for communal services and facilities in blocks of dwellings.

10. Special state banks established for the purpose.

11. Sometimes known as SA.HLM - Sociétés anonymes or limited companies.

12. There are 92 Départements in France which are the principal administrative units of the state at local level, each with a chief administrator known as a Préfet or Prefect. (Now subject to reform)

13. Until the 1977 Housing Act, the HLM movement built dwellings of different standards and hence rents to meet the varying ability of tenants to pay. The top two categories are Immeubles à loyer normal (ILN) (Normal - theoretically market - rent dwellings), and Immeubles à loyer moyen (ILM) (medium rent dwellings), and they were specifically built for the better paid, civil servants, professional people. Space and amenity standards are superior to those of the ordinary grade. Habitation à loyer modéré ordinaire (HLMO) (ordinary moderate rent dwellings) which make up the great bulk of HLM dwellings. The bottom two categories are the HLM des programmes à loyer réduit (PLR) (HLM dwellings at reduced rent) built to slightly lower standards than HLMO and seen as a stepping stone to that category. The HLM du programme social de relogement (PSR) (HLM dwellings for those displaced by clearance, redevelopment or eviction) have low rents but the space and amenity standards are very basic indeed. The 1977 Act seeks better standards for all, (all these categories have been abolished) and higher rents are offset by a new universal system of means tested housing assistance.

14. Crédit Foncier de France (CFF) Principal state credit bank responsible for financing most public works. It was reorganised in 1950 to finance and expand the home ownership sector of the housing market.

15. Comités Interprofessionnels du Logement (CIL) Para-public bodies responsible for the collection and distribution of employers' compulsory contributions to housing construction.

16. Le Participation des Employeurs à l'Effort de Construction (employers participation in the construction effort) colloquially known as the '1%' or alternatively le Pâtronal.

17.   Frequent changes in the titles, structures and responsibilities of French ministries, including those responsible for housing and planning, can be confusing. In the early 1950s it was the Ministère de la Construction et du Logement (construction and housing) whilst at the time of writing it is the Ministère de l'Urbanisme et du Logement (planning and housing.

18.   E. Preteceille, La Production des Grands Ensembles, (Ecole Pratique des Hautes Etudes, Mouton, Paris, 1973).

19.   Plans d'Aménagement. Land use management plans.

20.   Employment distribution in France, 1946-1975. (percentages)

	1946	1962	1975
Primary (agriculture, fishing extractive industry)	34	22	10
Secondary (manufacturing, etc.)	31	37	38
Tertiary (services, transport, etc.)	35	41	52
	100	100	100

Source: C. Dyer, Population and Society, p.192; J.W. House, France, p.178.

21.   Growth Rates of Gross Domestic Product 1950-1980. (percentages)

	France	W.Germany	U.K.	U.S.A.
1950-60	4.4	7.6	2.6	3.2
1960-70	5.6	4.1	2.5	3.8
1970-80	3.7	2.8	1.8	2.8

Source: OECD National Accounts
          OECD Industrial Production

22.   Occupancy Rate - Definitions
Acute over occupation - two or more rooms less than the norm for the household
Moderate over occupation - one room less than the norm for the household
Normal occupation - number of rooms accords with the household norm
Under occupation - one or more rooms more than the norm for the household
The norm - 1 room for a couple including head of household; 1 room for a person over 18 years of age (not head of household), 1 room for two children under 7 years of age, 1 room for two children of same sex 7-18 years of age, 1 room for domestic staff, and 1 living room for any household.

23.   Cités de transit - temporary quarters; Cité familiale - family quarters. These dwellings are managed and financed by the Ministère de la Santé - Ministry of Health.

24.   The PSD were replaced in 1971 by a similar

loan, the Prêt Immobilier Conventionné (PIC) -
Contractual house loan.

25. D. Combes and E. Latapie, L'Intervention
des Groupes Financiers Francais dans l'Immobilier
(Centre de Sociologie Urbaine, Paris, 1973).

26. DATAR. Délégation à l'Aménagement du
Territoire et à l'Action Régionale. Body attached
to the Prime Minister's office with the task of
giving areal expression to the objectives of the
National Plans. Today its role and influence is
very much less than in its early years.

27. Loi d'Orientation Foncière - Land use
planning law.

28. J. de Lanversin, La Région et l'Aménagement du Territoire, 3rd Edn. (Libraries Techniques
(LITEC), Paris, 1980). Excellent summary, with
comment, of all elements of French region and urban
planning with particular reference to administrative,
legal and procedural aspects; Y.M. Darnan, J.P.
Forget, J.P. Morel, J. Vidal, Procédures et
Institutions d'Aménagement et d'Urbanisme (2 Vols.,
Ministère de l'Environment et du Cadre de Vie, 1978).
Details of planning procedures; C. Sorbets, Control
of Urban Development in France in J. Lagroye and V.
Wright (eds), Local Government in Britain and France
(George Allen & Unwin, London, 1979). Useful
article on planning practice.

29. I am grateful to Chris Flockton of the
University of Surrey for this insight.

30. House, France, pp.134-140; J.F.Langumier,
Peri-urbanisation et Aménagement du Territoire
(SESAME - DATAR, PARIS, 1979).

31. S. Nora, B. Eveno, l'Amélioration de
l'Habitat Ancien (Ministère du Finance et Ministère
de l'Equipment, Documentation Francaise, Paris,1975).

32. Commission d'Etude d'une Reforme du
Financement du Logement (Ministère du Finance,
Documentation Francaise, Paris, 1975).

33. Taxe additionale au droit de bail An additional tax of 3.5% is levied on all rent income of
properties constructed pre-1948.

34. ARIM - Housing rehabilitation associations;
CAL-PACT - Housing improvement centres (associations).

35. L'Enquête Nationale sur le Logement
(INSEE, 1978). One of a series of housing surveys
carried out by INSEE at 4-5 year intervals; Le Parc
de Logements et son Occupation en 1978, Supplement
to No.41 Informations d'Ile de France, (Prefecture
de Région Ile-de-France, 1980). Detailed analysis
of housing in Paris and the Ile-de-France.

36. A. Massot, J-C. Toubon, Les Marchands de

FRANCE

Biens, Metropolis Vol.4, No.33/34 (1978), p.21.
37. A-M. Romera, A. De la Chaise, Bilan de
l'Acquisition - Amélioration HLM en Ile-de-France
(IAURIF, PARIS, 1978).
38. Vivre dans les Grands Ensembles. Cahiers
d'IAURIF, vol.45, March 1977; Les Grands Ensembles.
Résumés d'études, Cahiers du GRECOH no.7, March,
1975; P. Lucain, Peut-on renover les Grands
Ensembles? Metropolis, Vol.3, No.23 (1976) pp.24-31.
39. La Réhabilitation des Grands Ensembles;
l'Example des Opérations Habitat et Vie Sociale,
(Architecture et Construction, Ministère de
l'Environnement et du Cadre de Vie, Paris, 1980).
40. Plans de Référence Circular No.77 - 42 of
3 March 1977; J.L. Destandeau, Les Plans de
Référence, Metropolis, vol.3, No.26/27 (1977),
pp.22-29.
41. OPAH Circular No.77 - 34 of 3 March 1977;
Circular No.77-83 of 1 June 1977.
42. Une Politique sociale de l'habitat,
(UNOPHLM, Paris, 1975). The Livre Blanc (white
paper) a discussion document for developing a
socially oriented housing policy.
43. F. Schaufelberger, Guide du Financement du
Logement Neuf ou Ancien, (Editions de Moniteur,
Paris, 1980). The best and most comprehensive guide
to housing finance including the 1977 legislation.
44. The PLA much modifies and improves the
existing acquisition-amélioration scheme of the HLM
movement.
45. Normes Minimales d'Habitabilité NMH
(Minimal living norms). For a dwelling to reach NMH
it must have internal running water, toilet and bath,
and central heating. Rooms must be of a certain
number, type and size, and be adequately ventilated
and the structure must be sound and in good repair.
46. The so-called 'Loi Quiller' after the
Ministère de l'Urbanisme et du Logement.
47. Rapport de la Commission Habitat et Cadre
de Vie: Préparation du Huitième Plan 1981-1985,
(Commissariat Général du Plan, La Documentation
Francaise, Paris, 1980) pp.29-38.
48. Rapport de la Commission Habitat et Cadre
de Vie, pp.93-95.

ANNOTATED LIST OF ACRONYMS USED IN CHAPTER 2

AL   Allocation familiale de logement
          Personalised housing assistance.
ANAH   Agence Nationale pour l'Amélioration de
          l'Habitat

51

	National housing improvements agency.
APL	Aide Personalisée au Logement
	Personalised housing aid.
ARIM	Associations de Restauration Immobilière
	Building restoration associations.
CAL-PACT	Centres d'Amélioration de Logement-Protection, Conservation, Transformation de l'Habitat
	Housing improvement associations.
CDC	Caisse des Dépôts et Consignations
	State bank for funding communes, Départements and other public bodies.
CEL	Compte d'Epargne Logement
	House savings account.
CFF	Crédit Foncier de France
	State bank for funding public works.
CIL	Comités Interprofessionnels du Logement
	Organisations responsible for collection and distribution of employers contributions (the 1%) to housing finance.
CPHLM	Caisse des Prêts aux Organismes d'HLM
	State bank (offshoot of the CDC) for the distribution of public funds to the HLM movement.
DATAR	Délégation a l'Aménagement du Territoire et à l'Action Régionale
	Body responsible for co-ordinating the territorial aspects of the National Plans.
FAU	Fonds d'Aménagement Urbaine
	Funds for urban planning and infrastructure provision.
FNAH	Fonds National d'Amélioration de l'Habitat
	National funds for improving (private rented) housing. Replaced in 1971 by ANAH.
FNAH	Fonds National de l'Habitat
	National housing funds to finance APL.
HLM	Habitations à Loyer Modéré
	Dwellings at moderate rent.
HLMO	Habitations à Loyer Modéré Ordinaire
	Ordinary standard HLM dwellings.
HVS	Group Interministérial Habitat et Vie Sociale
	Interministerial group for Housing and Social Life.
ILN	Immeubles à Loyer Normal
	Dwellings at normal (market) rents.
ILM	Immeubles à Loyer Moyen
	Dwellings at medium rents.
LOGECOES	Logements économiques et familieux
	Economical family houses.
	(also "600s" cheaper versions of Logecoes)

FRANCE

NMH	Norme Minimales d'Habitabilité Minimum housing standards.
OPAH	Opérations Programmées d'Amélioration de l'Habitat Programmed operations for the improvement of dwellings and their environment.
OPHLM	Offices Publics d'HLM Public (non-profit making) organisations of the HLM movement.
OREAM	Organisation d'Etudes d'Aménagement d'Aire Métropolitaine Metropolitain area planning study group.
LE PATRONAL or 1%	La Participation des Employeurs à l'Effort de Construction Contribution of employers to the finance of housing.
PAH	Primes à l'Amélioration de l'Habitat House improvement grants.
PAHL	Primes à l'Amélioration de l'Habitat Locatif Improvement grants for rented dwellings.
PAP	Prêts à l'Acession à la Propriété House Purchase loans.
PC	Prêts Conventionnés Contractual loans (for house purchase).
PEL	Plan d'Epargne Logement House savings scheme.
PLA	Prêts Locatif Aidés Subsidised loans for social dwellings to rent.
PLR	HLM des Programmes à Loyer Réduit HLM dwellings in special, low rental construction programmes.
PME	Programmes de Modernisation et d'Equipment Programmes of public infrastructure investment and modernisation.
POS	Plan d'Occupation des Sols Local land use plan.
PSD	Prêts Spéciaux Différés Special differed loans.
PSI	Prêts Spéciaux Immédiates Special immediate loans.
PSR	HLM du Programme Social de Relogement HLM dwellings in rehousing programmes.
PUD	Plans d'Urbanisme de Détail Detailed (local) urban plans. (Replaced by POS)
SAHLM	Sociétés Anonymes d'HLM Limited companies of the HLM movement.
SCET	Société Centrale d'Equipment du Territoire State development and construction company.
SCIC	Société Civile Immobilière de la Caisse

	des Dépôts
	State development company.
SDAU	Schéma Directeur d'Aménagement et d'Urbanisme
	Long term land use structure plan.
SEM	Société d'Economie Mixte
	Joint private and public companies.
UNOFHLM	Union Nationale des Fédérations d'Organismes d'HLM
	National union of federations of HLM organisations.
ZUP	Zone à Urbanisé par Priorité
	Priority urbanisation zone (replaced by ZAC)
ZAC	Zone d'Aménagement Concerté
	Co-ordinated planning and infrastructure investment zone.

3. WEST GERMANY

by Declan Kennedy

The amazing re-building programme which was implemented after the Second World War in West Germany has
been seen as a model for many other countries in
Europe. This achievement has become somewhat of a
myth and has influenced opinions and politcal decisions in the Federal Republic of Germany itself, long
after discerning people had realised that this
country was heading towards a new housing crisis.
Now, in the beginning of the eighties, forty years
after the war, the poor state of housing in West
German cities is being recognised by all political
parties as an outcome not only of the general economic recession, but also of past housing policies.[1]

The Post-War Situation
The provision of housing immediately after World War
II faced the most difficult situation. About one
third of the housing stock in Germany was destroyed.
Large numbers of refugees from the East placed an
additional load on the already overcrowded western
zone (later to become the Federal Republic). The
whole specialized building trade had broken down.
There were no materials, no money, no skilled labour
and the ownership of houses and land was all too
often unclear.
        The congested conditions in the remaining
housing stock were gradually alleviated as the
building trade was taken over by the legendary
Truemmerfrauen (rubble women) who, more or less,
created the conditions for a re-building process
through their unsalaried work. Without hesitation
action was taken to eleviate the worst conditions:
roof repairs, temporary roofs, plastering up bullet
holes and boarding up the badly damaged windows.
Getting more organised, they began to heap the rubble

456WEST GERMANY

from the bombed buildings and later made building
blocks out of it.

Banks were reintroduced in 1949, but still only
a few loans were available on a short-term basis.
However the building activity sector began to show
signs of recovery. Private house owners with more
than one dwelling began to use their rare wealth.

In 1949, the newly organised 'Trust' system in
the housing sector was established and in 1950 the
first Housing Act was passed. As a result, the
number of newly built dwellings exceeded the number
of renovated dwellings for the first time in 1952.
In 1953, it rose to 73% in West Germany. Government
policy was twofold; firstly to support private sector
house building by tax incentives, and secondly to
provide housing for lower income groups through
'social' housing loans and subsidies. Of the 15
million housing units completed between 1949 and
1978, 6.5 million were in the 'social' housing categories.

Social Housing. The term 'social housing' is the
equivalent to 'public housing' (USA) and to 'council
housing' (GB) in as much as the goal was originally
to supply cheap housing for the poorer sections of
the population. In 1950, the population of the
Federal Republic amounted to 47 million people, consisting of 15.3 million households. These families
found only 9.5 million dwellings available - a
deficit of more than 6 million dwellings (Housing
Census 1950). Roughly 45% of the families were sub-
tenants, that is, more than one third of the households had no flat or house of their own. The
programme of social housing was passed in 1950,
introducing rent control, public allocation procedures, and tenants' rights both in privately
financed and publicly supported housing units. This
policy aimed at supplying reasonably priced dwellings
for all population groups. As a result, up to
300,000 social housing units per year (1950-59) were
built by private investors with public grants. But
still the need for housing was not being satisfactorily met. This need was not only a result of the
bomb damage, but also of the gap in building activity, during and immediately after the war, of almost
ten years (1939-1949).

New incentives were provided to private investment also. Thus the development of all new housing
averaged from 500,000 to 600,000 dwellings per annum
from 1950 to 1974.[2] This 'housing miracle' was part

56

of the 'economic miracle'. Beside the positive aspects, it is seen also as the source of many problems of today, the worst being speculation and the concentration of housing capital in the hands of a few. Considering the amount of tax monies that went into social housing, one might presume that most dwellings would be publicly owned, but this is not so. Social housing is predominantly privately owned. The proportion of housing directly built and owned by the government is still very small and, indeed, has decreased from 5% to just above 3% over the last 15 years. Social housing policy revolved around publicly subsidized loans to private investors who, in receiving these benefits, bind themselves to at least a 15 year social rent control, and to a system of allocation of the dwellings by state or local government agencies. The investors also subordinate their designs to minimal standards which, of course, (like the Parker Morris standards) became maximal norms. (Figure 3.1)

Figure 3.1   1950s Housing in Berlin-Kreuzberg.

The Housing Acts. Under the first Housing Act (1950),
financial support to house builders consisted of
grants and cheap or no-interest loans. In the early
1950s, 70% of all dwellings were financed in this
way. The ruling conservative government at that time
saw this as a temporary measure in a situation where
private capital was unable to get sufficient funds
through the usual credit systems.

The second Housing Act came in 1956. A new
direction in the financial programmes for social
housing was developed. Loans were not directly state
monies, but from the normal capital markets. The
government took on the guarantees for the investors
towards the banks. Grants were at first available to
counteract high interest rates, and to offset part of
the annual mortgage payments. But after 1972 only
the investment repayments were subsidised - mainly
to assure that rents remained reasonably low.

Despite these early changes in the original
supportive system in the fifties, a considerable
amount of public investment went into the provision
of housing. The policy was aimed at supporting a
market-oriented housing sector but a quantitative
goal was not defined, the underlying assumption being
that the market would regulate itself. Therefore,
the conditions attached to public funds were merely
regulative regarding size, accommodation and fittings
of the housing unit or, in the case of owner-
occupiers or housing associations, the amount of the
down-payment necessary.

Housing in a Period of Abundance

All through the 1960s and into the 1970s, the
housing market boomed. In the meantime, household
numbers had risen to 21.6 million (1966/67) and
housing units to 19.6 million. The deficit had
been reduced, but was still at 2 million units. Of
the 19.6 million dwellings, 12.6 were rental properties which had been built under very different conditions at different times: older flats from the
pre-war period, social housing with capital subsidies, social housing with interest subsidies,
unsubsidised free-market high-rent dwellings and, to
make things more complicated, there were different
kinds of owners in each category, with different
profit allowances and expectations. This was a
difficult point of departture for any policy aiming
at the preservation of the original goal: to provide
all sectors of society with reasonably priced
dwellings.

In many cases tenants (the largest part of the population) were left at the mercy of private land-lords after the restrictions had been lifted. Other examples showed that social housing units were mis-allocated and occupied by the affluent rather than those parts of the population most in need. A third factor which began to show clearly the limits of the 'free market mechanism' was the increasing destruc-tion of the city fabric.

Alexander Mitscherlich in his famous book Die Unwirtlichkeit unserer Städte (The unhospitability of our cities)3 criticised the programmes and forms of urban planning prevalent at that time, and their irrational characteristics. The author argued that without a sufficient grasp of social and psychologi-cal conditions, and without a re-organisation of ownership of property and land, urban planning would continue to destroy rather than improve cities. How-ever, the bombed out cities continued to be re-knitted along the pattern of neatly packaged land-uses - industrial, residential, recreational, insti-tutional, traffic etc. Monofunctional downtowns and monotonous suburbs and production areas were the result, and the number of square kilometers asphalted for private traffic doubled and quadrupled.

Mitscherlich's book does not strive to attack any particular culprit but attacks the whole postwar generation in respect to its lack of comprehension of the opportunity for effective change. The book, along with Jane Jacobs' The Death and Life of Great American Cities4 had an effect on planners and planning concepts. Since then, there has been a realisation that it was necessary to co-ordinate housing and urban development policies.

The Social Democrats, when they came into power in 1969, introduced new urban renewal and regional programmes. Their urban planning 'offensive', as they termed it at the beginning of the 1970s, included special programmes to meet the growing dis-satisfaction with urban development among large sections of the urban population. Municipal, regional and state development planning agencies were set up both within the local and the state levels of administration. This led to an enormous expansion of city bureaucracies. Urban development teams in many cities were given special powers through a direct link in the decision-making process with the mayor. New Federal laws were intended to co-ordinate municipal plans. In contrast to the original goal of creating strong local powers in a federal system, municipalities now had to apply for planning approval from regional, sometimes state, authorities. This led to more control from above. The Federal Building Act (1960) and the Federal Regional Planning Act (1965), passed under a conservative government, had respected the planning autonomy of the municipal councils. Now it was quite the contrary. The series of Acts that followed attempted to regulate and 'assist' urban development from above.

Following the passing of these Acts (which included the 1971 Urban Renewl Act), there was a considerable increase in the allocation of funds for infrastructure and environmental improvement. This led to numerous planning constraints which wiped out almost all possibilities of user participation in urban development, especially in housing, just at a time when this was being broadly advocated.[5]

Most planners felt that, at least, a rational approach to the improvement of the environment had been achieved; at last they had more statutory powers. They overlooked, however, that their power to determine the quality and the quantity of housing, to further new housing starts or to renovate the existing stock was still quite limited. The provision of housing and stimulation of building activities has always been an instrument for steering economic trends or, more precisely, for counteracting a general economic slump.

Each Federal Act passed contributed to the trend towards centralisation. Municipalities now had to submit almost every endeavour for approval by a higher power. With the exception of education, the Federal concept itself - which had been formulated by the three Western Powers in the 'Basis Law' (constitution) for West Germany after World War II - was being undermined. Federal Acts no longer provided a framework in which the state (Länder) and local parliaments made their decisions, but rather stipulated the details of how, when and why particular tasks had to be done. The vehicle for control was the tightly interrelated financing and subsidy systems. It can be said that the experiment of a federal state in Germany has been to some extent smothered by the planning and housing regulatory acts. This development was partly an answer to some blatant mistakes that had occurred at the municipal level, where small local governments had been subject to 'free market forces' at a time of fast economic growth.

In retrospect, the core of the problem was not at which level decisions were being made, but rather

the speed of implementation. The period of abundance during the 60s and 70s provided an opportunity
for both large scale production as well as large
scale mistakes. Certainly, more centralisation was
removing those responsible even further away from
the consequences of their mistakes. No wonder protests against the way in which housing was built
mounted, as people were shifted, infrastructure was
neglected and old areas were torn down. Resistance
against urban renewal methods became the order of
the day. Citizen action groups sprang up, especially
where urban clearance was proposed; apart from court
cases, demonstrations, go-ins and sit-ins, new more
radical forms of protest like squatting and street
fights were employed for environmental causes.[6]

Physical Design. The emphasis and layout of cities
during the post-war rebuilding period changed
several times. Reconstruction, and repairing the
existing stock, was largely concentrated within
existing city boundaries. To a large extent even
the pre-war uses were re-established; soon, however,
the prospering commercial and administrative uses
began to take over inner city housing areas and the
idea of the central business district was born.[7]
Formerly well-defined city districts changed not
only their character but also their boundary lines.
Residents were pushed out and with the migration of
the former residents and the demolition of the
buildings the identity of the place was lost.
     The wealthier parts of the population moved
into the newly built heavily subsidised, but still
expensive, suburban areas. The poorer part of the
population settled in the remaining older and slowly
deteriorating parts of the cities. Inexpensive
housing diminished and where it remained, slum
tendencies set in. This trend continued practically
until the end of the 70s and in its course destroyed
more urban fabric and historic areas than World War
II.
     Ironically the example exerting the strongest
influence on this trend originally aimed at demonstrating something quite different. The 1957 Berlin
Interbau in Berlin-West attempted to integrate the
restructuring of an older city area (the Hansa
Quarter) with new buildings, whilst at the same time
preserving a large open inner city park. 51 architects from 30 countries designed and built 45
buildings housing 8,000 people. Aalto, le Corbusier,
Niemayer, Vago (to name but a few) created 70 types

of model apartments as examples of modern living in
a large urban residential area. The Berlin planning
administration saw the Interbau as a contribution to
better environmental conditions in the inner city
area. However, a site like the Tiergarten next to a
very large and historic urban part seldom came up
again. The relationship of housing to immediate
recreational surroundings was unique.

As most other West German cities were lacking
similar sized inner city sites, the idea behind the
Hansa Quarter was subsequently transferred to peripheral locations. All too often, the park landscape
which could have been created in the new suburban
designs was confined to an arrangement of the regulatory spaces between the buildings, required by law
for day-lighting and sun-lighting purposes. The
versatility of design which had come about in the
Hansa Quarter, through the fact that many architects
had given their best (within the restrictions of
Federal German planning and building laws), was
unfortunately lacking in its successors. The result
is the one-off idea, multiplied hundreds of times,
maybe technically of high quality but environmentally
and aesthetically poor, monotonous, malfunctional
and badly connected to the rest of the city structure.

The largest and most well-known examples of
this type of design have been implemented in Berlin:
Gropiusstadt (in the south) and Maerkisches Viertel
(in the north); in Hamburg, there are Steilshoop
and Billwerder-Allermoehe; in Darmstadt: Neu-
Kranichstein; in Wolfsburg: Detmerode; and in
Munich: Fuerstenried and Perlach, to mention but a
few. Housing between 15,000 to 50,000 inhabitants
each, these were designed at the beginning of the
1960s and finished ten to fifteen years later.

Although the planners and architects believed
that they were treading new paths in design, the
concepts were revised so much in the process of
implementation, because of economic considerations
and building restrictions, that little of the
positive aspects of the Interbau model remained.
Both in Berlin (Maerkisches Viertel) and Darmstadt
(Neu-Kranichstein) for instance, the overall height
of the buildings was increased for these reasons
although the density in the original design was at
the maximum acceptable limit. The profits rose
accordingly, and by the time the residents arrived
the decision had become irreversible. In addition,
pre-fabrication, or even traditional building techniques, coupled with static plans of housing units,

Figure 3.2 <u>Block of flats in Berlin Kreuzberg.</u>

were difficult to change. While professional
journals spoke of 'interesting solutions' or of 'one
of the strongest expressions of post-war planning',
residents soon considered these grand-scale housing
estates as being inhuman, isolating, frightening,
unecological and unhealthy. Vandalism and crime
rates prove that these areas are not only unsocial
but also uneconomical in the long run. Not only in
West Germany did this mass housing catastrophe

happen. It seems as if wherever housing capital amassed, planners and architects were reduced to draughtsmen of the latest fashionable trend with a slide rule and a sociological flair.

The power of the economic 'free market forces' during this time of rapid expansion and building grants, and the equation of large scale solutions with 'progress', prevented socially oriented architects to implement their concepts. Although lip service was paid to conservation and rehabilitation, to citizen participation and grass roots involvement in the 1960s and 1970s, their wider acceptance and application set in only with the economic recession in the wake of the energy crises in the 1970s.

Heading Towards Austerity

The first economic recession in 1966/67 made it clear that growth was not guaranteed forever. In 1969, the Social Democratic Party (SPD) came into power together with the Liberals (FDP), and this new coalition, which remained in power until 1982, emphasised urban issues in its housing policy. Because it inherited the imbalance between supply and demand for dwellings from its predecessors, the new coalition did not change the housing programme which generally favoured the ownership of one-family houses (Table 3.1).

Table 3.1 Percentage of Dwellings built as One-Family Houses in Different European countries

	65	71	75
Great Britain	72.0	73.3	71.9
Denmark	69.2	58.9	73.4
Netherlands	61.0	73.0	76.0
Fed. Rep. of Germany	47.9	43.1	48.2
Sweden	28.5	31.3	63.6
France	26.9	38.1	46.0

Source: Annual Bulletins for Housing and Building Statistics for Europe (UN, Economic Commission for Europe, Geneva).

During the 1960s the proportion of owner-occupiers increased rapidly and continued into the 1970s. Whereas 26% of the population lived in their own houses in 1948, already the figure had risen to 33% in 1960, 39% in 1970 and in 1980 was estimated at 48%. However, as these figures include second homes and week-end houses of people in the higher income bracket, it is estimated that far more than half of the population (59%) still live in rental property. But, helped by special grants and tax benefits, the proportion of workers owning their homes rose from below 20% to over 40% between 1957 and 1978.[8] The proportion of self-employed owner occupiers, in comparison, remained at a constant of approximately 64% (Table 3.2).

Table 3.2   Households in owner-occupied Dwellings, according to Social Status of Head of Household, 1957-78.

				1978 %
Self-employed	64.6	66.8	66.8	63.6
Civil Servants	19.3	22.3	28.8	43.0
Employees	19.3	22.3	28.8	39.8
Workers	19.3	27.2	37.6	44.3
Without Employment or retired	25.6	28.1	30.3	34.5

Source: Wolfgang Glatzer, Wohungsversorgung im Wohlfahrtsstaat, (Frankfurt/New York, 1980) p.248.

While these results at first glance seem to suggest a move towards more equality between the different social strata it excludes a realistic picture of the price paid by different income groups for their home in comparison to the available income. This was estimated to vary between 24% and 40%, usually in inverse relationship to people's income, in 1979. In addition, these statistics do not take into account the quality of spaces, materials and location and, even more important, the age at which the average German family is able to afford its own home. Ironically this happens only when the children are about to leave the house; 40% of the people are 40-60 years when they become owner occupiers. Another 40% are between 30-40, and only 12% manage to occupy their own house before the age of 30.[9]

The policy of outlying municipalities to release large areas for new 'mixed' (i.e. flats and houses) or 'one-family' housing resulted in an in-

equality of housing supply within and between the
different regions of the Federal Republic of Germany.
The already rampant disparities between the inner
cities and outskirts were then augmented further by
the increasing supply of owner-occupied housing in
the countryside for the wealthier city commuters. In
a way, it can be said that urban sprawl is being
furthered, financially, by the same government that
has been concerned about how the open countryside is
being devoured and how inner cities are facing an
economic crisis. Of course, these decisions also
call for subsequent investment in traffic and infrastructure, in energy supply, and social networks.
Shopping facilities move from the inner city to outlying shopping areas, and a chain reaction is set up.
While wealthier city commuters may be able to afford
more time and money for their journey to work, the
poorer families feel the burden more severely.
Women, especially, are likely to feel isolated,
typically being left with small children, and without
car, in a satellite housing estate. At the same
time, the real cost of housing spiralled dramatically
through the sixties and seventies (Table 3.3), and

Table 3.3   Cost Index for Housing in the Federal
            Republic of Germany 1962-82 based on the
            DM at its 1950 value; adjusted to negate
            inflation.

(1950=100), Month=December	
1962	182.6
1964	201.1
1966	216.3
1968	220.7
1970	271.7
1972	320.1
1974	368.6
1976	390.4
1978	434.6
1980	534.4
1982	573.1

Source: Deutsches Architektenblatt, (Year 14, No.12,
          Forum-Verlag GmbH, Stuttgart, 1982).

the so-called 'social housing' has now become a
privilege of the middle class.

Rehabilitation. From the early 70s onwards, the
growing citizen's protest had an increased effect as
government policy began to emphasise modernisation
(comprehensive rehabilitation) and renewal, rather
than bulldozer clearance. However, the end result
was often similar as renewal agencies had to
rehabilitate according to standards which were set
up for new social housing. In most cases ground
floor plans of older tenement buildings had to adhere
to the standards of orientation and day-lighting of
new flats. Bathrooms had to be tiled, kitchens had
to be built in, balconies and elevators had to be
added, new piping and wiring and roofing were
installed, sometimes regardless of whether these
items had been built in by the tenants. The rents
soared, often doubling or tripling overnight.

Comprehensive rehabilitation produced - as did
urban clearance - a dispossession and displacement
of the original residents, especially of the low
income tenants. The rehabilitation movement had its
first peak in the European Conservation Year of
1975, when a rehabilitation competition between
major German cities was staged. In most cases,
comprehensive rehabilitation aimed at recreating the
historic scale or facade of old building. But in a
few exceptional examples, there was a conscious
attempt at planning with the inhabitants, and at
organising a change process in which the original
tenants remained in their social milieu.

Two of the prize winning schemes from Wiesbaden
and Berlin-Charlottenburg (Figure 3.3) then became
models for a third approach to the treatment of
decaying urban areas (after 'urban clearance' and
'comprehensive rehabilitation') - 'minimal maintenance and rehabilitation'. This approach, presently
being pursued in preparation for the 1984/87 International Building Exhibition in Berlin-Kreuzberg,
aims at alleviating only the worst conditions in the
run down housing stock in order to allow everybody
to remain in the area. Instead of applying new
building norms to old houses, only standards of
safety and health are rigidly adhered to. In addition, tenants and small property owners are given
advice and assistance in ways and means to help
themselves.[10]

This approach is keeping down rents, and preserving the identity of the Berlin city centre.
Although the goals of minimal standard rehabilitation
were clearly defined in 1979, it took the preparatory
group of the International Building Exhibition Team
three years to secure the possibility of their

Figure 3.3   Minimal Maintenance and Rehabilitation,
             Berlin-Charlottenburg, 1975.

implementation against the interests of the landlords
(in many cases non-profit housing associations partly
or totally owned by the City of Berlin). After many
deliberations and public debates, it has become clear
that the reason for the possible implementation of
this policy in Berlin is that the city is running
out of cheap housing areas for low income families
and foreigners. In other German cities, for
instance Stuttgart or Munich, low income and foreign
families move out to the surrounding villages, or
live in overcrowded conditions (where landlords will
allow this to happen), usually at an exorbitant price
in the city itself.

The Present Situation
The present housing situation in Germany is characterised by high building costs, low investment risks,
a stagnating market and an ever increasing deficit
in low cost accommodation. Scandals and embellish-
ment in the highest ranks of the largest social
housing association Neue Heimat have sensitised the
public to the danger which arises where vast amounts
of property are accumulated and administered by a
few.
    It has been estimated that the cost to the
government of incentives and subsidies for new house
building since 1978 exceeds the total promotion and
construction costs, and yet the government has no
part in their ownership. These subsidies include
capital loans, tax rebates, low interest arrangements
and rent subsidies and allowances (Table 3.4). It
has been suggested that it would be cheaper for the
government to supply the low income recipients
directly with no-cost housing than to go through the
rigmarole of all the different systems of housing
finance and tax reliefs.[11]
    Government housing policy is based on providing
incentives to individual home owners through subsidies and tax rebates, and the following summary
provides an overview of the major programmes and
their effects. Every wage-earner who saves a
certain minimum per year in his building savings
account can benefit from tax reliefs or can get a
premium (since 1969). The premium has been claimed
mainly by small wage-earners who accept a government
grant with little paperwork. This sum does not only
add to their capital; it allows the person to get
low-interest credit when the process of building
starts. As wages and savings increased, the total
amount of savings earmarked for building accumulated,

Table 3.4   The Distribution of Housing Subsidies
from the Federal, State (<u>Laender</u>) and
Local Levels in the various support categories, 1978.

Expenditure for	in Bill. DM	in Bill. $	in %
Social Housing Subsidies	4.70	2.35	23.4
Income Tax Rebates (§7b Income Tax Act)	4.76	2.38	23.7
Income Tax Rebates (§7.5 1 ITA + §82 Income Regulations)	0.90	0.45	4.5
Land Acquisition Tax Rebates	2.30	1.15	11.5
Annual Land Tax Rebates	0.89	0.44	4.4
Rehabilitation Programme + Energy Savings Grants	0.79	0.39	4.0
Urban Renwal Act	1.09	0.55	5.4
Total	15.43	7.72	76.9
Buildings Savings Premiums + Tax Savings	2.69	1.35	13.4
Rent Allowances	1.95	0.98	9.7
Grand Total	20.87	10.44	100.0

Source: Bundesbauministerium (Federal Ministry of
Building).   The table includes the cash
value of the subsidies in 1978 and the subsidies for which legal guarantees were
given in 1978. $ translations on the basis:
1$=DM2.-approx. the mean value of 1978. 1
Billion=1 Milliard, i.e. a thousand million.

causing a peak in building activity in the mid-70s.
With the general cut-backs in 1980, the premium was
reduced from 18% to 14%.   The general readiness to
save was dampened accordingly, and new building has
more or less stopped.
     Over and above the yearly savings premium
every home-owner can take advantage of tax reliefs
once the building is started or bought.   At present,
this second form of subsidy costs the government
more than twice the first.   Known as '7b', this part
of the legislation allows a tax deduction over eight
years, covering up to 40% of the building costs of a
home (house or flat).   If owner-occupiers own more
space than they need themselves, even a one-room
flat, a further deducation on this investment is
possible, because this is seen as a contribution to
the general provision of housing.

A group, rather than individual, endeavour is the Bauherrenmodell - in order to build a block of flats or houses small investors form a building society. The building costs, over and above the so-called representational and advertsing costs, can be declared as tax-deductable under company law. This third category is interesting for wealthy people who pay more than 48% in taxes. It is usually taken advantage of by people who invest in a flat for leasing or letting purposes. It combines both a reasonably high return in the invested money with massive tax savings. It is seen by many as a new system of government sponsored speculation.

This trend has wide-ranging social and political repercussions. Its speculative aspect has commanded such widespread practice that we can now speak of a shift from federally sponsored social housing towards the federal support of private property ownership in the hands of the wealthy, half of the tax benefits going to the upper third of the income scale, only 20% going to the lowest third.

New Policies for the 1980s. In the light of what has been said above, tax reliefs and subsidies to high income recipients must be brought down to a level which is socially and economically feasible. Then, housing for the lower and middle classes has to be re-organised along the lines of self-help and co-operative building societies, in order to pull down costs and to re-establish a more direct responsibility of residents for their homes. Proposals for decentralising the large scale housing associations on a regional basis aim in a similar direction. Since this in quantitative terms would be the most significant change it will be discussed in more detail below.

Housing for the poorest section of the population needs a completely new orientation. Government housing policy and housing programmes have to make sure that this area is not subject to speculation but rather part of government infrastructural planning. The validity of a policy to radically reform and restructure the German Federal 'social' housing system in the direction of council-owned or municipalised housing can be further argued from the standpoint that the existing forms of municipalised housing in other West European countries arose out of similar 'crisis' development.[12] The rise in building costs, in financing costs, in interest rates were determinants which led to unacceptable rents.

A large part of this type of housing provision will probably remain in the hands of the housing associations, but there is currently much discussion about reorganising present housing associations into new housing co-operative societies. It is argued[13] that housing associations in the 'public benefit' or 'trust' categories should be phased out in their present form, and dwellings currently under their management would be pooled with other government owned housing and handed over to newly formed co-operatives. These would be much smaller organisations and would be area based, having responsibility for public housing, particularly the older stock, in specific neighbourhoods. Some associations would remain, under the control of local councils, to manage newer stock, again on a local area basis, and new regional housing associations would carry out new building and the rehabilitation of older buildings. After the building operations are finished, the dwellings would be handed over immediately to the co-operative society of the respective tenant members. This would mean that the housing associations would be seen more as a service company than as an owner (as is presently the case). No housing associations should control more than 2,000 units in order to avoid new tendencies towards concentration.

Concluding Remarks

This chapter concentrates on housing policy in the Federal Republic of Germany, its background, its financing, its laws and some of its implications. It tries to show how an originally socially oriented programme, harnessing private initiative with public support, can change into a speculative process over the years. It demonstrates how, within a relatively well-to-do society, this process destroys the human aspects, thus failing to create a dignified living environment for everyone. Without allowing people to participate in the planning process, especially in those areas which affect them most, housing policy is easily turned into an instrument of profit making, ignoring the interests of the individual.

It is not possible to cover all the aspects which contributed to this development. Hardly anything has been mentioned about aesthetics or the design of housing. The immediate surroundings, ancillary facilities and the urban aspects have only been touched upon. Nor does it cover the movement

which demands a new integration of the man-made and
natural environment.
    At the core of the present housing crisis
quantitative and qualitative demands converge.
People in urban areas want more indoor space and
more open space. They want greener cities and less
energy-consuming homes. They want better access to
their work, social services and shopping facilities.
However, they don't expect these changes to happen
through political action and bureaucratic channels
any more. Self-help is becoming a viable answer not
only for dissatisfied resident groups but also for
some political decision-makers. The politicians'
insight into the value of grass-roots democracy is
helped by an ever deepening hole in the public purse.
    These qualitative changes which are appearing
in both urban and rural settlements may assist in
counteracting the former one-sided emphasis on
quantity and lack of service infrastructure in the
housing sector. By establishing their own facilities for children and elderly citizens, for women
and for foreigners, by planting trees, they add
colour and local character and begin to create an
identity which is severely lacking in the monotonous
post-war housing areas.
    It is almost impossible to make up for the lost
chance in rebuilding residential areas in Germany
after the war. The environmental crisis, the lack
of jobs and reduction in public spending may,
finally, lead to a more appropriate model of
housing provision, based on small steps, self-help,
self-reliance and the re-integration of nature and
social functions.

NOTES AND REFERENCES

    1.   Renate Petzinger & Marlo Riege, Die neue
Wohnungsnot, (VSA-Verlag, Hamburg, 1981).
    2.   Bundesbaublatt No.7, (Statistisches
Bundesamt, Wiesbaden, 1978).
    3.   Alexander Mitscherlich, Die Unwirtlichkeit
unserer Staedte, (edition suhrkamp 123, Frankfurt
am Main, 1965).
    4.   Jane Jacobs, The Death and Life of Great
American Cities, (Jonathan Cape, London, 1962).
    5.   Declan & Margrit Kennedy (eds.), The Inner
City, Architects' Year Book XIV, (Paul Elek,
London, 1974).
    6.   Heinz Grossmann (ed.) Buergerinitiativen,
(Fischer Buecherei, Frankfurt am Main, 1971) and
Roland Guenter & Rolf Hasse, Handbuch fuer

Buergerinitiativen, (VSA-Verlag, Berlin, 1976).
    7.   Margrit & Declan Kennedy, 'The regeneration
of Regensburg' in David Lewis (ed.) The Growth of
Cities, Architects' Year Book XIII, (Elek Books,
London, 1971), pp.150-171.
    8.   Wolfgang Glatzer, Wohnungsversorgung in
Wohlfahrtsstaat, (edition, suhrkamp, Frankfurt am
Main, 1980), p.248.
    9.   'Finanzierungsverfahren von Bausparen' in
Der langfristige Kredit, No.6, (1980), p.176.
    10.   Uli Hellweg (ed.), Selbsthilfe im Altbau,
(Internationale Bauaustellung GmbH & Compress-Verlag,
Berlin, 1982).
    11.   Franzika Eichstaedt-Bohlig, 'Die
Mietpreisbindung und die subventionierte
Wohnungswirtschaft' in Arch. +, No.54, (Klenkes
GmbH, Aachen, 1980).
    12.   Stefan Kraetke, Kommunalisierter
Wohnungsbau als Infrastrukturmassnahme, (Verlag
Peter Lang, Frankfurt am Main, 1981).
    13.   Peter Soetje, 'Zur Situation der
Staedtischen Wohnungsgesellschaften', working paper
for an SPD Conference on the reform of housing
associations in the FRG, unpublished, Berlin 1982.

Photographs reproduced courtesy of the Neue Heimat
Housing Association, Berlin & Hamburg, and the
Senator for Building and Housing, Berlin West.

4. GREAT BRITAIN*

by Roger Smith

Introduction

There is a well established dogma found within the
British Conservative Party that the working of the
free market is the most efficient method of creating
and distributing wealth.[1] Accordingly the most
effective way of providing housing is to leave it to
the market. A free market philosophy does not necessarily provide all with the goods and services they
need at any moment in time. Rather, it is justified
on the grounds that, overall, the free market can
create and distribute wealth more efficiently than
state agencies. The justification of state involvement comes only at that point when it becomes necessary to assist the casualties of the free market.[2]
Thus the state's concern with housing is limited to
providing the minimum necessary assistance to those
incapable, for one reason or another, of meeting the
exigences of the market. As far as housing is concerned, exponents of the market view would argue
that this is the most socially desirable of housing
policy options because, being the most efficient way
of providing housing, it provides the maximum number
of families with the highest quality housing they
can afford.[3]

* To an extent this is a misleading title. In many
areas of housing Scotland has had separate legislation which in broad principle generally mirrors
English legislation but differs in detail. Space
prevents this from being taken into account here.
However, Glasgow makes a useful case study of the
relationship between housing and urban change. This
Scottish example has, therefore, been included and
it is this which broadens the essay into a British,
rather than simply an English, study.

75

A contrary dogma is to be found within the British Labour Party.[4] The starting point here is that all citizens have a right to decent housing, irrespective of the individual's ability to pay. The role of the state is thus to obtain sufficient resources to enable it to provide the necessary number of dwellings to meet the nation's housing needs. Within this philosophy housing provision becomes a part of the welfare state. Just as the state becomes the major supplier of health care, so the state becomes the dominant supplier and manager of housing.[5]

Since the end of the Second World War the control of central government has alternated between the Conservative and Labour Parties (the Labour Party has won six general elections and the Conservative five). As far as housing policy is concerned attempts can be observed to implement these two extremes of policy. But no party in power, at least since 1945 (apart perhaps for the present Government), has been able to sustain a partisan housing policy for long. Historically the Conservatives have had to contain their attempts to extend the domain of the free market in the face of considerable housing need. In practice the 'safety net' role of the state has had to be more extensive than the free marketeers would have liked. The Labour attempts at securing a greater degree of collectivisation in the supply and distribution of housing has had to be modified on two major counts. One has been a strong desire on the part of a large proportion of the electorate to either become owners of their own houses or to remain in this sector. It has not taken politicians long to learn that they cannot afford to alienate votes of the owner-occupiers. Housing policy has to take this into account. The other has been the necessity to contain the volume of public resources devoted to housing during times of national economy difficulties. This has meant that the scale of public investment in housing has had to be limited on occasions and with it the degree of collectivisation.

This essay, then, examines in outline changing housing policy in Britain since 1945, highlighting the ideological differences between the two major political parties and demonstrating how in practice such views have been modified in face of the need to secure electoral support and to contain public expenditure. Also evaluated here is the impact of these policies on the changing morphology of British cities over the past fifty years. The final section draws out some general lessons that can be learned from this retrospective study.

Pre-1945 Housing Policy and the First Post-War Labour Government

By 1945 many important strands of current British housing policy had already been established and, in varying degrees, accepted by both political parties. At the end of the First World War (1918) it was believed that the private market could not provide enough houses at a sufficiently cheap rent to meet the housing needs of the time.[6] Consequently the government charged local authorities to build high quality working class housing and, to ensure that rents were kept down to an acceptable level, the 1919 Housing and Town Planning Act enabled the Treasury to grant subsidies to those local authorities which were engaged in such programmes. The occupiers of these council houses were expected to pay a rent which it was thought the working classes could afford. This, it was recognised, would not cover the full costs of building and maintenance. To cover part of the deficit those local authorities with housing pro- grammes were required to levy a penny rate (i.e. all property owners in their area were expected to pay an extra penny for every pound for which their proper- ties were assessed). Any deficit still remaining on the costs of the council houses was to be covered by a grant from the Treasury. In other words, the Treasury had an open ended commitment to meet any costs that could not be met by a combination of rents and a modest contribution from the local autho- rity rate fund. This situation was changed under the 1923 Housing Act which determined the level of Treasury grants to approved local authority house building activities by fixing monetary amounts per dwelling over a stated period of time - £6 per year for each dwelling for twenty years. This principle of housing subsidy generally held good until 1967 with only minor variations, although the two minority Labour governments of the 1920s did much to make the scale of these subsidies more generous. It was the second of these governments which also introduced the principle of allowing local authorities to fix the rent levels of their houses provided that rent in- come, central government subsidies and rate contribu- tion equalled costs. Thus, any local authority had the right, if it chose to exercise it, to subsidise council house rents from the rates. During the inter war period, the local authorities of England and

Wales built 1.1 million houses.

The 1920s was a period when housing policy was geared to add to the overall housing stock of the country. The subsidy system, largely harnessed to the building activities of local authorities, was one way to do this. Yet within the Conservative Party the view could be found that the free market was still the best mechanism for providing working class dwellings for renting. Housing subsidies should be seen as temporary expedients to deal with short run imperfections of the market, and it was this line of argument which encouraged the Conservatives to give subsidies to private house builders as well as to local authorities. Under the 1923 and 1927 Housing Acts, private builders were given £75 and £50 respectively for each approved working class house they built.

During the 1930s there was every indication that the advocates of the free market were correct in their analysis. Building costs fell relative to income and both land prices and interest rates were low. The situation created something of a social revolution by not only stimulating a house building boom but also by making owner-occupation a feasible proposition for the middle classes as well as for many of the working classes. Of the 3.8 million dwellings built in England and Wales between 1914 and 1938, 1.8 million were built for owner-occupation.

Rent control had first been introduced in 1915 as a war-time measure. There were those in the Conservative Party who were naturally anxious to remove this impediment to the operation of the free market. But because of the housing shortage following the end of World War I, the rent controls continued, and it was not until 1925 that the Rent and Mortgage Interest Restriction Act made tentative attempts to decontrol rents. This Act allowed any 'controlled housing' which became vacant and reverted to the landlords' possession to be freed of any further restriction. In 1931 the government set up the Marley Committee to examine the working of the rent acts.[7] The committee found that the systems of decontrol by possession had worked well as far as medium sized houses were concerned, but too quickly with regards to the smallest houses. The process of decontrol amongst the small houses was therefore causing real hardship amongst the poorest families. These findings formed the basis of the 1933 and 1938 Rent Restriction Acts. Decontrol by change of tenancy for small houses was stopped. The decontrol of medium sized houses remained as under the 1925

Act; and all control was removed from the largest houses.

Primarily because the free market was working better in supplying homes during the 1930s than ever before, the predominantly Conservative Governments of the period found themselves able to concentrate public resources in those areas of housing which exhibited the greatest need. Henceforth housing subsidies were regarded almost exclusively as a tool for getting rid of slums and overcrowding. The 1933 Housing Act, building on the 1930 Housing Act, provided subsidies to local authorities on the basis of the numbers of families displaced and rehoused as a result of clearance operations. Up to 1938 some 300,000 slum dwellings were pulled down in England and Wales - 4 percent of all housing stock of the country at the beginning of the First World War. On the question of overcrowding, the Housing Act of 1935 gave it a statutory definition and made it an offence on the part of landlords and tenants to allow it to continue. Additional subsidies were given to local authorities engaged on programmes for rehousing those living in overcrowded conditions.

The innovations in housing policy which were introduced during the 1920s and 1930s had a profound impact on the morphology of British industrial cities and towns. The case of Birmingham can be used to illustrate what was happening more generally.[8] Birmingham was developed as a light engineering centre in the early nineteenth century. The first great wave of migrant workers came during the period 1780 to 1850 and these workers and their families rented the back-to-back dwellings provided by speculative builders who crowded as many houses as possible onto these sites. These houses were built in a double row under a single room, one row facing the street and the other looking onto a paved courtyard. Thus almost every house was surrounded on three sides by a dwelling of similar type, thereby preventing any through ventilation or adequate daylight. Most of the houses contained three rooms, one above another. The houses were originally built without internal water supply or sink. Even by the 1930s many still had only one standpipe in the court to serve all the houses. The net housing density was often about 60 houses or 200 persons per acre. (Figure 4.1)

From the 1850s onwards a combination of higher real earnings amongst the artisans and black coated workers, and national and local legislation led to a new housing type for the working classes - the terraced house. In Birmingham they encircled the

Figure 4.1 <u>Back-to-back court dwellings in central</u>
            <u>Birmingham.</u>

back-to-back houses. Generally speaking these were
three bedroomed houses, with parlour, living room and
scullery. Being built in rows, with the front facing
onto the road and a garden at the back, they provided
air space on at least two sides of each dwelling.
The density was usually between 20 and 30 houses per
acre, but it was noted in the 1930s, still too high
to permit convenient planning and adequate daylight
illumination.
      The 1920s and 1930s witnessed the creation of a
third 'housing ring' within the city - the result of
the development of private and local authority
housing estates. It was the Birminghal City Council
which initiated this aspect of the city's physical
development. In 1918 the city council acquired 400
acres for house building and 100 acres were assigned
for immediate development. Within four years of the
passing of the 1919 Housing and Town Planning Act
over 3,000 local authority houses had been built in
the city. By 1938 Birmingham had built over 40,000

council houses. Some of the larger estates, such as
Kingstanding and Lea Hall, were as big as small
towns. The houses were predominantly semi-detached,
and at the low density of twelve houses to the acre.
They had at least three bedrooms and had separate
bathrooms and WCs. A number of the estates were
laid out with churches, schools, playing fields,
libraries, baths and shopping centres but this was
not always so. Some such estates, lacking social
facilities, became soulless.

One can detect during these years a movement of
population away from the central areas of back-to-
back houses, and what became known as the 'middle
ring' of terraced houses, into the council houses in
the outer ring. A parallel movement can also be
observed of some of the Birmingham population moving
into the private estates which began to develop in
this outer ring from the 1930s onwards, as lower
building costs for the first time encouraged some of
the working classes in Birmingham to become owner
occupiers. Between 1935 and 1938, 7,000 houses were
built each year for owner occupation on the outskirts
of the city.

This suburban pattern of development was very
marked and obvious in the case of Birmingham, but
variations on this pattern could be found in most
industrial cities and towns in Britain during the
1920s and 1930s.

Considerable progress was made during the latter
part of the 1930s in clearing slums and reducing
overcrowding. Nonetheless, by the end of the Second
World War, the incoming Labour Government was con-
fronted with major housing problems. There had been
virtually no house building during the war years,
many dwellings had been destroyed in the blitz, many
other dwellings had fallen into decay, and an upsurge
in marriages and births, which accompanied the end
of hostilities, added to the demand for more homes.
The Labour Government (1946-51) saw its main task as
encouraging the local authorities to provide as many
houses as possible. The system of building licenses,
which had been introduced during the war, was
retained and used to contain private house building
activities, and a new local authority subsidy
system was introduced in the 1946 Housing Act, which
worked in a way very similar to the system introduced
in 1923. Subsidies were once more to be given to
those authorities building to satisfy a general
housing need - that is to say the subsidy was not
limited to those authorities involved specifically
in slum clearance activities or the relief of over-

crowding, as had been the case in the immediate pre-war years. Furthermore, unlike earlier housing legislation, the government's second housing act of 1949 did not charge local authorities to provide specifically working class dwellings, reflecting a more collectivist view of housing. Ultimately local authorities would be expected to provide houses for all sectors of society, and in so doing would help to destroy class barriers. Housing supply and egalitarian principles would go hand in hand.

Because of the pressing need for housing in the immediate post-war years, temporary prefabricated dwellings were introduced. They were financed by the Exchequer and allocated to local authorities to manage. It was anticipated that they could relieve any temporary hardship whilst individual local authorities made progress in the provision of permanent dwellings. Many were still occupied in 1981. In all, some 902,000 dwellings were built in England and Wales under the Labour administration of 1946-51, 78 percent of them by local authorities. (Figure 4.2)

Figure 4.2 <u>Outer periphery council housing in Nottingham.</u>

As far as the urban morphology was concerned, local authority estates continued to be built on the fringes of the towns and cities, (although without accompanying social facilities) and to the casual observer it is often impossible to distinguish between council houses built in the years immediately prior to 1939 and those built in the late 1940s and early 1950s. There were, however, certain policies which were assembled during 1940s which related to housing and urban planning which were to have a profound effect on the subsequent growth patterns of towns and cities. Essentially they were concerned with the containment of urban sprawl.[9] In 1940 the Royal Commission into the Distribution of the Industrial Population (the Barlow Report) was published. It argued that the larger cities, like Birmingham, should not be allowed to expand without control on their peripheries. The trend during the 1930s, as was discussed above, was for a gradual thinning out of the congested urban centres and a redistribution of population in the low density suburbs. According to the Barlow Report this trend was unacceptable. Peripheral growth meant a substantial separation of place of residence from place of work and shopping and leisure facilities, with a consequent strain on transport provision. The Barlow Report agreed that residential densities in the inner cities should be drastically reduced, but that a limit should be placed on urban peripheral growth, as had been the case in London which had been surrounded by a statutory green belt in 1938. Those moved from the inner city should be relocated in smaller expanded or new settlements in which a full range of jobs and community facilities would be available.

The Barlow Report exercised considerable influence, and the Labour Government was anxious to see it implemented. A number of regional reports were issued during the 1940s which incorporated this mode of thinking. The Greater London Plan, the Clyde Valley Regional Plan (covering the Glasgow region of Scotland) and the West Midland Plan (covering the Birmingham region) all recommended in their differing ways policies of urban containment and overspill.

Central Government, for its part, passed two significant acts to enable such policies to be implemented. The 1946 New Towns Act gave the Ministry of Town and Country Planning and the Scottish Office powers to build new towns to receive overspill population. The 1947 Town and Country Planning Act, amongst other matters, gave local authorities powers to zone land for green belts.

During the Labour administration eight new towns - Stevenage, Crawley, Hemel Hempstead, Harlow, Hatfield, Welwyn, Basildon and Bracknell - were designated to receive overspill population from London. East Kilbride was designated to receive overspill population from Glasgow. In addition five other new towns were designated to house workers in newly opened coal mines, and other remote areas of industrial activity.[10]

Conservative Housing Policy 1951-1964

A Conservative Government was returned to power in 1951 on a programme of relaxing governmental controls and intervention. The Labour Government during its later years had produced an average 170,000 dwellings per annum; the Conservatives maintained they would ensure that 300,000 dwellings were completed each year. Initially this was to be achieved largely through the efforts of local authorities, although their white paper of 1953, Housing the Next Step,[11] argued that the government saw the market as the main mechanism to provide houses and that its principle concern, therefore, should be in dealing with older and obsolete houses. Here we can catch echoes of the housing policies of the 1930s - let the market predominantly provide the houses, and let the state act simply as a safety net.

By 1954, the Conservatives had pushed the total annual house completion figures in England and Wales to over 300,000, nearly 200,000 of which were built by local authorities (Figure 4.3). Simultaneously the Conservatives set about freeing the market by abandoning building permits, and then repealed the 'betterment' clauses in the 1947 Town and Country Planning Act, which had ensured that all profits involved in land deals were to go to the state. The Conservatives had made the point that such measures dissuaded owners from putting land onto the market, and that removing such a 'tax' from land transactions owners had a greater incentive to release land for housing purposes. From 1954 to 1964 the annual number of private houses completed in England and Wales rose from 88,000 to 210,000.

The more selective approach to housing was demonstrated by the 1956 Housing Subsidies Act, which introduced a general reduction of Government subsidies for council housing and a concentration on housing built to re-accommodate those from slum areas. Indeed local authorities had begun to engage

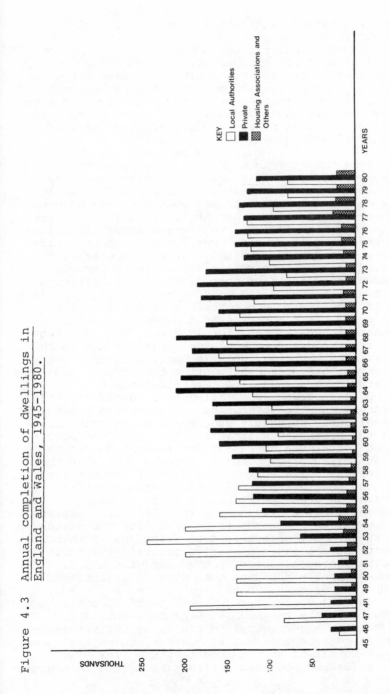

Figure 4.3   Annual completion of dwellings in England and Wales, 1945-1980.

in slum clearance activities from 1954 onwards. The
procedure was clarified under the 1957 Housing Act,
although some authorities preferred to use the
powers given to them under the 1947 Town and Country
Planning Act (passed by the Labour Government) which
enabled them to declare Comprehensive Redevelopment
Areas. As will be seen from Figure 4.3 there was a
steady decline in the annual completion of council
houses. The highest ever recorded output of 250,000
came in 1953, and between 1959 and 1963 the figures
varied between 93,000 and 105,000. By the end of
the 1950s the government was optimistic about its
housing policies, and it was anticipated that the
slums would soon be cleared. Between 1951 and 1960,
363,000 slums had been pulled down (mostly between
1956 and 1960), and it was argued that full employment and rising income levels would ensure that free
enterprise would provide improved housing standards.
There was even a belief that, provided controls were
relaxed, the private rented sector would have a new
lease of life and take over from the public rented
sector.

The post-war Labour Government had strengthened
the rent control system of the 1920s and 1930s, and
at the outbreak of war, the 1930 and 1938 Rent Acts
were retained until six months after the end of the
hostilities. In the immediate post-war, the Labour
Government had kept rent control in force through
the 1946 Furnished Houses (Rent Control) Act, which
set up rent tribunals in respect of furnished
lettings, and the 1949 Landlord and Tenant (Rent
Control) Act, which extended the scope of rent control to unfurnished lettings. As far as the private
rented sector was concerned, the Labour Government
saw the first priority as protecting the interest of
the tenants. The Conservatives, on the other hand,
saw rent control as a disincentive to investment in
housing for rent. By allowing rents to find the
level of the market, and so allowing the owners to
obtain a reasonable return on their investment, an
incentive would be provided to encourage further
new investment in this housing sector. The first
move in the decontrol of rents came with the 1954
Housing Repairs and Rent Act, which allowed landlords to undertake limited rent increases to meet
the mounting costs of repairs. The big breakthrough,
however, came with the 1957 Rent Act, which started
the process of decontrol in earnest. Ultimately the
aim was to decontrol all rented properties and to
allow the market to fix rent levels in the private
sector, as had been the case before 1915. This was

to be achieved in two ways. All dwellings of higher rateable value were to be decontrolled 'at a stroke', so that tenants would start paying the new rents at the will of the landlord. This was known as 'block' decontrol. The other form of decontrol, relating to properties with a lower assessed rateable value, was to be introduced at that point when the tenancy changed hands. This process, known as 'creeping' decontrol, was to protect the poorest tenants from immediate rent increases.

Thus during the 1950s the Conservatives, through limiting access to central government subsidised council housing, encouraging speculative builders to cater for the growing demand for owner occupied properties, and removing rent restrictions on privately rented accommodation was attempting to shift housing supply and management into the hands of the private sector. Even so the presence of central and local government intervention in the inner cities was strong and the strands of the Barlow philosophy were very much in evidence. The central areas of the inner cities were undergoing marked changes as a result of slum clearance activities. Again Birmingham can be selected as an example of what was happening in many other industrial parts of the country.12 The main thrust of the city's slum clearance schemes came with the designation of five central redevelopment areas. The areas, all within the core of the Victorian city, housed over 100,000 people in some 30,000 houses, nearly half of which were built back-to-back. The redevelopment areas also contained over 2,000 shops and over 2,000 commercial and industrial premises. Although the clearance activities during the 1950s were not as rapid as had originally been anticipated, the residential central parts of Birmingham began to be transformed. New road systems in the central redevelopment areas were established, new council houses, in the form of industrial dwellings, maisonettes and high rise tower blocks began to appear. (Figure 4.4) However the rebuilding and redevelopment activities were hindered by a lack of building land on the outskirts of the city. The central areas were redeveloped at lower residential densities than had formerly prevailed because of the need to provide extra open space, playing areas, car parking areas and school play grounds. One solution was to extend the city's boundaries. But both Labour and Conservative Governments were committed to the concept of containment. The Conservatives stressed this point nationally in a circular issued

Figure 4.4 <u>High-rise flats in Birmingham.</u>

in 1957. If this policy were adhered to, where
would those moved from the central areas be
reaccommodated? This was a matter of great concern
to Birmingham and other cities like it at the end of
the 1950s. To an extent Birmingham was suffering
from its generous use of land in building low
density peripheral housing estates in the immediate
post 1945 years. Furthermore much building land on
the edge of the city was being taken up by private
builders. The answer Birmingham found was to save
land by building tower blocks in the suburbs.
      The Barlow philosophy was, of course, to re-
house substantial proportions of the population in
new towns. But shortly after coming into office the
Conservative Government announced that it intended
to designate no more new towns; they were seen to be
too expensive. In their place, under the 1952 Town
Development Act, cities needing to shed population
were encouraged to make overspill arrangements with
smaller settlements. Birmingham attempted to do
this, but due to financial difficulties, the schemes

were less than successful. Birmingham was not alone
in experiencing this. Indeed by the early 1950s,
Glasgow, which was about to embark on a massive
programme of clearing 100,000 dwellings, found that
it was essential to have more overspill outlets than
could be provided at East Kilbride, and in 1956 the
government had to change its policy and designate a
second new town for the city at Cumbernauld.[13]

As far as Birmingham was concerned, the Government was forced to designate a new town for it at
Dawley (later renamed Telford) in 1963 and then one
at Redditch in 1964. Liverpool and Manchester were
also experiencing similar land shortages for
housing, and new towns were designated for them at
Skelmersdale in 1961 and Runcorn in 1964. The
pattern was set for a more vigorous overspill policy
to be pursued by a succeeding Labour administration.

Labour Housing Policy 1964-1970
Even before the Conservatives left office in 1964
there were disquietening signs that the government
was being too complacent over housing policy. In
1960, J.B. Cullingworth's book Housing Need and
Planning Policy,[14] argued convincingly that the local
authority statements of housing unfitness were 'a
gross underestimate' and that the process of decay
would itself require the replacement of 141,000
dwellings each year. Other independent inquiries
supported this view, as did the report commissioned
by the Ministry of Housing and Local Government -
The Housing Situation in 1960.[15] In addition,
increasing population and rising expectations were
adding to the pressure for housing. Indeed this
point was recognised in one of the last white papers
of the Conservative government - Housing in England
and Wales[16] - issued in 1963. It argued that house
production and slum clearance would have to be
prosecuted with much greater vigour.

The Conservatives were thus forced to modify
many of their ideological stances in the early 1960s.
More public resources had to be given to local
authorities to encourage them to increase their
house building targets. The Housing Act of 1961
attempted to do this through a very complex mechanism whereby the subsidy given by the Treasury for
each house depended upon the needs of individual
authorities. Those authorities which had to draw
heavily on their rates to balance their overall
housing revenue accounts were to receive higher
proportions of Treasury subsidies, and there were

additional subsidies to cover such matters as
building on poor land, or providing high rise and
deck access blocks. However, subsidies were only
available for those dwellings built under the 1956
Act referred to above. When Labour came to power
the major solution to the housing issues of the day
was seen in dramatically increasing the number of
council houses built, which would provide accommodation for newly married couples and enable the slum
clearance rate to be quickened. To encourage local
authorities once more to take a more comprehensive
view of their housing responsibilities, they were
again provided, in 1965, with subsidies to meet
general housing needs, which, it was hoped, would
help to ensure 500,000 dwellings were completed each
year.

A major problem was how this could be done
against the background of a deteriorating economic
climate in which building costs were rising. One
measure which was tried was an overhaul of the subsidy system, introduced in the 1967 Housing Subsidies
Act, which took into account both building costs and
interest rates. The basic subsidy and additional
subsidies at fixed monetary rates under the 1961 Act
were retained, but the difference between loan
charges at four percent per annum, and what the
local authorities were having to pay, was to be met
by the Treasury. In this way local authority
housing costs were being offset by an 'open ended'
government grant which was reminiscent in this respect of the financial provisions in the 1919 Act.
But this time there were safeguards on the 'open
ended' commitment with the introduction of the
'housing cost yardstick'. The yardstick, to be continually updated in the face of rising costs, was a
financial measure against which local authority
requests for house building permission were judged.

If, by this measure, a local authority's scheme
was judged to be too expensive, it would be returned
for amendment. The standards used to fix the yardstick were based upon a report issued by the
Ministry of Housing and Local Government in 1961 -
Homes for Today and Tomorrow (the Parker Morris
Report).[17] The report argued for high quality local
authority housing on the grounds that there was
enough inferior housing available, and the housing
cost yardstick was seen as a mechanism for ensuring
that local authorities built high quality dwellings
at the most economical price. In order to ensure
that sufficient land was available for house construction, the Labour Government introduced the Land

Commission Act in 1967. The Commission was empowered
to buy land through agreement or compulsorily, which
could be sold or leased to public or private bodies.
    As can be seen from Figures 4.3 and 4.5, the
Labour Government did manage to increase the output
of local authority houses and increase the rate of
clearance.
    Despite the economic difficulties of the mid
sixties, the government felt sufficiently confident
in its ability to ensure that enough local authority
houses were built to make a major attack on what it
saw as profiteering private landlords. It had become
clear that the Conservatives' 1957 Rent Act had not
brought more privately rented houses onto the market.
Indeed, during the last years of the Conservative
government there had been a number of scandals
involving landlords driving out tenants through
various forms of harassment in order to decontrol
the property, which led to the setting up of a
government committee under the chairmanship of Sir
Milner Holland to investigate the London housing
situation. The Holland Report,[18] published in 1965,
demonstrated that housing squalor in the capital was
considerable and that many tenants were clearly being
exploited by these landlords. The 1957 Rent Act
needed revising.
    The Labour Government responded with the 1965
Rent Act, by which control was once more established
on decontrolled property and the 'fair rent' concept
was introduced. The concept of a fair rent was
difficult to define, but it was based partly on prevailing rent levels and the conditions of the area.
The fair rent was to be fixed either by a local rent
officer, or in the event of an appeal, by a local
rent assessment committee, drawn from a panel of
people appointed either by the Ministry of Housing
and Local Government or the Lord Chancellor. These
provisions, which were consolidated in the 1968 Rent
Act, added to the decline of the private rented
sector (Figure 4.6). The landlords argued that rent
control made it impossible for them in many instances
to make even a modest profit and some private rented
property was sold to sitting tenants at a relatively
cheap price; a larger proportion of private property,
however, went off the market as a result of clearance
operations.
    At no time between 1964 and 1970 was anything
like the 500,000 dwellings per annum target reached,
although 1968 did witness the highest number of
annual completions ever for England and Wales at
372,000, principally because of the very high number

GREAT BRITAIN

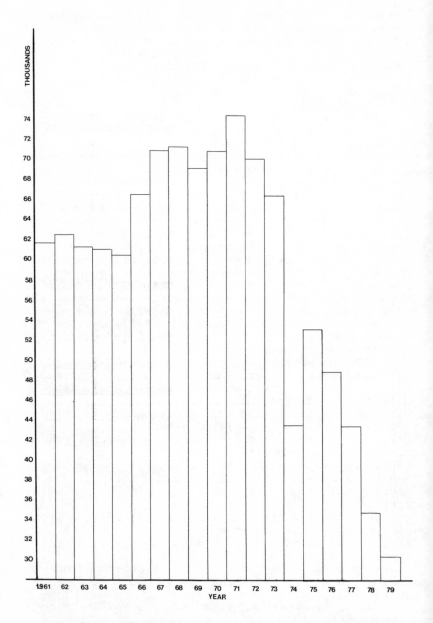

Figure 4.5   Total dwellings cleared or demolished by
             Local Authorities in England or Wales,
             1961-1979.

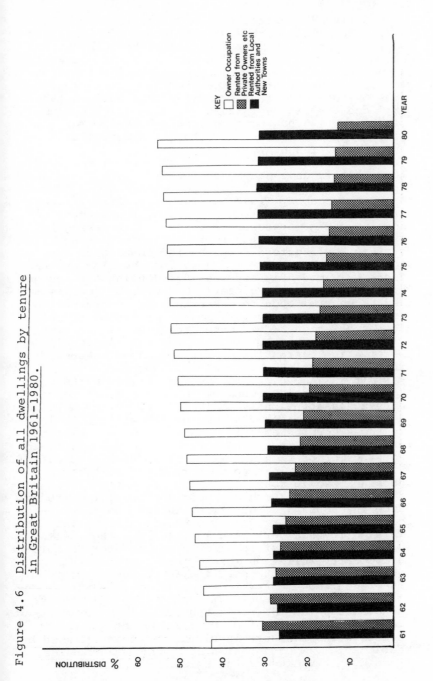

Figure 4.6 Distribution of all dwellings by tenure in Great Britain 1961-1980.

of dwellings completed in the private sector (Figure 4.3). Nonetheless, the annual number of houses completed under the Labour administration built either privately or by the local authorities was somewhat higher than the average yearly completion rate for the last seven years of the previous government. (The average number of council houses built between 1957 and 1963 in England and Wales was 107,000 compared with 140,000 between 1964 and 1970. The comparable figures for owner occupation were 152,000 and 194,000 respectively.)

The housing associations, which form the voluntary sector, have had a lengthy history in Britain.[19] During the nineteenth century the efforts of Octavia Hill, the Peabody Trust and the Bournville Village Trust were all experiments to demonstrate that good housing could be provided by non-profit making private bodies charging rents that the working classes could afford. During the opening decades of the twentieth century the number of housing associations grew modestly and the 1936 Housing Act recognised the National Federation of Housing Societies as the central body representing and co-ordinating the work of the voluntary movement. Under the act, the associations could enter into formal agreements with the local authorities in their areas and receive the appropriate government housing subsidies that were available for council houses.

It was, however, the Conservatives in the post 1951 period who did much to encourage 'cost rent' housing associations. In 1961, through the Housing Act, they established a fund of £25 million to loan to those housing associations which were registered as charities. Then, under the 1964 Housing Act, the Housing Corporation was established with a budget of £100 million to loan to cost-rent and co-ownership housing associations. The associations could receive up to a third of their borrowing requirements from the Housing Corporation, whilst the rest was expected to be borrowed from Building Societies. This policy was very much in line with the 'self help' philosophy often associated with the Conservative Party whilst on ideological grounds, the voluntary sector at that time found less favour by the Labour movement which saw direct state intervention as a more effective method of providing houses. Nonetheless the 1964-1970 Labour administration used Conservative legislation concerning the voluntary sector with considerable vigour to offset the decline in the private rented sector. Indeed the lending activities of the Housing Corporation were extended under Labour's 1969 Housing Act, and building activities in the voluntary sector increased somewhat from 1965 onwards (Figure 4.3).

The 1960s was thus typified by vigorous slum clearance and redevelopment programmes and private and public building schemes and it was during these years that the urban fabric of British cities changed most dramatically. Many of the urban renewal schemes developed in the 1950s were realised. High rise blocks appeared with increasing frequency in the urban area.[20] The technology was available, especially with the use of industrialised building. From a production point of view building systems were developed which meant that the high rise blocks could be built with great speed. Indeed in 1956 10.6 percent of all dwellings erected by local authorities in England and Wales were in buildings of fifteen or more storeys. But, of course, these tower blocks were not restricted to the central areas. The urban containment policy was still being vigorously pursued and most cities were experiencing land shortages even more acutely than had been the case in the late 1950s. Consequently there was considerable pressure to build high rise blocks of flats wherever land became available. Nowhere was this more evident than in the case of Glasgow.[21] By the early 1960s Glasgow had begun the process of declaring twentynine clearance areas, entailing the demolition of 100,000 dwellings. By 1971 Glasgow had built 208 tower blocks containing 20,836 flats principally to accommodate those who had been cleared in slum clearance operations. Many of the tower blocks were built in the redevelopment areas, but many were erected indiscriminately throughout the city where pockets of land could be found.

Building 'high' did not remove the necessity of overspill arrangements. Such was the pressure for publically provided dwellings that the overspill programme had to be increased. More overspill outlets had to be found to enable the redevelopment of London to continue. Milton Keynes was designated as a new town - or rather a new city - in 1967 to accommodate a quarter of a million persons from London. The new towns mechanism was also used to accommodate Londoners in the ancient towns of Northampton and Peterborough. Glasgow had had a further new town designated for its use in 1962 at Livingstone and towards the end of the 1960s plans were being prepared for a further new town at Stonehouse.

There was also pressure to find land for housing to be built by the private developers. Increasingly villages surrounding the industrial towns and cities were being expanded to form commuter settlements for the owner occupiers. Indeed much of regional planning and the 'structure' planning which was introduced in 1968 was concerned with finding suitable new sites for public and private housing developments.

Towards the end of the 1960s the Labour Government, however, had to rethink its slum clearance policies. The policies of extensive slum clearance activities accompanied by massive local authority rehousing schemes were increasingly seen to be not only unworkable and financially burdensome, but also socially harmful. Too many properties which could be improved were being demolished because they did not meet the high standards that were thought proper for every family. Furthermore there was growing disquiet about the sort of accommodation which local authorities were providing. It was quicker, although by no means cheaper, to provide systems built high rise and deck access housing, which also facilitated relatively high density development - an attractive attribute for local authorities increasingly finding themselves experiencing land shortages. The number of flats built by local authorities increased steadily in the 1960s, constituting almost 50% of total council house construction in the decade as a whole (Figure 4.7).

High rise flats were criticised for being ill constructed - many were damp, partly because tenants could not afford to use the expensive forms of electrical heating, - whilst the architectural forms isolated families, encouraged vandalism and generated neurosis amongst tenants. At the same time, clearance programmes were breaking up communities, and paradoxically moving people who did not want to move into dwellings which they did not like.[22] There is little wonder that by the end of the 1960s there was a pronounced shift towards rehabilitation, at a time when the Labour Government was also beginning to appreciate that owner-occupation should be encouraged. There were two reasons for this shift in attitude: owner-occupation could take some of the pressure off the local authorities, whilst there was a growing number of Labour supporters who were either owner-occupiers or who wanted to be owner-occupiers.

Early attempts at encouraging local authorities to bring about housing improvements were made in 1949

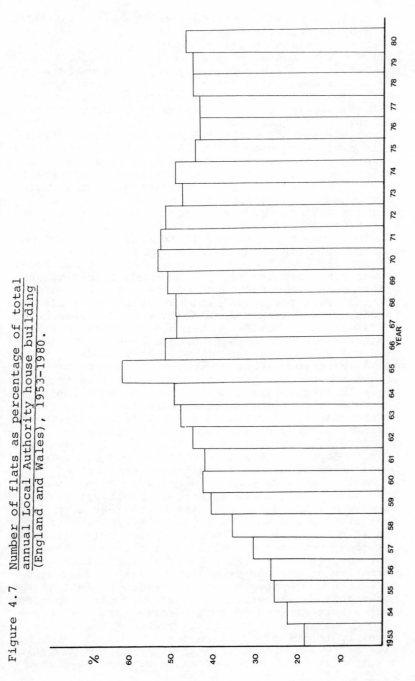

Figure 4.7   Number of flats as percentage of total
             annual Local Authority house building
             (England and Wales), 1953-1980.

and 1964. The major move forward, however, came with the publication by the Ministry of Housing and Local Government of the Deeplish Study: Improvement Possibilities in a District of Rochdale, in 1966.[23] On the basis of this report, a survey was mounted which led to the 1968 White Paper, Old Houses into New Homes.[24] It was demonstrated that the scale of the national clearance programme was too ambitious. It was not just a question of a hard-core of slum houses to be dealt with, - in addition to 18 million unfit dwellings, some 4.5 million dwellings required either £125 or more spent on repairs or at least lacked one basic amenity. Resources were not available to clear these properties during the next seven years, and so the government announced a switch of public investment from new house building to improving older dwellings.

This was done principally through the 1969 Housing Act. In order to make improvement as financially advantageous to local authorities as new development, discretionary and standard improvement grants were increased, and a further grant - a special grant for installing the standard amenities in houses in multiple-occupation where self-contained units were not provided - was added. This meant that grants could be used for approved rehabilitation work, providing up to half the cost of the whole operation. Furthermore, the Minister had powers to increase the amount of grant over the limit in areas where the incidence of bad housing was especially high. Housing associations also became eligible for this financial help if they acquired old houses for improvement or conversion. The 1969 Act also introduced the concept of the General Improvement Areas (GIAs) to contain between 200 and 300 older dwellings, capable of being brought up to a reasonable standard. In other words, they were not to be dwellings which were ripe for immediate clearance, but rather dwellings which, if neglected, would soon fall into that state. The significant point about houses in potential GIAs was that they should contain a high proportion of dwellings in owner-occupation. In fact, Local Authority grants had been made available for owner-occupiers to improve their properties since 1949; but with the GIA mechanism, owner-occupiers in older houses were encouraged to invest in their own homes through making even higher improvement grants available, up to 60% of total costs. The local authorities would also be given extra funding to undertake environmental improvements in an effort to restore public confidence in the area.

Towards the end of the 1960s, then, the Labour government was rethinking its position over owner-occupation, and this also led to new subsidies for house buyers. The most significant assistance given by governments to house buyers had taken the form of tax relief allowable on the interest paid on the mortgage. Such relief has a long history, but the starting point of the present system goes back to Conservative legislation introduced in 1963. The Labour government attempted to encourage a greater degree of owner occupation in 1968 when it introduced an option mortgage scheme to help those whose taxation levels were too low to enable them to benefit from relief. Those who applied for the scheme could repay the building societies who lent them their money at between two and three percent below the borrowing rate, but no tax relief was to be available to those in the scheme. The building societies then recouped their return so lost from central government.

The Return of the Conservatives 1970-1974

The Conservatives were returned to power in 1970 intent on stimulating private initiative which it was believed had been constrained under the socialists. The new government believed that too many public resources were being devoted to housing, especially council housing. There was no need, it was argued, to 'featherbed' local authority tenants, at the expense of those in other housing sectors. Many council tenants, it was said, did not need subsidising from taxes and rates. The rhetorical question was posed: why should those on slender incomes in the private rented sector subsidise through the rates the well paid local authority tenants? The 1972 Housing Finance Act was passed to deal with what was thought to be this major anomaly in the housing system. The aim of the act was to enable central government to drastically reduce its commitments to paying subsidies, and at its core was the desire to ensure that local authority tenants paid a 'fair rent'. The Conservatives used the concept of the 'fair rent', which had been employed in the 1965 Rent Act for tenants in private property, for those in the publicly rented sector as well. For the purposes of the 1972 Act, the determination of what constituted fair rents in the public sector for each area was to be the responsibility of a local Rent Scrutiny Board. Rents in the

local authority sector were normally required by the
act to rise by £26 per annum until a fair rent was
achieved, this had wide implications on two issues.
Firstly, it was in direct opposition to the principle
that local authorities had autonomy over fixing rent
levels; and secondly, the act drastically altered
the subsidy system.

All subsidies payable under earlier acts were
withdrawn and replaced by a new provision. Any gap
between a local authority's 'reckonable' housing
revenues - that is to say steadily rising rents
culminating in the 'fair rent' - and expenditure was
to be met by central government and the local authority in agreed proportions. Ultimately it was
expected that most authorities would find their
housing revenue accounts in balance, and that in
those cases there would be no further central
government subsidies. Some authorities, it was
anticipated, would even show a profit. After making
allowance for working balances, such profits were to
be paid to the Department of the Environment and
distributed to those authorities which were
experiencing heavy losses. But, true to the element
of paternalism implicit in much of Conservative
thought, in order to prevent hardship to individual
tenants, all local authorities were required to
introduce rent rebate schemes. When surpluses on
the housing revenue accounts were exceeded by the
amount of rebates paid, the Secretary of State for
the Environment was to repay one half of the excess
to the authority for the benefit of the general rate
fund. Through the act such rebates were also made
available to tenants in privately rented properties.

The Conservatives also addressed the problem of
housing improvement areas. A concern with those in
the greatest housing need can be observed in the
1974 Housing Act, which allowed local authorities to
declare Housing Action Areas (HAAs); these were to
contain properties which, although capable of being
improved, were nonetheless in a worse condition than
those in a general improvement area. In addition
HAAs were to exhibit features of social stress and
would normally contain a high proportion of
privately rented dwellings. Dwellings in a HAA
would receive a higher level of improvement grants
than in a GIA but would carry a lower percentage of
grants to improve the general environment.

The annual rate of local authority house
building had begun to fall under the previous
government from 1968 onwards. This fall continued
under the Conservative administration (see Figure

4.3), and in 1972 a decline in the clearance rate
began to be apparent also (see Figure 4.5).

The Labour Government 1974-1979
A Labour Government was returned in 1974 against the
backcloth of a worsening economic climate of
increasing inflation, rising interest rates and
balance of payments difficulties. To combat these
problems, the government was forced by the International Monetary Fund to adopt deflationary
economic policies, principally through reductions in
levels of public expenditure. But allied to this,as
a means of controlling inflation, the government
attempted to establish an incomes policy with
voluntary agreements with the trade unions. A
crucial element in this was the concept of a 'social
wage' - effectively, that element of goods and
services provided by the welfare state - which was
to be used to compensate workers for any drop in
real earnings that may have resulted from the
voluntary incomes policy. To an extent such an
agreement ran counter to the policy of containing
public expenditure, especially so far as housing
policy was concerned. More precisely, local authorities needed to continue to build and improve
houses. At the same time the government could not
allow rents in council houses to rise, as would have
happened through the 1972 Housing (Finance) Acts,
whilst at the same time exhorting workers to moderate
their pay claims. To deal with these issues the
government quickly passed the 1975 Housing Rents and
Subsidies Act. The act discarded the 'fair rent'
principle in the public housing sector, although the
compulsory rent rebate provisions were retained. As
far as the subsidies paid by central government to
local authorities were concerned, the following
measures were introduced:-
1. a housing subsidy was to be paid to each local
    authority at the same monetary rate as was
    established for the financial year 1974/75,
2. a new subsidy called a 'capital cost element'
    was to be paid on all new investment i.e. on
    land, new building, improvement and acquisition -
    given at a rate of sixty six percent of the
    interest which had to be paid on borrowing for
    all such new investment,
3. a supplementary element at the rate of thirty
    three percent paid on any increase in loan
    charges on pre 1975/76 housing debt resulting
    from an increase in interest charges,

4. a 'special element' paid only for the years
    1975/76 and 1976/77 to authorities which would
    otherwise have been obliged to impose sharp
    increases in rents.
During the period when this legislation was being
prepared, there was a growing concern that a rigid
central control over local authority housing programmes was undesirable. To promote greater sensi-
tivity over housing policy, a programme of housing
strategies and investment policies was introduced in
1977 and during the succeeding four years a number
of further changes were introduced.

The Housing Investment Programmes and Strategies
(HIPS) were to establish a new relationship between
central and local government. Central government
had an obligation to lay down an overall national
policy framework, but

> the key to the success of national housing
> policy now lies in the development of effec-
> tive local housing strategies, planned and
> carried out by local authorities with the
> minimum of detailed intervention from the
> centre.25

There was thus a recognition that the local authorities were the only agencies capable of assessing the
full range of housing requirements in their areas.
By the same token local authorities ought to be the
most effective agencies for drawing up their own
strategic housing policies and programmes for
proposed housing investments.26

In doing this, local authorities were expected
to link in their housing policies with other areas
of concern, such as transport, employment, health
and social services. More significantly, in preparing their housing policies, local authorities
were expected to orchestrate the activities of the
public, private rented and voluntary sectors of
housing. Through the work of the Housing Corporation, local authorities could collaborate with the
work of housing associations. The 1975 Housing
Subsidies Act, for example, included provisions to
enable local authorities to set up housing co-
operatives. This meant that a local authority
could loan money to prospective occupiers to purchase properties to be managed and owned collectively
by the occupiers. Such a body thus became a type of
housing association. The Labour Government was at
this time also beginning to work closely with the
building societies; an attempt was made to stabilise

the flow of mortgages for home ownership by the government's £500 million loan to the building societies. Furthermore, local authorities were encouraged to grant mortgages to those who could not get them from the building societies. It was this sort of lending which was to go primarily to those who wanted mortgages on the pre 1914 properties, perhaps in GIAs or HAAs. In this situation there was a clear need for the local authorities to work in close harmony with the building societies in their area.

The previous administration had got rid of the Land Commission; but in order to ensure that a plentiful supply of land was available for building purposes, at a price that was not pushed up through speculation, the new Labour administration passed the 1976 Community Land Act.[27] This act gave local authorities the powers to purchase land, compulsorily if necessary, and to use it for the general good of the community. Such land could be used for the construction of council houses or owner-occupied houses, with land sometimes being leased or sold to private builders to develop according to the brief drawn up by the local authorities. By using the Community Land Act, local authorities were in a very strong position to formulate and implement comprehensive housing strategies for their areas. As far as the financial side was concerned, each year local authorities were required to make bids within a rolling programme to central government on the basis of their overall strategies. Central government would then inform the local authorities about what they could have within the overall framework of the national spending priorities. Given this allocation, the local authorities had some discrepancy in switching resources from one heading to another and from year to year, according to changing circumstances.

Whilst simultaneously dealing with immediate housing issues, the government also began in 1975 a comprehensive review of housing policy in England and Wales. Initially, the review was restricted largely to financial issues, but it was later decided to widen its scope to include the social aspects of housing. A consultative document, Housing Policy, was issued in 1977.[28] It was clear that the government was moving from a fixed ideological stance to a more flexible approach. Thus, although it was noted that the traditional aim of a decent home for all families at a price within their means must remain the primary objective,[29] it also

103

stressed that, since the war, much progress had been
made in dealing with unfit and overcrowded dwellings,
and that there was no longer an overwhelming absolute shortage of housing everywhere. Consequently it
was recognised that a purely national approach could
draw attention and resources away from areas with
the most pressing needs. This was the justification
for giving local authorities more autonomy over
housing, and, it was suggested, greater encouragement ought to be given to widening owner-occupation,
especially to those on moderate incomes wanting to
buy older properties. Existing measures should be
strengthened to enable building societies to do
this. Furthermore, local authorities should compli-
ment the work of building societies by providing
topping up loans, by providing improvement and
repair grants in respect of older houses bought for
home ownership, and by guarantees that they would
cover costs should mortgages default on payment.
The government itself should ensure that building
societies and local authorities had sufficient funds
to allow them to lend for socially desirable purposes. The consultative document also recognised
that the various rent acts could do harm to the
supply of privately rented accommodation. It was
thus thought desirable that the letting by resident
landlords and temporarily absent home owners should
be encouraged by speeding up the procedure for
obtaining repossession, and that lettings of flats
over shops and other accommodation normally associated with a business should not in future give the
tenants full security of tenure under the rent acts.
As for improvement policies, the government was
anxious to take measures that would encourage more
people to take up improvement grants, especially
where landlords were unwilling to do so, or in
cases where dwellings were in multiple-occupation.
    The consultative document also recognised the
need to become more sensitive to specific types of
housing need. These included the homeless, who
were later given legislative recognition in the
Housing (Homeless Persons) Act, one parent families,
battered wives, disabled and handicapped people, old
people, single people, mobile workers and ethnic
minorities.
    A noticeable change could be found in the inner
cities as a result of these policies. The bulldozer, as the phrase of the time had it, 'had been
pensioned off'. Comprehensive clearance had all but
stopped. It was replaced by 'selected' clearance.
This meant that local authorities selected small

pockets of the very worst properties to be pulled
down. There was also a marked reduction in the number of high rise blocks that were being built.

This is not to say, however, that there was no
new house building being undertaken within the inner
city. Far from it. For the first time there was a
considerable volume of private development being
undertaken. There was a growing demand for new
owner occupied premises within the centre of the
cities. This partly reflected the growing shortage
of 'green field' sites. It also partly reflected
the high cost of commuting from outlying villages
following on from the increased oil prices of the
early 1970s. The private developers initially were
not willing to risk their capital on inner city
ventures of the kind so that a number of authorities
released some of their vacant inner city land to
them at below market value. These experiments
generally proved to be successful and increasingly
builders began to seek out such sites. Other vacant
sites in the inner city were released to housing
associations for their new build activities.

But possibly even more noteworthy was the
improvement to older inner city properties. Housing
associations were buying up blocks of older houses
from private landlords and improving them. GIAs and
HAAs were beginning to make an impact on the town-
scape. Private individuals were beginning to take
up improvement grants, encouraged by the confidence
that local authorities were now taking in such areas.

This growing concern with the state of the
inner cities was related at central and local
government level to a re-evaluation of overspill
policy. Glasgow makes a useful case study which
starkly demonstrates what was happening in London,
Birmingham, Manchester and Liverpool.

In 1973 the Secretary of State for Scotland
confirmed the designation order for Stonehouse, the
fifth new town to receive Glasgow's overspill population.[30] In May 1976 it was announced that the
further development of Stonehouse would no longer
proceed. Between these dates detailed studies had
shown that too many people were leaving Glasgow and
that the formal overspill policy was simply rein-
forcing a trend that was underway. Indeed, it was
argued, that if the rate of emigration was to continue then Glasgow would find that it had a surplus
of municipal houses. Furthermore those who were
leaving Glasgow tended to be the younger and more
skilled of the population. Policies now had to be
re-directed to encourage the population to stay. The

priority now, therefore, was to improve the quality of the existing housing stock and the overall housing environment of the city. The de-designation of Stonehouse was a part of this policy. To help with this improvement the Scottish Office set up the Glasgow Eastern Area Redevelopment Team (GEAR) and made £120,000,000 available to regenerate and rehabilitate the East End of Glasgow. Thus here, as elsewhere, rehabilitation was taking over from comprehensive redevelopment.

In England the Secretary of State for the Environment directed that overspill policies should be similarly rethought and that resources should be switched from new town policies to inner city rehabilitation. In 1976 the Secretary of State for the Environment set in motion a policy which under his government and the Conservative one which followed effectively put an end to formal overspill policies. In future the solutions to inner city issues, including inner city housing issues, were to be situated within the inner cities and not in overspill settlements. Target populations for the new towns were reduced and provision was made under the 1976 Town Towns (Amendment) Act to transfer the assets of the new town development corporations directly to the local authorities.

A Return to the Freemarket: The Conservative Government, 1979

Although the consultative document on housing was criticised for not being comprehensive or radical enough, it did represent a positive move towards more sensitive local housing policies, which recognised the distinctive contributions that could be made from the various housing sectors.[31] In practice, however, the Labour Government had to implement its policies within a difficult economic climate. Thus, although annual house completion rates between 1974 and 1979 did tend to fall in England and Wales in all but the voluntary sectors (Figure 4.3) under the circumstances the record was a fair one, and efforts were made to protect housing from the worst consequences of reductions in public expenditure. When the Conservatives were returned to power in 1979, a very different attitude to housing could be observed. The new administration was committed to stimulating economic growth through a greater reliance on market forces. The government saw its principal role as implementing an anti-inflationary policy largely reliant on increased

GREAT BRITAIN

control of public expenditure. The argument was that
inflation was fuelled by excessive public expenditure,
and so the imposition of tight monetary limits on
public expenditure would reduce the level of inflation, and also switch national resources from the
public to the private sector.

During its last months the Labour Government had
drafted a housing bill to implement many of the
proposals in the consultative document, but the Conservatives scrapped this and began to prepare new
housing legislation. Meanwhile, the Conservatives
introduced an emergency budget in June 1979 in which
the previous Labour government's allocation of
£2,862 million for housing was reduced to £2,554
million - an arbitary cut of £308 million. Then in
the budget of April 1980 the government announced
its future financial allocation for housing. At
1979 survey prices, public expenditure on housing
was to be reduced from £5,372 million in the year
1979/80 to £2,790 million in 1983/84. In real terms,
this represented a cut of 48%.32 The Secretary of
State for the Environment noted that the emphasis of
public sector housing policy now must be to meet
particular needs, such as those of the elderly and
the handicapped. Home ownership and the private
rented sector was to be encouraged. In order to
encourage private builders by ensuring a plentiful
supply of land, the Community Land Act was scrapped
under the 1980 Local Government Planning and Land
Act, and a circular was issued instructing local
authorities to ensure that adequate supplies of land
were available for private development over the
following five years.33

It was clear that the reduction of public
expenditure on housing was being used as a principal
vehicle to achieve wider national economic goals,
and that such reductions were harsher than in other
areas of government expenditure. In 1980, it was
envisaged that all public expenditure should be
reduced by four percent and by October 1980 the
government argued that the local authorities were
exceeding their spending on housing by some £180
million.

A moritorium was thus put on local authorities
issuing any more contracts until the end of the
financial year, and, in order to tighten the control
of central government over local government spending
on housing a new subsidy system was introduced in
the 1980 Housing Act. In future, local authorities
were to be given their allocation based on the
formula 'Base Amount' plus 'Housing Cost Differen-

tial', minus 'Local Contribution Differential'. The
'Base Amount' was the figure payable to the authority
during the previous year. The 'Housing Cost Differential' was the amount by which the reckonable
expenditure for that year exceeded the reckonable
expenditure for the previous year. The 'Local Contribution Differential' for any year was the amount
by which reckonable income for the preceeding year
exceeded reckonable expenditure. If the final
figure came to nil or a negative amount, then no
subsidy would be paid to the authority that year.
What the Act did was to give the Secretary of State
for the Environment considerably more powers to
directly intervene in local authority housing
finance. He obtained the powers to adjust the Base
Amount for each authority by increasing or reducing
it as he thought fit, determine what he thought was
reckonable expenditure, and determine reckonable
income by including any contribution made by the
authority out of its general rate fund as well as
any modified rent rebate subsidy.

As regards the extension of private owner
occupation, the 1980 Act gave all local authority
tenants and most housing association tenants[34] who
had held their tenancies not less than three years
the right to buy their dwelling at a discount of
between 33% and 50% of the value. The purchaser was
also to have the right to a mortgage. The Act gave
tenants in the public sector broadly the same pro-
tections to those given to the private sector under
the 1977 Rent Act, although the 1980 Act made it
somewhat easier for the private landlord to increase
rents or make shorthold tenancies. In effect, landlord and tenants could mutually agree to contract
out of the security of tenure provisions under the
1977 Rent Act; a form of exercising decontrol was
thus reintroduced.

The Conservative Government attempted to induce
more private investment in housing and to diminish
the public sector contribution. Arguably this
policy has been pursued more rigorously by this
Government, than any other in the post war period.
Certainly the post-1979 Conservative Government has
drastically reduced central government resources
going into housing, both for new build and improvement purposes, although it should be noted that
receipts of money from the sale of council houses
can be spent on local authority house building and
improvement activities. The overall picture, however is one of constraint and restriction in the
public sector and the 1980 Housing Act, and subse-

quent changes in the block grant system for overall
local authority expenditure, have ensure that any
deficiency in housing expenditure now be made up by
the local authorities drawing in their rate funds.
In this way local authority autonomy has been
reduced, and by giving council house and certain
housing association tenants the right to buy their
dwellings irrespective of the wishes of the individual authorities or associations, the government is
ensuring that the owner-occupier sector increases
and the role of the public sector diminishes.

To what extent is this policy working? It is
too early to judge, but as can be seen from the
Table 4.1 there has been a substantial reduction in
local authority 'starts' between 1979 and 1981 on a
half yearly basis. The number of renovation grants
also declined between 1980 and 1981, although the
1981 situation seems better than that in 1979
(Figure 4.8).

Table 4.1   Housing Statistics, England and Wales,
            1979-1981.

	Local Authority 'starts'	Private sector 'starts'	Renovation Grants
1979	24,234	55,921	55,774
1980	17,069	48,322	72,031
1981	10,621	53,937	62,839

On the basis of the figures provided, it is clear
that the initial impact of the government's
policies on housing has not been beneficial. Reduction of public expenditure has dramatically reduced
the number of local authority houses started, but
there is little indication that this is being offset
by houses built by developers for owner occupation.
Why this is so, is debatable. There is the argument
that high interest rates have meant that developers
have not been able to afford to raise capital,
whilst others would say that there is a shortage of
land for the private developers. Furthermore, the
1976 English House Condition Survey indicated that
911,000 houses in England and Wales were fit but
needed repairs in excess of £3,000 (at 1979
prices).[35] On the basis of these figures and taking
into account the reduction of cental government
funds to be devolved to housing the Association of
Metropolitan Authorities noted that:

Figure 4.8 Number of dwellings renovated with aid
of grants and subsidies in England,
1961-1980.

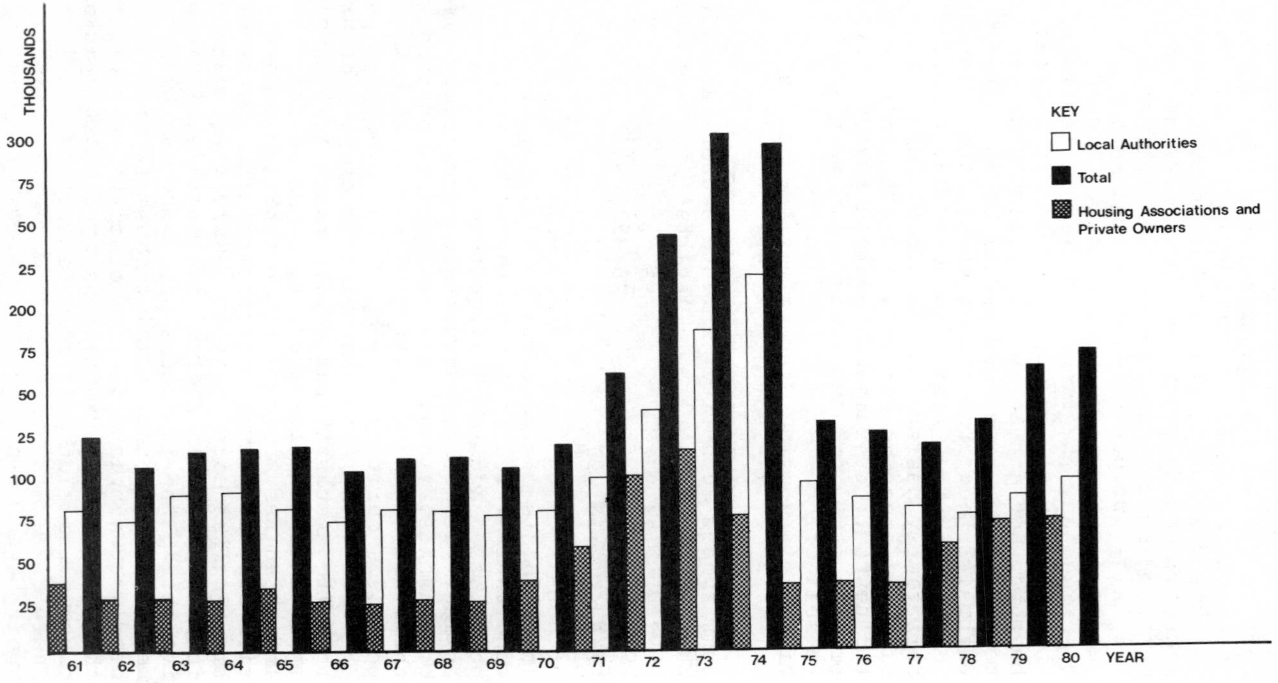

At a time when the older housing situation
is getting considerably worse, existing
policies and efforts to deal with it have
been slowed down considerably....On current
trends therefore, present policies have
little effect on the older housing situation
and suggest the necessity for a substantially increased level of replacement at some
point in the future.[36]

As yet, however, and despite this point having
been made to the Secretary of State for the Environment,[37] the current government shows little
enthusiasm for recognising such needs (Figure 4.9).
As far as the new towns were concerned, the Conservative Government effectively put an end to the
official overspill roles of new towns. The work of
the new town development corporations was prematurely
brought to an end and legislative provision was made
to sell off commercial, and indeed housing, assets
of the new towns to the private sector.

Summary and Reflections
What can we learn from this review of British
housing policy and its implementation? The first
point that stands out is that the problems of providing the right mix of housing types in the right
proportion of tenure groups to meet the full range
of housing needs and requirements in a complex
industrial society cannot be achieved by a slavish
adherence to either a free market or a collectivist
political philosophy. Indeed it can be argued that
as many problems are created as are solved when
governments attempt to take housing policy outside
the framework of a mixed economy and pluralistic
political structure.
The fact that many families do live in houses
that they own and that many council tenants are
anxious to purchase their home can be taken to
indicate that a very large proportion of the population wish to become owner occupiers. The contrary
argument from the political left, that all this
indicates is that in reality there is little effective choice and that many are owner occupiers simply
because they cannot obtain a council house, is
hardly convincing. The free market advocates are
thus in tune with a post-war need which welcomes
owner-occupation. It also makes electorial sense.
There is a clear psychological satisfaction in
owning one's own home. The growing popularity of

Figure 4.9   Housing Action Area improvement in Nottingham.

'Do-it-Yourself' activities bears witness to the
enjoyment people derive from undertaking improvements
to their own properties. A recent feature of local
authority housing estates has been the obvious signs
of external changes to those properties which have
gone into owner occupation. This commitment on the
part of the owner-occupier to his house is not a
trivial concern, but is something very deep rooted
which should be taken very seriously be politicians.
        The paradox is, of course, that owner-occupation
cannot be brought about simply be freeing up the
market. It needs considerable governmental intervention. Unless there were to be a drastic reduction
in the tax threshholds in Britain - which would
presumably mean a drastic lowering of public services
across the board - the maintenance of owner-occupation is dependent upon giving subsidies in the form
of tax relief or through the option mortgage scheme.
Furthermore if more older houses are to be available
for sale then government - working largely through
local authorities - has to ensure that improvement
policies be pursued with the aid of public money in
order to maintain confidence in the older parts of
urban areas. Once this confidence has been established then it is essential that mortgage funds be
available to enable people to purchase these older
properties and then to improve them.
        Throughout much of the post 1945 period very
few private builders were prepared to risk building
houses for sale in the inner cities even if local
authorities were prepared to release land for these
purposes. Apart from a few die hard collectivists,
few would now question the wisdom of encouraging some
new build owner occupied houses being provided in the
inner city. If this is to be done, however, local
authorities have to minimise the financial risks to
the speculative builder by offering subsidised land
or guarantees that they will purchase the properties
if they are not sold. Again, the housing market
cannot operate properly unless there is considerable
state underpinning.
        It is in the area of rent control and security
of tenure where the policies of the advocates of the
free market have done the greatest harm. The theory,
as we have seen, is that by removing controls over
rent levels and by making it easier for landlords to
end tenancies, more investment in the private rented
sector will take place and more privately rented
dwellings will come onto the market. Yet in practice
this seems not to have happened. The general result
of attempts to free up the rented sector has been to

impose rent increases on those least able to afford
them and to make their tenure less secure.

If a free market approach in housing can only
yield beneficial social results provided that it is
carefully controlled and regulated by central and
local government, what faith can we have in the
ability of central government to do the job?
Certainly we have good grounds for being sceptical.
The building of large peripheral council housing
estates on the outskirts of industrial towns and
cities with few social facilities and remote from
places of work, the whole fiasco of high rise flat
building, the wholesale clearance programmes without providing adequate replacement buildings, the
long term planning blight which settled on older
areas and which discouraged private housing invest-
emtn, all points to deficiencies in the collectist
policy for housing.

Having made these points, however, it would be
wrong to argue that governmental intervention on a
large scale in housing in Britain has been so
insensitive that there is nothing to be done but to
rely on the market despite its imperfections.   In
the early 1960s there were many dwellings that were
in such bad order that no other course was open but
to pull them down. At a very basic level high
infant mortality rates and ill health abounded in
many of these areas. By demolishing them and rehousing the populations many lives, especially the
lives of children, were saved.

What went wrong was that the speed of clearance
went ahead at a rate too fast to facilitate rehousing at the highest possible standards.   Thus
high rise redevelopment was undertaken largely under
pressure to provide new accommodation at the fastest
possible rate without allowing time to pass to learn
the technical and social lessons from the earlier
schemes. Many of the problems of the peripheral
council housing estates were also the result of
pressure to provide houses as quickly as possible.
Available resources went into providing the maximum
number of dwellings to the detriment of social
facilities.

A further criticism that can be levelled at the
comprehensive redevelopment schemes of the 1960s and
early 1970s is that too many improvable dwellings
were pulled down. The motives underlying the situation were good. Labour Governments have been traditionally concerned that all should have housing of
the highest standard. Consequently a belief was
generated that local authorities had the capacity to

provide as many of these high quality houses as
would be needed. Older houses which although capable of being made sound were therefore to be pulled
down. The clearance operations and the uncertainty
that lay over many older housing areas outstripped
the local authorities organisational and financial
capacity to build these high quality replacement
dwellings.

The 1970s can be seen as a period when both
central government and local authorities learned
their lessons. The move towards housing improvement
areas is a major example of this. Indeed Labour
Government activities during the second half of the
1970s can be seen as marking a mature phase in
attitudes towards housing policy. Government had
come to accept that there was a legitimate and
important role to be played in the provision and
management of houses by private builders, building
societies, housing associations, private landlords
as well as the local authorities working in collaboration. A crucial role for the local authority was
to orchestrate these activities. Central government
came to recognise that the housing problems of individual towns and cities differed and that, within
broad financial parameters, local authorities should
be given the maximum freedom to design policies to
match the needs of their own areas. This led to
the HIPs system. The discussion document on
housing that the government issued contained much to
indicate that a more subtle awareness of the nature
of housing need was taking place at the most senior
levels.

By 1979 there was still much to be done in
implementing many of the housing objectives of the
government, but the achievements were impressive,
especially when seen against the backcloth of a
difficult economic climate. There was, however,
considerable optimism about the future. This was
rudely shattered with the policies of the new
Conservative Government which was to ensure a
return to crude market forces in many areas of the
nations life, including housing. Draconian reductions in public money given to housing activities,
reduced discretion on the part of local authorities
in determining their housing policies, attempts to
undermine rent controls and security of tenants in
the private rented sector have resulted in dismantling what the previous administration had
achieved. There is still considerable housing need
in Britain, new houses in the public and private
sectors are still required, older houses still have

to be maintained and improved. The ability to deal with these issues now seems in jeopardy because of a revival of a partisan approach to housing policy.

Despite this pessimistic conclusion, housing conditions have improved considerably over the period we have been discussing, although arguably a decline has been apparent since 1979. For good or ill, however, the implementation of the various strands of housing and planning policy has had a significant impact on the morphology of British towns and cities. This essay has shown that the industrial revolution left a legacy of back-to-back housing, which by the 1930s, had left a core of slums in the inner areas. Late nineteenth century national and bye law housing legislation resulted in these slums being surrounded by rows of working class terraced housing.

During the 1920s and 1930s a third housing ring appeared, made up principally of housing estates, built at low densities and in which semi detached dwellings predominated. A large proportion of these estates were built by local authorities, availing themselves of the central government grants which became available after 1919. Many of these council estates were built to reaccommodate those moved from the inner city slum areas which were gradually being cleared. Other peripheral housing estates were the result of speculative developers responding to the demands of potential owner occupiers. Thus by the end of the 1930s outer peripheral housing estates were a common feature of the outskirts of industrial cities, whilst in the centres could be found cleared sites on which were built low rise council flats.

These trends, interrupted by the war, and its aftermath, continued into the late 1950s. From that point onwards dramatic changes could be observed. The speed of slum clearance activities quickened. Not only were the back-to-back houses cleared but many of the bye law houses too were being declared unfit. Inner city comprehensive redevelopment schemes were resulting in high rise blocks of flats being built. Furthermore green belt policies containing peripheral urban growth were beginning to create shortages of building land within the cities. This had a number of significant consequences. It meant that local authority housing development on the outskirts of the urban areas resulted in high rise flats being built. It also meant that house building activities had to take place beyond the green belts. As far as many of the local authorities were concerned this meant making overspill agreements with

other local authorities which had a capacity to
accommodate more population or encouraging some of
their population to move to overspill new towns. The
speculative builders, for their part, were forced to
build in what were to become commuter settlements
surrounding the industrial towns and cities. A
settlement pattern was thus becoming established in
which a series of smaller satellite settlements,
public and private, were set round the parent cities
which themselves were typified by high rise buildings
in their centres and on their peripheries.

This trend did not continue during the late
1970 and early 1980s. The large scale redevelopment
of older areas ceased, to be replaced by much
smaller pockets of redevelopment either on sites
cleared during the 1960s and early 1970s or on
smaller areas of cleared properties which were in
such a poor state of repair that improvement was out
of the question. No more public high rise blocks of
flats were built and the growth of new towns and
'official overspill' expanded towns were drastically
reduced. The appearance of the inner parts of the
cities began subtly to change. General Improvement
Areas and Housing Action Areas resulted in the
improvement of housing conditions and the environment in which the older houses stood. There was,
nonetheless, as has already been stated some house
building within the central urban areas, but this
was increasingly being undertaken by the speculative
builder and by housing associations, (which, of
course, were also very much involved in improvement
work as well).

What of the future? During the 1980s and 1990s
are we likely to see these trends continuing? Is
public and private building on green field sites
likely to be diminished as the number of new households being formed contracts? Is new building
likely to be concentrated on smaller sites within
the older areas? Is there likely to be a continuation of the improvement of older properties? The
answer to these questions depends partly on the
future state of the British economy and partly upon
governmental housing policies. If the economy picks
up, then government clearly has the option of increasing public expenditure on housing. If the
lessons of the 1960s have not been learned this
could result in the appearance once more of large
scale clearance operations. Indeed this option
might be forced on a government if currently
improvement is neglected to a degree that results in
older housing falling into such a state of disrepair

that clearance becomes inevitable. Alternatively
such a government may be able to increase expenditure on improvement. If the national economy does
not drastically improve, which seems more likely
from this vantage point of 1982, the paradox is can
government not afford to increase expenditure on
older housing, even if this means shifting spending
from other budgetary heads, such as defence or even
education? Without decent housing, it might be
argued, many other areas of public expenditure, no
matter how desirable in themselves, may simply be
wasted.

NOTES AND REFERENCES

1. Russell Kirk, The Conservative Mind,
Gateway Editions, South Bend. Indianna, 6th Edition
1978 Chapter XI: James Prior, 'The Conservative
Party', in How shall I vote?, ed Hardiman Scott.
The Bodley Head. 1976, esp p.58.
2. Lord Blake, 'A Changed Climate', in The
Conservative Opportunity, ed Lord Blake and John
Patten, Macmillan. 1976, esp pp.10-12.
3. John Patten, 'Housing and Society' in Lord
Blake and John Patten (eds); and Anthony Steer, New
Life for Old Cities, Aims of Industry, 40, 1981.
4. R.J. Tawney, Equality (1931) pp.63-72 and
189-192, quoted in English Party Politics, ed Alan
Beattie. Weidenfeld and Nicolson, 1970, pp.498-502.
5. The Labour Party Council Housing Working
Group, A Future for Public Housing, 1981.
6. For a general historical survey see J.
Burnett. A Social History of Housing. Methuen,
1980; for a more detailed study of housing policy
during the nineteenth century see Enid Gauldie.
Cruel Habitations. Allen and Unwin. 1974; for the
period 1919-1939 see M. Bowley, Housing and the
State, Allen and Unwin, 1947.
7. Interdepartmental Committee on the Rent
Acts, HMSO, 1931.
8. Bournville Village Trust, When we Build
Again, George Allen and Unwin, 1941.
9. This is very extensively discussed in Peter
Hall et al., The Containment of Urban England, Allen
and Unwin, 1973.
10. For general studies of British new towns
policy see, F.J. Osborn and A. Whittick, The New
Towns: The Answer to Megalopolis, Leonard Hill, 1969;
Frank Schaffer, The New Town Story, MacGibbon and
Kee, 1970.
11. Housing: The Next Step, Cmnd 8996 HMSO 1953.

12.   See Anthony Sutcliffe and Roger Smith, Birmingham 1939-1970 Oxford University Press, 1974, esp chaps. IV and VII.

13.   Roger Smith, 'The Politics of an Overspill Policy', Public Administration, Spring 1977.

14.   J.B. Cullingworth, Housing needs and Planning Policy, Routledge and Kegan Paul, 1960.

15.   P.G. Gray and R. Russell, The Housing Situation in 1960 Social Survey 1962.

16.   Housing in England and Wales, Cmnd 1290 HMSO 1961.

17.   Central Housing Advisory Committee, Homes for Today and Tomorrow HMSO 1961.

18.   Report of the Committee on Housing in Greater London (The Holland Report) Cmnd 2582, HMSO 1965.

19.   Central Housing Advisory Committee, Housing Associations HMSO 1971.

20.   For studies of high rise flat development during this period see E.W. Corney 'High Flats in Local Authority Housing in England and Wales since 1945', Anthony Sutcliffe, A Century of Flats in Birmingham, 1875-1973 and Roger Smith, 'Multi-dwelling Building in Scotland' in Multi-Storey Living ed Anthony Sutcliffe, Croom Helm, 1974.

21.   See Smith, op.cit.

22.   For criticism of clearance programmes see especially Jon Gower Davies, The Evangelistic Bureaucrat, Tavistock, 1972.

23.   Ministry of Housing and Local Government, The Deeplish Study: Improvement Possibilities in a District in Rochdale, HMSO 1966.

24.   Old Houses into New Homes, Cmnd 3602, HMSO 1968.

25.   Housing Policy - A Consultative Document, Cmnd 6851, HMSO 1977 p.42.

26.   Housing Strategies and Investment Programmes DOE, Circular 63/77, HMSO 1977.

27.   Brian Waters, Leslie Robinson, Jonathan Lucas, The Community Land Act Explained, Boisot Walters Cohen Partnership, The Architectural Press, 1976.

28.   Housing Policy: A Consultative Document, Cmnd 6851, HMSO 1977.   In addition three technical volumes were published.

29.   Housing Policy, p.7.

30.   For a study of Stonehouse see Roger Smith, 'Stonehouse, an Obituary for a new town', Local Government Studies Vol.4, No.2, 1978.

31.   For criticisms see J.B. Cullingworth, Essays on Housing Policy, Allen and Unwin, 1979.

32.   Quoted in Planning, 29th February 1980.

33.   Land for Private Housebuilding, DOE Circular 9/80, HMSO, 1980.

34.   Excepting those tenants in associations registered as charities or where the association did not hold the freehold.

35.   Housing and Construction Statistics No.29 HMSO, 1980, Table XVI.

36.   Association of Metropolitan Authorities Housing in the Eighties: An Analysis of Prospects in the Public and Private Sectors AMA, 1980, p.6.

37.   House of Commons Environment Committee, Session 1979/80 Enquiry into the Implications of Government's Expenditure Plans 1980/81 to 1983/84 for the Housing Policies of the Department of the Environment First Report HC 714, p.8, HMSO, 1980.

5. SPAIN

by Martin Wynn

This chapter discusses housing policy and construction in Spain in the post (Civil) War era. An
attempt is made not only to discuss the evolution of
Government policy in the housing field, but also to
discuss the impacts housing deficits and house construction have had on the growth and everyday life
of the country's main urban areas.
     The chapter comprises four main sections. The
first of these focuses on the immediate post-war
(1939-53), when the early state Housing Acts were
approved, the housing deficit grew and construction
figures remained low. Then, the new era of housing
policy dating from the passing of the 1954 Housing
Act is examined; private sector construction
increased rapidly,first relying upon the support of
State subsidies and then boomed in the non-aided
sector. The third main section looks at the decline
of production in the seventies and the unsuccessful
attempts of post-Franco Governments to introduce a
new loan system for house buyers. Finally, some
concluding comments are made.

The Post-War Housing Shortage and the 1939 and 1944
Housing Acts (1939-53)
In April, 1939, the Spanish Civil War ended. War
damage was severe (192 settlements had suffered
destruction of 60% or more of their buildings), and
the Franco Government set about creating the insti-
tutional and legislative machinery to facilitate new
house building and administer the reconstruction
effort in general. The National Institute of Housing
(Instituto Nacional de la Vivienda - INV) was
founded in 1939, followed by the Syndical Housing
Authority (Obra Sindical del Hogar - OSH) in 1942,
the former within the Ministry of Work, the latter

responsible to the Home Office. The INV was to develop and direct State housing policy throughout the post-war era (from within the Ministry of Housing after its creation in 1957) whilst the OSH became a second State housing construction body (along with the INV), constructing over 300,000 dwellings in all Spain in the post-war.[1]

At the same time, a number of other authorities acting within different ministries were charged with certain reconstruction duties and responsibilities, divisions which inevitably brought about certain conflicts and contradictions. These bodies included the General Directorate of Devastated Regions (Home Office), the General Directorate of Architecture (Home Office), and the National Institute of Reclamation (Ministry of Agriculture). More important, however, was the generally low level of house construction in the forties, and the consequent increase in the housing deficit.

During the first 40 years of the century annual house construction figures in Spain remained relatively low (Figure 5.1). The cheap Housing Acts

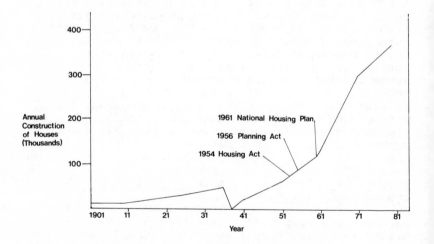

Figure 5.1 House Construction in Spain this Century
Source: Instituto Nacional de la Vivienda, Memoria de
        Actividades, INV, 1976.

(Leyes de Casas Baratas) of 1911 and 1921 offered rate exemptions and low interest loans to co-operatives building low cost dwellings for renting

out. These measures, to be administered by Local
Authorities, had little overall impact because of
the scant resources of such co-operatives and
general lack of support from the Savings Banks and
other credit organisations.

Within two weeks of the end of the war,
Franco's Government passed its first Housing Act,
which apart from indulging in the customary demo-
gogic rhetoric,[2] attempted to centralise the administration of state aid to house constructors. The
newly formed INV was made responsible for admin-
istering a new system of state aid to the constructors of 'protected houses' (viviendas protegidas).
Incentives included 90% exemption of local rate
payment (contribución urbana) for 20 years, interest
free loans to cover up to 40% of the construction
costs of public or syndical housing authorities, and
grants to cover up to 20% of constructions costs for
housing co-operatives (Table 5.1).

Emphasis was placed on public and syndical
authorities as the main house constructing agencies –
the OSH, Provincial Governments, the Savings Banks
and the newly created Municipal Housing Foundations
(Patronatos Municipales de la Vivienda). Private
constructors could benefit from the 90% rate exemption, but they were not seen as the major agencies
to implement the Act. All dwellings built within
the framework of the Act had to meet technical and
economic requirements, including a low rent level
which was not to exceed more than "a fifth of the
monthly salary of the user";[3] and they could not be
sold.

The 1939 Housing Act had very little positive
effect. State house construction agencies were slow
to take-up the incentives offered by the Act, and
the private sector chose to invest in more profitable sectors of the economy, or in housing for the
middle and upper income brackets. This latter tendency was in fact encouraged by the Urban Rent Act
(Ley de Arrendamientos Urbanos), approved in 1946.
This froze rents in the main urban areas in an
attempt to prevent private investment in housing and
channel resources into the production section of the
economy.

Nevertheless, the 1944 Housing Act (Ley de
Viviendas Bonificables) did provide some stimulus to
private house building, although its major objective
was to create new employment. It introduced a new
system of aid for subsidised houses (viviendas
bonificables) to run in parallel with the system
introduced in the 1939 Act. The two systems were in

Table 5.1 Benefits and Incentives Offered to House Constructors in 1939, 1944, 1954 and 1957 Housing Acts

Benefit/ Incentive	Legislation			
	1939 Housing Act	1944 Housing Act	1954 Housing Act	1957 Housing Act
Local Rate Exemption**	90% exemption for 20 years	90% exemption for 20 years	90% exemption for 20 years	–
Low Interest loans to cover Construction Budget	Interest free loans* for up to 40% of construction budget	4% annual interest rate on loans of up to 60% of construction budget	Interest free loans up to 75% of construction budget	900 pts/m^2 if more than 75m^2 floorspace; 600 pts/m^2 if less
Complementary Loans	–	–	Complementary loans also available (for Group II only)	
Grants	Up to 20% of construction** budget to housing co-operatives	–	Grants of* up to 20% of construction budget	'Fixed Subsidy' of 30,000 pts per dwelling
Others	–	–	Supply of Building Materials	

* To public and syndical agencies only.
** Members of co-operatives must use their own labour in housing projects.
*** Fiscal Exemptions in the 1939, 1944 and 1954 Acts also included exemption from Land and Property Transfer Taxes, and from Business Trade taxes. The 90% rate exemption was in fact a 90% discount on the tax base for calculating the contribución territorial urbana and other municipal taxes for a 20 year period. 'Rate Exemption' is thus a loose translation only. For a more detailed account of the incentive system, see J. Rafols, 'Evaluación Economica de los incentivos fiscales a viviendas de protección oficial' Hacienda Publica Española, No.47 (1977).

fact quite similar (Table 5.1) with loans being increased to cover up to 60% of the construction
budget, (at 4% annual interest rates, to be paid off
over 50 years) for viviendas bonificables. More
importantly, however, sale of these houses became
technically possible, and was made easier still
after the Act was amended in 1948. Incentives
offered thus became more attractive to both public
and private agencies, and state-aided house construction figures rose dramatically from 3484 in 1946 to
over 30,000 in 1951 (Table 5.2).

In the decade 1941-50, however, overall state-
aided house construction figures remained low, there
being only 44,000 such dwellings completed, out of a
total house construction total of 509,000. The
nature of house supply was often inappropriate to
the solvency of demand, and certain areas of the
country (notably the Catalan and Basque regions)
were largely overlooked by State housing authorities.
A generally anti-urban ideology[4] was pursued in the
forties, in which concentration was focused on the
'devastated regions' of the south and west, where
whole villages had been destroyed in the war. In
Barcelona, for example, only 15,000 houses were
built in the 1940s, of which 13,000 were financed by
the private sector.

Yet it was in the country's major cities that
the housing deficit was most acute. In Barcelona,
100,000 migrants arrived there in the first post-war
decade, swelling a housing deficit of 20,000 in 1940
to 80,000[5] by 1950 in the Barcelona municipality
alone. Many of these migrants were forced into
taking overcrowded sub-let accommodation, or building
their own dwellings in the rapidly expanding shanty
towns, which had sprung up in the green zones and
hitherto empty tracts of land in the city periphery
and in the adjoining municipalities. By the end of
the 1940s an estimated 26,000 people were living in
the Barcelona shanty towns alone and by 1954 the
figure had doubled.[6] (Figure 5.2 & 5.3). And in
Madrid, a 1950[7] report found that 6071 families were
living in 'shanties, caves or ruined houses' in the
city outskirts. The population of the city was
growing annually by 30,000, and the housing deficit
was put at 20,000. By 1955 the national housing
deficit was estimated at 1.5 million.[8]

It is against this background that the increase
in house production figures in the early fifties
must be seen. Far from declining, the housing
deficit was reaching unprecedented levels, and the
masses encamped in the shanty towns represented an

Table 5.2 House Construction in Spain 1943-60

	State-Aided Houses (see Table 5.1)						Non State-Aided Houses	Total Houses Constructed
	'Protected Dwellings' (1939 Housing Act)	'Subsidised Houses' (1944 Housing Act)	'Group 1 Houses' (1954 Housing Act)	'Group 2 Houses' (1954 Housing Act)	'Fixed Subsidy Houses' (1957 Housing Act)	Total State-Aided Houses		
1943	80	–	–	–	–	80		
1944	595	–	–	–	–	595	464870 con-structed 1941-50	509235 constructed 1941-50
1945	1326	–	–	–	–	1326		
1946	2701	783	–	–	–	3484		
1947	4120	2051	–	–	–	6171		
1948	5736	3108	–	–	–	8844		
1949	5429	4100	–	–	–	9529		
1950	5822	8514	–	–	–	14336		
1951	12898	17760	–	–	–	30658	26300	56958
1952	8766	16994	–	–	–	25760	37200	62960
1953	9711	15971	–	–	–	25682	41300	66982
1954	14844	15598	–	–	–	30442	56600	87042
1955	27537	18184	–	–	–	45721	66300	112021
1956	45238	30578	98	1812	–	77726	44300	122026
1957	30741	25802	4080	6115	–	66738	41300	108038
1958	30413	21826	12093	31488	137	95957	33400	129357
1959	32105	16062	23280	36749	16979	125175	12500	137675
1960	18589	6199	26591	32605	43534	127518	16800	144318
TOTAL 1943-1960	256651	203530	66142	108769	60650	695742	840870	1536612 (1941-60)

Source: Instituto Nacional de la Vivienda, Memoria de Actividades, INV, 1976.

Figure 5.2 Shanty Dwellings (Barracas) on the beach at
Somorrostro in the 1930s. 7000 shanty dwellers lived in this
area by the late 1940s.
Source: Archivo Historico Municipal de Barcelona.

Figure 5.3 Descendants of the Somorrostro shanty dwellers at
Camp de la Bota in the 1970s. In 1958, Barcelona Council
cleared the Somorrostro shanty town and rehoused inhabitants a
kilometre away in Council built prefabs. Over 600 people
remained living there in the late 1970s. Photo: M.G. Wynn.

127

ever present threat to law and order. The General
Strike of 1951 in Barcelona was repeated in other
major cities in the early 50s; the resistencia de la
población demanded more effective intervention by the
Government in the housing field. In Madrid, the Sub-
Regional Planning Authority embarked upon the planning
of 8 'overspill estates' (including San Blas - Figure
5.4) comprising 27,000 dwellings in the city peri-

Figure 5.4 San Blas, Madrid. San Blas, 7 kms to the east of
Madrid, was one of the earlier public housing estates built in
the periphery of the capital. Most of the estate and its 1960s
addition,Gran San Blas, were built and administered by the OSH.
Photo: M.G. Wynn.

phery,[9] specifically to rehouse shanty dwellers; and
in Barcelona, the early public housing estates of the
OSH (e.g. at Verdun - Figure 5.5) and the Municipal
Housing Foundation[10] epitomized the modest internal
dimensions, rationality of street layout, and general
low rise development (3-4 storeys) that typified these
early public estates, and set the planning and design
standards for state subsidised housing, in both pub-

Figure 5.5 Verdun, an OSH estate built in the north-eastern
limits of the Barcelona municipality in 1954. Verdun (1,460
houses) was one of the first OSH estates of such size built in
the Barcelona Sub-Region. Photo: M.G. Wynn.

lic and private sectors, for the next decade.
      At Central Government level, with economic reco-
very well under way and trade relations with other
countries returning to normality after the 'autachic
period' of the forties, a new housing policy was
being formulated to boost housing production and
give private sector agencies the dominant role in
implementing this policy. It is to this that we now
turn.

State Aid to the Private Sector and the Construction
Boom of the Sixties (1954-71)

The Content and Functioning of the 1954 and 1957 Acts.
The 1954 'Limited Rent' Housing Act followed the
pattern of the 1939 and 1944 Acts in offering financial benefits and incentives to house constructors

(see Table 5.1), but the 1954 Act put emphasis, for the first time, on the leading role that the private sector should play in state-aided house construction. The ensuing period up to 1971 may be characterised as a boom period for the construction industry, and can be divided into two phases. In the first of these (from 1955 to 1962), the private sector thrived on the incentives offered by the state and were responsible for 80-90% of state-aided house construction, which increased threefold in this period (Tables 5.2 and 5.3). Then, in a second phase from 1962-1971, the non-aided private sector boomed after having declined throughout the fifties. Construction figures as a whole doubled in the period 1961-1969, and construction of non-aided private sector dwellings increased tenfold between 1959 and 1968, coinciding with the rapid demographic growth in the country's major urban and industrial centres, where in some years house construction outstripped new housing demand (e.g. in Barcelona - Figure 5.6).

The 1954 'Limited Rent' Housing Act specifically mentioned the 'construction firm' and 'development company' as major implementation agencies, reflecting a change in government thinking as regards the nature of State intervention in housing. Housing policy also became an end in itself (rather than satisfying other political-economic objectives as it had in the 1940s), and corresponding political administrative change culminated in the creation of the Ministry of Housing in 1957. Before considering the functioning of the 1954 Act, let us first consider its main provisions and those of the 1957 Amendment Act.

The 1954 Act divided state-aided houses into two groups. Group I houses could have a usable floorspace of between 50 and 200 m^2, and could be sold off by developers without price restrictions. For this type of dwelling, no grant was offered, but rather the established 90% rate exemption, loans of up to 60% of construction budget, and supply of certain building materials. Rents were controlled in Group II houses, but these could also be sold off, although sale price could not exceed a 5% capitalisation of gross annual rent (i.e. gross annual rent x 20); and construction costs (per square metre) could not exceed 'model levels' set by the INV for different house categories, based on floorspace (again 50-200 m^2) and design. In addition to 90% rate exemptions, Group II houses could receive interest free loans to cover up to 75% of

Table 5.3   House Construction in Spain, 1961-1976

Year	Programmed House Construction in the 1961 National Housing Plan	Total House Construction	STATE AIDED HOUSING						Non-aided private sector dwellings
			'Protected Houses' (39 Act)	'Subsidised Houses' (44 Act)	'Group I Houses' (54 Act)	'Group II Houses' (54 Act)	'Fixed Subsidy Houses' (57 Act)	TOTAL	
1961	125,085	148,000	13,194	3,167	28,109	37,235	52,771	134,476	13,544
1962	139,603	162,445	2,096	2,685	24,453	36,042	82,558	147,833	14,612
1963	150,518	206,703	2,250	1,024	33,870	32,772	117,968	187,885	18,818
1964	162,144	256,894	3,461	775	57,668	26,319	142,928	231,205	25,689
1965	175,051	283,285	1,086	428	79,334	19,229	140,716	240,793	42,492
1966	188,392	268,366	902	78	88,429	17,189	104,768	211,366	57,000
1967	210,577	204,471	38	179	51,553	12,233	68,093	132,093	72,375
1968	216,623	248,089	344	41	43,724	26,831	62,430	133,398	114,719
1969	232,627	270,254	–	171	42,465	17,960	97,373	157,969	112,285
1970	249,258	308,049	–	346	54,826	17,043	113,079	185,294	122,755
1971	265,920	318,941	–	–	54,033	34,935	101,726	190,694	128,257
1972	285,018	336,309	–	–	51,075	35,450	103,889	190,404	145,610
1973	303,719	348,548	–	–	49,932	28,266	99,125	177,323	171,225
1974	323,900	358,460	–	–	51,373	24,039	100,371	175,783	182,677
1975	340,955	374,391	–	–	66,384	26,370	103,712	196,466	177,925
1976	353,510	*319,825	–	–	*58,408	*15,733	* 88,153	*162,294	*157,531
TOTAL	3,713,900	4,197,415	23,371	8,894	835,636	407,913	1,579,714	2,855,528	1,341,887

Sources: Instituto Nacional de la Vivienda, Memoria de Actividades, INV, Madrid, 1975; and
* J. Rafols Esteve, 'La Crisis de la Politica de Vivienda en España' Arquitectura No.213 (1978), p.64.

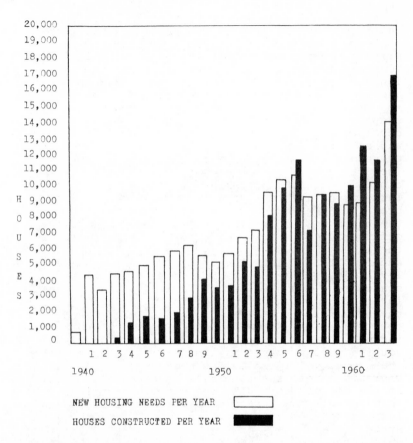

Figure 5.6 Housing Needs and House Construction in the Munici-
pality of Barcelona 1940-63.
Source: M. Sala Schnorkowski 'El Sector Inmobiliario en
Cataluña', Ciudad y Territorio, No.3 (1977) p.61.

construction costs, repayable over 50 years, and
complementary loans for a further 15% could also be
negotiated. Grants to cover 20% of the construction
budget were also available to Local Authorities,
State or Syndical organisations (Table 5.1).
    In 1957, a further Act introduced a new incen-
tive for house constructors. A 'fixed subsidy' of
30,000 pesetas per unit was made available for
dwellings of 50-150 m^2 floorspace, plus loans of 900
and 600 pesetas per m^2 of floorspace, depending on
whether floorspace was more or less than 75 m^2. Rent

levels were fixed as a function of floorspace and
amended annually to accord with cost of living fluctuations. By the late 1950s, then, five separate
state-aid systems were in operation for public and
private house constructors (Tables 5.1, 5.2, 5.3).
(Certain incongruences in the disparate pieces of
legislation were ironed out in the 1963 Housing Act[11]
and the accompanying 1968 Regulations.)
     From the late fifties onwards, the 'fixed sub-
sidy' system tended to be favoured by private sector
developers, whilst the restrictions on rent levels
and sale price for Group II houses discouraged the
private sector from participating in this system
(see Tables 5.2 and 5.3). Indeed, the INV itself,
along with the OSH and other public bodies, built a
large number of the Group II dwellings. It was the
profit expectations of the private sector, then, and
their response to different financial incentives
offered by the State, which in many ways controlled
the rhythm of house construction through the forties
and fifties. In the immediate post-war, the low
level of economic activity, the rent freeze and
scarcity of materials had discouraged private sector
investment in housing; but in the fifties, the
normalisation of economic relations with other
countries, the general economic recovery and the new
incentives offered by the 1954 and 1957 Acts saw the
housing sector emerge as a major growth area within
the economy, fuelled by the ever present flow of
migrants[12] into the country's major cities. Then,
in the mid sixties, with the construction industry
well established, private sector developers began to
increasingly forego the incentives offered by the
State, in exchange for the higher profit margins
which non-aided construction offered. By 1968 non-
aided construction figures (114,719 dwellings) were
on a par with those of the private state-aided
sector, for the first time since the mid-fifties.

Related Political-Administrative Change (1955-71).
The approval of the 1954 and 1957 Housing Acts was
complemented by a series of governmental initiatives
and administrative measures in the housing field.
In July, 1955, the first National Housing Plan was
put into effect, with the objective of building
550,000 state-aided houses in the period 1956-1960.
(80% of these-493,000-were in fact built, see Table
5.2). Then in 1956, a Decree was issued setting out
the guidelines for collaboration between the INV and
the General Directorate of Architecture and Urban

Planning (GDAUP) on the acquisition and preparation
of urban land to be used for the construction of
State housing estates. This function was reinforced
by the creation of the Ministry of Housing in 1957
and the removal of the GDAUP from the Home Office to
function within the new Ministry as two separate
Directorates - the General Directorate of Architecture and the General Directorate of Urban Planning.
The INV was taken from the Ministry of Work to become part of a General Directorate of Housing, and in
1959 the National Institute of Urban Development
(INUR) was created as a fourth division within the
Ministry, specifically to undertake land acquisition
and preparation tasks for State housing and industrial programmes.[13]
    It is worth noting here that the removal of the
General Directorate of Architecture and Urban
Planning from the Home Office, and the land acquisition and planning responsibilities for housing
estates with which it was charged in its new guise
after 1957, undoubtedly contributed to the failure
of the national planning machinery created in the
1956 Land and Urban Planning Act. It was the General
Directorate of Urban Planning (GDUP), which (along
with other central planning authorities which were
never created) was charged in the Act with the overall management and regulation of a planning system
consisting of a tiered hierarchy of urban plans and
planning authorities. But whilst the GDUP was
increasingly concerned with State housing programmes
in the Ministry of Housing, the Local Councils (the
lowest-tier planning authorities) remained answerable
to the Home Office and failed to receive (or, indeed,
ask for) the necessary guidance on the technical and
procedural provisions of the new Act. Upper tier
plans and planning authorities either did not exist
or failed to function as envisaged in the Act, and
the resultant chaos and general bastardisation of
the planning machinery at municipal and local levels
is well documented.[14]
    The lack of credibility afforded the planning
system was made worse by the fact that central and
local housing authorities (such as the OSH and
Municipal Housing Foundations) frequently by-passed
statutory planning procedure, and resultant housing
developments often contravened approval urban plans[15]
We will return below to discuss in more detail the
part housing estates had in shaping the form of urban
growth in these years.
    The programming of house construction by the
Ministry of Housing was extended to individual metro-

polises with the approval of the <u>Planes de Urgencia Social</u> for Madrid (1957), Barcelona (1958) and Asturias and Bilbao (1959). These 'plans' contained housing construction targets, and also (unsuccessfully) attempted to halt migration into these areas and consequent urban sprawl. Arrese, the Minister of Housing, asserted that these plans should encompass "restrictive measures, which by closing the door on new in-migration, will limit the problem to its present bounds...if we do not introduce measures to prevent the abnormal growth of cities, we shall achieve very little, and in the end find that although we might have built the programmed number of houses, new housing needs will have arisen in the meantime".[16]

These measures, as applied in Madrid, included the delimitation of a green belt and the designation of new satellite settlements beyond[17] (features of previous plans for Madrid since the 1920s,[18] and incorporated into the 1964 Madrid Metropolitan Area Plan). Shanty settlements were also periodically cleared, the existing communities broken up and inhabitants usually rehoused in various peripherally located public estates.[19] Indeed this policy had been formally developed in the 1957 Cabinet Decree on clandestine settlements which introduced measures "to regulate the uncontrolled migration to the capital, prevent abnormal land development and impede land speculation in areas of the Madrid periphery which should be classified as agricultural".[20] Anybody wishing to move to Madrid had to inform the authorities of their place of residence in Madrid, and Madrid companies were instructed not to employ anybody not officially residing in the capital. The immediate destruction of all shanties and other buildings without a building permit was authorised and inhabitants were to be returned to their town of origin.[21]

In 1961, the National Housing Plan was launched by the Ministry of Housing with the objective of constructing 3.7 million new dwellings over a 16 year period. The existing housing deficit was estimated at 1 million dwellings, with the remaining 2.7 million dwellings being assigned to meet new needs created by population increases, migratory movements and renewal of existing stock. The annual construction targets (see Table 5.3) were also linked with future estimates of gross national product and investment in housing, as expressed in the 4 yearly National Development Plans[22] of the periods 1964-7, 1968-71 and 1972-75, which were based very much on the French 'growth poles' model. As Table 5.3 shows, in quantitative terms alone, the construction targets were, in fact, exceeded, although there were important discrepancies between the nature of the supply and the purchasing power of the demand. We shall return to discuss this later.

Housing and the Urban Growth Process. The Land and Urban Planning Act of 1956, as well as the Sub-Regional Plans for Madrid (1946) and Barcelona (1953), placed considerable emphasis on the estate (poligono) as the major morphological unit of urban growth, for which Local Plans (planes parciales) and corresponding Roads and Services Projects (proyectos de urbanización) were to be drawn up, and approved by the public authorities. Throughout the fifties and sixties, then, the housing estate (of both public and private promotion) was one of the dominant physical forms of urban growth in Spain's major cities.

Over the period as a whole, these estates tended to become larger, in terms of dwellings constructed, and higher, as regards the number of floors per block. A survey[23] of public housing estates in Barcelona, for example, has shown that all those built in the early fifties (e.g. Verdun, Figure 5.5) comprised less than 1,000 dwellings, whilst those dating from the sixties (e.g. La Paz[24] - Figure 5.7) were of 1,000 units or more (Table 5.4), reflecting

Table 5.4   Public Housing Estates built in the Municipality of Barcelona 1950-69.

Year	Dwellings built by public promotion	Floor Space Built (m^2)	Average Floor Space per Dwelling (m^2)	Size of Promotion
1950-54	3,667	207,634	56.2	All less than 1,000 dwellings
1955-59	7,078	513,895	72.60	Between 1,000 and 1,500
1960-64	8,398	587,510	69.96	All above 1,500
1965-69	8,055	578,779	71.85	All above 1,500
TOTAL	27,198	1,887,818	69.4	

Source: J. Borja, E. Llexia, M. Sola-Morales and J. Verrie, 'El Habitat en Barcelona', Construcción, Arquitectura & Urbanismo, No.10 (1971).

Figure 5.7 The 'La Paz' Housing Estate (2,499 houses) in the
Municipality of Barcelona. This estate was built between 1963
and 1966 by the Syndical Housing Authority (OSH) at an average
density of 591 inhabitants per hectare. Photo: M.G. Wynn.

in part the introduction of industrialised building
techniques[25] and the economies of scale they offered.
This increase in estate size culminated in the construction of the 5,300 dwelling OSH estate Can Badia,
30 kms outside Barcelona in 1971, and the designation
in 1970 of eight new towns (only one of which – Tres
Cantos outside Madrid - was ever built).[26]
    Another significant factor in determining estate
dimensions was the set of norms introduced in the
National Housing Plan of 1961 to act as guidelines
for estate construction; 500 inhabitants per hectare
was seen as the 'optimum average density for Spain'
and the value of land required for estate construction
was fixed at 15% of total estate valuation (including
the land), once completed. To comply with these
requirements meant not only that estates had to be
compact but also that it was unrealistic to attempt
to reserve large areas within housing estates for
collective service infrastructure (green zones, medical facilities, schools, etc.) as the same norms

had suggested. The need, also, to provide more space for parking and traffic circulation, led the Ministry of Housing to subsequently abandon these guidelines and plan estates at lower residential densities.

Parallel changes occurred in private sector estates (both aided and non-aided), and the general inadequacy or absence of service infrastructure and chaotic nature of accompanying smaller scale developments (often illegally constructed) gave the city periphery a grotesque overall appearance (Figures 5.8 and 5.9). The local plan mechanism was regularly

Figure 5.8 The Bellvitge ('Beautiful View') Housing Estate outside Barcelona. This estate of 3000 housing units was built by private developers in the mid-sixties. Note the contrast in the scale of construction when compared with an early fifties estate such as Verdun (Figure 5.5). Photo: M.G. Wynn.

misused (often with the blessing of the town hall) to change land use classifications from agricultural, service or recreational functions to residential uses.[27] Spain's major cities grew radiocentrically and anarchically, with housing development of one sort or another[28] featuring centrally in the urban growth process. The Land and Urban Planning Act of 1956 had failed to effectively control the urban growth process - and State housing policies, directly

SPAIN

Figure 5.9 Part of Hospitalet, to the south-west of Barcelona
The population of Hospitalet increased from 51,000 in 1940 to
284,000 in 1975. The photograph reveals the typically haphazard
nature of peripheral growth in the 1960s. The major priority
for many local authorities was to get as many dwellings built
as quickly as possible, often at the expense of adequate
services and infrastructure. Photo: M.G. Wynn.

and indirectly, had been a major reason for this
breakdown.

The Decline in Production in the 1970s and Failure of Social Housing Policy

The Emergent Problems, 1972-76. The advent of the
1970s marked a deceleration in growth in total housing
construction in Spain and a decline, in numerical
terms, in state-aided construction (Table 5.3). The
number of projects licenced by the College of Architects[29] - the best indicator of developers' expectations - dropped from 1973 onwards, above all in Madrid
(Table 5.5). Many of these licenced projects were

Table 5.5   Housing Projects licenced by the
            Colleges of Architects 1971-76

	Thousands National Total	Madrid
1971	357.7	55.7
1972	598.1	139.8
1973	696.4	222.2
1974	570.1	202.0
1975	388.8	96.9
1976	376.0	44.4

Source: J. Rafols Esteve 'La Crisis de la politica
          de vivienda en España: elementos para un
          debate' Arquitectura, No.213 (1978) p.63.

never built, in part because of the ensuing recession
and in part, because some were secured for speculative purposes only (i.e. a plot with licenced plans
for construction is worth more than without).

There were several reasons for this decline in
the construction industry, but essentially it reflected a crisis in demand rather than supply, although
the cost of materials and limited credit facilities
were hindrances to developers. Rural-urban migration
was less marked from the early seventies onwards, as
economic growth in the country's main industrial
centres slowed and job opportunities increased.
There was also a reduction in general purchasing
power of the middle and lower classes with house
prices rising[30] more quickly than salaries. Economic
expectations dropped and the scarcity of loan facilities for house buyers further limited demand. The
inadequacy of credit arrangements for house buyers
is in fact a critical issue, as we shall see later.
Suffice it to say here that lending to buyers is
generally only available, if at all, for the short
term (up to 15 years), for insufficient amounts, and
at high interest rates.

These factors contributed, then, to a drying up
of demand for housing at the middle to lower end of
the market. The housing policy born in the 1950s
had become obsolete and inappropriate. It had been
framed in an era of massive housing deficit, with
the objective of maximising housing production, and
thereby stimulating supply. This, however, had been
achieved by the mid-seventies: almost 375,000 houses
were built in 1975, compared with 87,000 in 1954.
The target figures contained in the National Housing
Plan had been met and exceeded, and the 1970 census
of population and houses showed there to be more

houses than families in Spain, although over 1.1
million dwellings (10.6% of total) remained vacant.
There remained, in fact, an urgent need for certain
categories of dwelling, which the available supply
failed to meet.

These were by and large low cost dwellings
required by those still living in shanty towns,[31]
and in old decaying dwellings with inadequate
services. As late as 1975, 48.6% of dwellings in
Spain still lacked a bathroom, 17.6% were without an
indoor lavatory and 13.2% did not have running water.
Most of these deficiencies were in the 42.3% of
stock built prior to 1942 (Table 5.6), and inhabitants could generally only afford to pay for a new

Table 5.6 Age of Housing Stock, 1975

Date of Construction	% of Total Stock
1960-1975	43%
1943-1959	15%
1942 or Before	42%

Source: J. Rafols 'La Crisis de la politica de
vivienda en España: elementos para un
debate', Arquitectura, No.213 (1978) p.68.

dwelling below the base price at which the private
sector were prepared to build and sell. A study in
Vigo in 1973, for example, revealed that 54% of
families could not afford to pay more than 600,000
pesetas for a new house, but that this was below
the base price at which housing promotors would
operate.[32] A similar study in Barcelona showed that
37% of families could only afford a 425,000 peseta
home,[33] this again being below the base price for
private promotors.

The failure of the housing market to adequately
meet the demand for low-cost housing was exacerbated
by the lack of appropriate selection and vetting
procedures for applicants to both state-aided
private construction and direct state construction.
It is perhaps first worth stressing that, although
in overall quantitative terms construction targets
contained in the 1961 Housing Plan were met, the
objectives as regards subsidised housing were not,
the overall excess being achieved by the massive
over construction in the private non-aided sector
(Table 5.7). On top of this, however, state-aided
houses were by and large going to middle class
families. The INV Vigo study concluded that "the

SPAIN

Table 5.7   Housing Targets and House Construction in
            the first 3 Development Plans (1964-67,
            1968-71, 1972-75).

	A Houses Constructed	B Target	Implementation Rate A/B x 100	
Free Mkt	197,556	72,715	271.7	1st Dev Plan
	477,979	130,000	367.7	2nd Dev Plan
	691,252	353,000	195.8	3rd Dev Plan
Gp. 1 &	733,543	526,559	139.1	1st Dev Plan
Fixed Subs	589,656	806,577	70.6	2nd Dev Plan
	624,265	720,000	86.7	3rd Dev Plan
Gp. 2 &	81,917	127,880	64.1	1st Dev Plan
Dir. Const	97,671	195,923	49.8	2nd Dev Plan
	105,755	270,000	39.2	3rd Dev Plan
Total	815,460	654,449	124.6	1st Dev Plan
state-aided	667,327	1,002,500	66.6	2nd Dev Plan
	730,020	990,000	73.7	3rd Dev Plan

Source: J. Rafols 'La Crisis de la politica de
          vivienda en España: elementos para un
          debate', Arquitectura, No.213 (1978) p.71.

socio-economic categories which provided the most
inhabitants of state-aided houses were... officials,
technicians and employees on the one hand, and
teachers, professionals and non-managing lettered
people on the other ... One may conclude that the
middle class have been the major beneficiary of state
housing policy in Vigo".[34]
     One reason for this is that state-aided private
sector houses have not generally been sold or rented
out at prices lower than corresponding dwellings in
the private unaided sector, with state subsidies
being 'absorbed' by developers as part of an
increased profit margin. At the same time, the means
test for applications for 'Group I' and 'Fixed Subsidy' dwellings concern only their capacity to pay
the rent or sale price. And even in 'Group II'
dwellings, which include most of the publicly
promoted estates of the INV, the OSH and other public
bodies, the vetting of applicants is minimal with no
real means test. Further, even the publicly
promoted houses can be sold off by the occupant after
5 years of residence, at market prices.
     By the mid-seventies, then, it became clear that
a revision of housing policy was required that would

abandon the indiscriminate incentives to house constructors and provide instead subsidies to house
buyers, above all to those on lower incomes. At the
same time, direct public promotion of dwellings was
still required, but the existing machinery and its
functioning needed improving so that public funds
could be more fairly and sensibly used.

The 1976 'Social' Housing Act. In July 1976, the
'social' Housing Act was approved,[35] whereby the new
category of 'social housing' was introduced to
replace 'Group II housing' as defined in the 1954
Housing Act. It was an attempt to radically modify
the state subsidy system by making loans directly
available for the first time to the house buyer,
rather than to the developer. All economic benefits
to constructors were abolished, barring the 20 year
rate exemption. That the Act failed in its objective
of stimulating demand was largely due to the lack of
co-operation from existing credit organisations in
making money available, as envisaged by the legis-
lators.
     The benefits to house buyers introduced in the
1976 Act varied according to family income, house
price, and family size. Certain income limits were
set, above or below which applicants were ineligible
for loans. Above the income maximum of 2.5 times
the statutory minimum salary of the day, it was
suggested applicants could get a 'Group I' house or
buy in the free market without state aid; and below
the minimum income of 11% of the sale price of the
house in question, it was thought that applicants
would not be able to manage the necessary repayments
and should therefore apply for a state house through
the INV or other public body. For those between
these income brackets, five different loan systems
were introduced, providing finance for up to 95% of
house price, to be repaid over a period of up to 25
years, at 4% interest rate. Repayment quotas would
always be between 18% and 25% of family income.
     These loans were to be provided by private
banks and the Savings Banks (Cajas de Ahorro), with
the INV subsidising credit arrangements to keep
interest rates down to 4% and extend loans up to 25
years, making them cheaper and longer than would
otherwise have been the case. At the same time, the
state controlled loans[36] given by the Savings Banks,
which had previously been used to finance all types
of housing, including luxury homes and secondary
residences, could now only be made to the promotors

or buyers of state-aided dwellings. In general
terms, then, the Act attempted to introduce mechanisms that would make loans directly available to the
purchaser; under the old system, buyers accrued, if
they were lucky, some knock-on benefits only, from
the subsidies made available to developers.

Following the passing of the 1976 Act and the
regulations for design and quality standards
approved the following year, the rush for 'social
housing' applications started. By mid-1978, there
had been 350,000 applicants for loans, yet only
53,000 'social' housing qualifications had been
issued and only 9,000 new 'social' houses constructed. New construction was limited, partly because
of the large number of unsold houses built in the
early seventies; but the major reason for the overall
failure of the Act was that sufficient finance was
not made available by the credit organisations, even
given the state subsidy of interest rates. These
loans were intended for low-income families, which
presented a high risk to lenders, and the 95% cover
on sale price was far in excess of normal arrangements. The Savings Banks normally lent up to 30% of
sale price, to middle and upper-middle-class
borrowers, and rarely more than one million pesetas.
The potential increase in the costs of management
and administration incurred by the new system also
discouraged credit-giving bodies from lending their
support.

By 1977, the Ministry of Housing, and then its
successor, the Ministry of Public Works & Urban
Affairs (MOPU), were beginning to reconsider the new
system in light of its evident failings. In March
1977, all financial incentives to house constructors
were reintroduced, and then in August, 1977, the
five loan categories were abolished in favour of a
simplified unified system for the house buyer. The
Savings Banks (and other credit entities) were
authorised to provide loans of up to 85% of sale
price, repayable over 15 years, at an 11% interest
rate, with the INV paying on average 26% of the
annual repayment and interest charges, and the house
buyer the rest. Restrictions on Savings Bank
lending were also modified enabling loans to be made
for the acquisition of free market housing of up to
120 m^2 floor space.

These measures, in fact, only served to make
the situation worse, because many of those for which
the system was devised (i.e. with incomes between
11% of sale price of house and 2.5 times the minimum
salary) had to use more than 30% of their incomes to

cover mortgage repayment quotas. Yet most of the
credit giving bodies used a 30% of income cut-off
figure as a major criterion for deciding on whom to
give loans to; and despite the subsidies and
guarantees provided by the INV, credit bodies were
still not inclined to make the necessary finance
available to stimulate demand at the lower end of the
market. What the failure of the Act has demonstrated
is that it is not easy to make such organisations act
against their own interests. Either far greater
financial incentives for credit bodies are needed, or
else state loans should be introduced direct to the
house buyer.

Initiatives in Renewal and Rehabilitation. As the
INV struggled in the late seventies and early
eighties to oil the country's reluctant credit-giving
machinery and stimulate new construction, significant
initiatives at the local level were being made in the
fields of housing improvement and renewal. Spain
has one of the most organised and activist Resident
Association movements in Europe,[37] and their
campaigns, above all in the worst state housing areas
and in the shanty towns, have produced innovative
improvement and renewal solutions. These are
characterised by the participation of residents in
the design process, the employment of their own
architect planner consultant teams, and the ad hoc
nature of securing the necessary funding from the
INV and other public agencies.
    A number of such schemes have now been completed
or are underway, above all in Madrid and Barcelona
(Figure 5.10), and these act as useful models[38] for
subsequent initiatives in this field. Similarly, the
conservation of historically significant housing
(usually in the old city centres) has become a
politically delicate issue, and certain areas (e.g.
La Corralla in Madrid - Figure 5.11) have been saved
from the bulldozer, although the wanton destruction
of architecturally valuable buildings was a sad
feature of the seventies as a whole.[39]

Concluding Remarks
Spain entered the post-war era with an acute housing
shortage in its major cities and in the rural regions
devastated in the Civil War. By the mid-fifties
this deficit had worsened, reaching an estimated 1.5
million in 1955. In quantitative terms alone, this
deficit had been turned into a surplus by the early

Figure 5.10 San Cosme, near Barcelona, 1976. A block of
houses in the GSH 'overspill estate' built in the mid-sixties
to house the inhabitants of shanty towns cleared from
Montjüich, a hill area overlooking the city. By the early
seventies cracks had begun to appear in most of the 1500
dwellings. The estate is now being demolished and rebuilt in
four phases. Photo: M. Wynn.

seventies, and this in itself is a considerable
achievement. Nevertheless, certain reservations and
qualifications need to be expressed.

   Although direct public investment in housing in
Spain has been relatively low, this has been offset
to some extent by the indirect costs, and above all
local tax (rates) exemptions. Thus, whilst direct
state expenditure on housing equalled only 0.6% of
Gross National Product in 1978 (cf. 1.0% in Italy,
3.8% in G.B., 1973), indirect expenditure through
fiscal exemptions (totalling 3.5% of tax income of the
state in 1974) exceeded direct expenditure in one of
the two studies undertaken in the sixties.[40] This has
had a significant effect on municipal budgets, with
lost revenue exceeding 50% of investment in urban
development and services, in certain municipalities
(in Barcelona, for example - Table 5.8). This has only
exacerbated the poor quality environment which was

Figure 5.11 La Corrala in the Lavapies district of Madrid.
These two buildings comprise 65 houses in which over 500 people
live. They are made of adobe brick and based on a wooden
structure, and were declared a ruin (thus facilitating demolition) by their owner in 1975. They were only saved after a
long campaign by the residents and the Madrid Architects
College. Photo: M.G. Wynn.

characteristic of many of the housing estates built
in the post-war anyway, in that it has removed a
source of revenue desperately needed by local authorities to provide the roads, services, schools, green
zones and health centres that many estates still lack
(Figure 5.12). The resultant mix of low construction
standards and service deficits fuelled the residents'
association movements of the seventies, and has resulted in new housing and planning problems costly to
resolve.
     Further organisational, economic and policy prob-
lems have now arisen with the faltering attempts of
post-Franco governments to introduce loan facilities

147

Table 5.8   State Subsidised Housing: Impact on the Municipal Budget of Tax Exemptions* in the Barcelona province, 1975.

Municipality	Estimate of Municipal Income Lost in Tax/Rate Exemptions for State Subsidised Housing (A) (Millions of Pesetas)	Municipal Budgets		Percentages	
		Ordinary Budget (B)	Investment in Urban Dvpmt. (C)	$\frac{A}{B}$	$\frac{A}{C}$
Barcelona Municip.	752	11,950	1,110	6.3	67.8
Badalona	25	572	94	4.4	26.8
Corella	47	252	76	18.6	61.9
Hospitalet	79	820	227	9.6	34.7
Santa Colomo de G.	21	260	45	8.1	46.9
Province of Barcelona	1,084	20,215	2,360	5.4	45.9

*   Includes only exemptions from 'Urban Land Tax' (Contribución Territorial Urbana).

Source: J. Rafols: 'Evolución economica de los incentivos fiscales a viviendas de protección', Hacienda Publica Español, No.47 (1977).

Figure 5.12 <u>Can Serra, Hospitalet, Barcelona.</u> Lack of local
authority finances have often prevented the provision of service infrastructure contained in Local Plans for housing areas.
Here, children play in an area in which a sports centre, public gardens, health centre and school should have been built.
Photo: M.G. Wynn.

for buyers. With the Spanish economy in recession
since 1974, the housing industry has suffered more
than most, and 200,000 construction workers were laid
off in 1978 alone. In 1980, MOPU ushered in a new
three yearly housing programme which aimed to create
a quarter of a million jobs, through the construction
of 571,000 new dwellings. Again, however, the plan
has been hampered by the lack of support from the
credit institutions, in part due to the rapid inflation rate of 15-16% annually, and the consequent
problem of keeping interest rates down. The success
(or otherwise) of existing policy, then, remains very
much linked to the financial markets and the state of
the economy as a whole, and would seem inadequate in
the long run. New mechanisms and institutions for
providing credit are needed, together with a more

rational use of public funds, involving a greater
involvement of locally based housing authorities.
With the first Socialist government since the Civil
War recently installed in power, new political initiatives in the housing field should soon be forthcoming.

NOTES AND REFERENCES

1.   The OSH ceased to exist as a house construction authority in the mid-1970s, and administration
of its housing estates has subsequently passed to the
INV.   Although in absolute terms the total house construction figures (300,000) were low, the activities
of the OSH were of significance because of the minimal
dimensions and generally low standards of their
estates.   For a detailed examination of the origins,
evolution and significance of the OSH, see: 'La Obra
Sindical del Hogar: El barraquismo vertical legiti-
mado' Cuadernos de Arquitectura y Urbanismo, No.105
(1974), whole edition; and V. Segui 'OSH, oración,
despedida y cierre', Construcción, Arquitectura y
Urbanismo No.44 (1977).   For a detailed case study of
the history of an OSH estate, see M. Wynn, 'San Cosme,
Spain: Planning and Renewal of a State Housing Area',
Journal of the American Planning Association, January
(1980). See also the detail on the OSH Gran San Blas
estate in J. King, 'Housing in Spain', Town Planning
Review, Vol.40, 2 (1971) pp.381-403.
2.   In the introduction to the Act, for example,
it is asserted that 'to provide hygienic and pleasant
housing for the working classes is a demand of social
justice which the National Syndicalist State cannot
deny ...' etc. etc. (Boletin Oficial de Estado,
20-4-39, No.110).   For more detail see J. Sole and
J. Vilagut, 'De la Vivienda Protegida a la Vivienda
Social', Construcción, Arquitectura y Urbanismo No.
52 (1978) pp.16-17.
3.   'Reglamento que desarrolla la Ley de Viviendas Protegidas', Boletin Oficial del Estado
(2-10-39, No.275).
4.   For a discussion of how this affected
Barcelona, see J. Borja 'Planeamiento y Crecimiento
Urbanos de Barcelona 1939-58', Construcción,
Arquitectura y Urbanismo, No.22 (1973).
5.   According to Borja, 'Planeamiento y
Crecimiento', p.90.
6.   According to a survey carried out by the
Colegio Oficial de Arquitectos de Cataluña y Baleares
(COACB), quoted in M. Galera, S. Tarrago, F. Roca,
Atlas de Barcelona (COACB, Barcelona, 1972).
7.   Report of the Comisaria para le Ordenación

Urbana de Madrid, cited in F. de Teran Planeamiento
Urbano en la España Contemporanea (Gustavo Gili,
Barcelona, 1978), p.288.
    8. Idem, p.342. This may seem a rather high
estimate compared with the deficits of 80,000 and
20,000 for Barcelona and Madrid in 1950. There are
likely several factors here. The housing crisis did
worsen considerably in the major cities in the early
fifties as country-city migration continued apace.
There are also several ways of computing the deficit,
and the 1.5 million figure probably takes into
account all possible definitions of deficit - sub-
letting, house-sharing, old decaying housing, shanty
towns etc. etc.
    9. The eight estates were built by public
housing authorities in the mid-fifties at Penagrande,
Mantoeras, Canillas, San Blas, Vicalvaro, Palomeras,
Villaverde, and Carabanchel.
    10. For a review of the construction activi-
ties of the Barcelona Municipal Housing Foundation
(and the OSH in Barcelona), see F. Carreras and J.
Vilagut 'La Obra Sindical del Hogar y el Patronato
Municipal de la Vivienda en Barcelona: 2 ejemplos de
ineficacia' Construcción, Arquitectura y Urbanismo
No.52 (1978) pp.31-34.
    11. Decreto 2131 of 24-7-63, Boletin oficial
del Estado (6-9-63, No.124).
    12. It has been estimated that between 1955
and 1959, 4 million people left the Spanish countryside, most of which came to live in the country's
major cities and towns.
    13. By 1976, the National Institute of Urban
Development (INUR) had 128 residential and 46 industrial functioning estates throughout Spain,
occupying 7,000 hectares, with a further 7,000
hectares under construction. INUR's role has
largely been restricted to land acquisition and the
provision of basic service infrastructure, and
serviced sites have been leased to other state
agencies (e.g. OSH) or to the private sector. See
INUR - La Creación de suelo urbanizado - informe,
(ARCE and Potti S.A. (for INUR), Madrid, 1977).
    14. See, for example, M. Wynn (ed) Planning
and Urban Growth in Southern Europe (Mansells,
London, forthcoming) Chapter 5 - Spain; M. Wynn 'The
Residential Development Process in Spain - A Case
Study' Planning Outlook, Volume 24, No.1 (1981); M.
Wynn, P. Portilla and J. Urena, 'The Port Service
Area Project, Santander: Central State and Local
Authority Intervention in the Planning and Develop-
ment of a Port-side Industrial Zone' Planning and

Administration, No.1 (1980) pp.6-21.
    15. See, for example, M. Wynn 'San Cosme,
Spain: Planning and Renewal of a State Housing Area';
and M. Wynn 'Peripheral Urban Growth in Barcelona in
the Franco era' Iberian Studies Vol.8, No.1 (1979)
pp.13-28.
    16. Jose Luis Arrese, speech made at formal
creation of Interministerial Commission for the
Decongestion of Madrid in March, 1959, cited in
Politica de Vivienda, Madrid, 1959.
    17. For more detail on decongestion policies,
see M.G. Wynn and R.J. Smith, 'Spain: Urban Decentralisation' Built Environment March (1978), pp.49-54.
    18. See M. Wynn (ed) Planning and Urban Growth
in Southern Europe, Chapter 5.
    19. For an example of the socio-cultural prob-
lems associated with rehousing shanty dwellers, see
W. Cernlyn-Jones 'Home is where the donkey is'
Guardian, 19th August 1978; for a study of shanty
development in the post-war in Madrid, see J. Montes
Mieza, M. Parades Grosso and A. Villanueva Parades,
'Los Asentamientos Chabolistas en Madrid' Ciudad y
Territorio 2/3 (1976) pp.159-172.
    20. Decree of 23-8-57 by the Presidencia del
Gobierno, Madrid; see Teran, Planeamiento Urbano,
pp.352-356.
    21. For more information on 'repatriation
schemes' for immigrants in Madrid and Barcelona, see
Teran, Planeamiento Urbano, pp.356-358.
    22. The history of National Development
Planning in Spain is dealt with fully in H.W.
Richardson, Regional Development Planning and Policy
in Spain (Saxon House, 1975).
    23. J. Borja, E. Llexia, M. Sola-Morales and
J. Verrie, 'El Habitat en Barcelona' Construcción,
Arquitectura y Urbanismo, No.10 (1971).
    24. For a study of the 'La Paz' estate, see J.
Ignacio Llorens, C. Diaz, F. Anguita and F. Lopez
'Tres Realizaciones de la OSH - Trindad, La Paz and
Can Badia', Cuadernos de Arquitectura y Urbanismo
No.105 (1974) pp.63-68.
    25. For a discussion of changes in building
technology in house construction in Spain in the
sixties, see I. Paricio, 'Las Razones de la forma en
la Vivienda Masiva' Cuadernos de Arquitectura y
Urbanismo No.96 (1973).
    26. For a detailed examination of Can Badia,
see 'Ciudad Badia - un modelo con futuro?',
Construcción, Arquitectura y Urbanismo, No.43 (1977),
whole edition. For studies on the Spanish new towns,
see Ciudad y Territorio 4/73 and 1/74 (combined ver-

sions 1974) - whole edition. See also M. Wynn
'Gallecs, Spain' Town and Country Planning Nov.(1980).
        27. On the use and abuse of the local plan
mechanism, see A. Ferrer, Presentacion y Estadistica
de los Planes Parciales de la Provincia de Barcelona
(COACB, Barcelona, 1974); and M. Wynn 'Peripheral
Urban Growth in Barcelona in the Franco era',
Iberian Studies, Vol.8 No.1 (1979), pp.13-28.
        28. For a classification of the different
types of residential peripheral growth see, (for
Madrid) R. Lopez de Lucio 'En torno a los procesos
reales de desarrollo urbano. Las tipologias de
Crecimiento en la formación de la periferia de
Madrid', Ciudad y Territorio No.2/3 (1976), pp.153-
158; (for Barcelona) J. Busquets Grau 'La ciudad y
la versión social de su crecimiento', Construcción
Arquitectura y Urbanismo, No.42 (1977), pp.56-61.
        29. All plans and accompanying documentation
for house construction had to be officially stamped
(visado) by one of the Colleges of Architects, the
official bodies of the profession, before planning
approval could be given by the local (or upper-tier)
authorities.
        30. In the municipalities of the Madrid Metro-
politan Area, for example, house prices rose at percentages varying from 32% (Getafe) to 48% (Torrejon)
in the period 1974-77.
        31. In Barcelona there remained 3-5,000 shanty
dwellings in the early seventies. For a detailed
breakdown of the different estimates for this period
see, J. Alibes, M. Campo, S. Tarrago, 'Barraquismo',
Construcción, Arquitectura y Urbanismo ('La
Barcelona de Porcioles'), No.21 (1973), pp.35-36.
        32. Instituto Nacional de la Vivienda,
Analisis del Mercado de la Vivienda en el Municipio
(INV, Madrid, 1974).
        33. CYNAM Demanda de Viviendas en el Area
Metropolitana de Barcelona (Barcelona, 1971).
        34. Instituto Nacional de la Vivienda
Analisis del Mercado, p.73.
        35. For the full text of the 1970 Act and sub-
sequent regulations and amendments, see Anexos Nos.
11 and 12 (1976), and No.22 (1977), COACB,
Barcelona, whole editions.
        36. The Savings Banks (Cajas de Ahorro)
emerged in the sixties and seventies as the major
credit giving entities for housing construction. A
part of their loan funds were regulated by the INV
to be made available at relatively low interest
rates (8½% up to 1977), and for a relatively long
term (up to 15 years). The other major sources of

public funds for housing were the INV itself and the two official Credit Banks - the Banco Credito de Construcción (BCC) and the Banco Hipotecario de España (BHE). These sources (INV, BCC and BHE) collectively contributed 5-15% of all investment in housing, whilst the Savings Banks contributed 45-55% in the seventies.

37. See J. Borja 'Urban Social Movements in Spain' in M. Harloe (ed), Captive Cities (Wiley, London, 1977).

38. See M. Wynn, 'San Cosme Spain: Planning and Renewal of a State Housing Area' Journal of American Planning Association Jan. (1980); M. Wynn, 'The Residential Development Process in Spain: a case study' Planning Outlook Vol.24, No.1 (1981); P. Reyes 'Public and Private Co-operation in Low-Income Housing in Madrid' paper presented at OECD Seminar on 'Methods of Improving Public/Private Co-operation in Urban Development and Investment' OECD Paris, (Ref. CT/LGM/548/3D).

39. See M. Wynn 'Conserving Madrid', Town and Country Planning, Feb. (1980); P. Sanchez et al 'La Lucha por el centro Urbano - Plan para el Casa Antic de Barcelona' Construcción, Arquitectura y Urbanismo, No.55, (1979), pp.33-54; and 'Arquitectura en peligio', Construcción, Arquitectura y Urbanismo, No.33 (1975) whole edition.

40. These showed a 'direct' total expenditure of 7.7 and 12.1 milliard pesetas in 1967 and 1969 respectively, (by the INV) compared with 'indirect' expenditure of 6.1 and 19.8 milliard pesetas in 1967 and 1969 through tax and other fiscal exemptions. See J. Rafols 'La Crisis de la politica de Vivienda' Arquitectura No.213 (1978), p.72.

YUGOSLAVIA

by Peter Bassin*

Introduction

The organisation of housing production usually directly reflects the socio-political organisation of the society in question and the organisation of its economy as a whole. This is certainly true of Yugoslavia's rather individualised socio-political and governmental system which has experienced continuous evolution since the national and social revolution during and immediately after the World War II. Throughout the last four decades, Yugoslav society has been deeply involved with housing and its related problems in all the major urban centres. Political and financial commitment has changed with the different stages in the development of Yugoslavia. At the same time, the nature of change in housing policy has varied slightly within and between the six federal republics and two autonomous regions. Notwithstanding these variations and changes, the main goal in all the different development periods has been to increase construction of new housing in urban centres, to cope with the housing needs created by rural-urban migration, rapid city growth and the fast industrialisation of Yugoslavia (Tables 6.1 and 6.2).

Because Yugoslavia's governmental system (as a federal republic) is decentralised, responsibility for housing lies with the governments of the six republics and two autonomous regions. Furthermore, the responsibility to fulfill the plans and demands

* The author wishes to express his special thanks to TOMO STEFE, of the Agency for Societal Planning of the Socialist Republic of Slovenia, who contributed to the discussion of sociological aspects of housing, and whose assistance and support in preparation of this chapter was invaluable.

Table 6.1 Population growth in major urban centres
          1953-81

City	(Population - in thousands)			
	1953	1961	1971	1981
Beograd	593	942	1209	1470
Zagreb	456	459	733	855
Split	98	132	185	235
Ljubljana	157	206	257	305
Sarajevo	-	213	359	448
Skopje	168	270	388	556

Source: Statistični godišnjak Jugoslavije, Beograd
         1954, 1962, 1972, 1982

Table 6.2 No. of households living in major urban
           centres, 1953-81 (in thousands)

City	1953	1961	1971	1981
Beograd	137	310	401	484
Zagreb	104	164	249	288
Split	14	40	214	246
Ljubljana	-	69	88	109
Sarajevo	-	64	101	136
Skopje	27	58	96	123

Source: Statistični godišnjak Jugoslavije, Beograd
         1954, 1962, 1972, 1982

for new housing is even more decentralised within
republics and regions, and left in the hands of the
communes (local authorities), their assemblies and
executive committees, and other operational institutions within the communes. There are also certain
basic assumptions concerning housing which derive
directly from the Yugoslav socialist socio-political
system. According to the 1958 Act of Nationalisation
of Urban Dwellings and Building Plots, no Yugoslav
is entitled to own, in principle, more than two
dwellings. 'The dwelling' was defined as a consumer
good, which can also be privately built, owned,
bought and sold, but all land within urban areas was
nationalised, with existing owners being granted
only the right to use (rather than own) the land.

Historical Background. Yugoslavia was founded in
1918, after the end of World War I, as a union of

different nations with diverse cultural, religious, developmental and political backgrounds. The Austro-Hungarian and Ottoman empires reigned in nearly all the regions of the future Yugoslavia till the very beginning of this century, but the Kingdoms of Servia (including Kosovo and Macedonia) and Montenegro (both formerly in the Ottoman empire) became independent before World War I, and they, together with newly liberated Slovenia, Croatia, Bosnia and Hercegovina and the northern part of Serbia-Vojvodina (all parts of the ex-Austro-Hungarian empire) formed a new state in 1918. This was first named the Kingdom of Serbs, Croatians and Slovenes, and later renamed the Kingdom of Yugoslavia. In 1939 Yugoslavia remained one of the most economically backward countries in Europe, with its economy based upon agriculture (that accounted for 55% of national income), and with only 15% of national income created by the industrial sector.

In World War II, even this poor economy was mainly destroyed. War damage included the total or partial ruin of 300,000 farms, one third of all plant and equipment, most mines, and most of the transport system. Over 20% of the housing stock was destroyed and 3.3 million people were left homeless.

Economic and Demographic Contexts. Post-war Yugoslavia has undergone major changes in all spheres of life: social, political and economic. Rapid industrialisation in the larger urban centres throughout the country started the movement of the pre-war rural under-employed to the cities. By 1978 over 50% of the 21 million population were living in urbanised areas, and less than 40% of the total population was still working in agriculture.[1] Such significant change clearly required new housing policies.

Within this chapter, it is not feasible to give a description of the eight slightly differentiated policies in the Yugoslav housing economy (i.e. one for each of the six federal republics and the two autonomous regions). Rather, a more generalised description of the overall situation of housing in Yugoslavia is given. To help understand this complex situation some data concerning certain broader aspects of economic development, demographic growth and migration flows are provided (Table 6.3).

It is evident that post-war trends in uneven regional development largely persist, in spite of the considerable efforts made to change this situa-

Table 6.3   Percentage share of gross material product (by Republics and Autonomous Regions; Yugoslavia = 100%)

Year	% of gross material product in							
	Slo-venia	Cro-atia	Bosnia & Her-cegovina	Monte-negro	Vojvo-dina	Ser-bia*	Kosovo	Mace-donia
1947	14.9	24.0	13.8	2.2	10.5	26.2	2.3	5.1
1960	15.5	26.8	13.4	1.6	10.8	25.2	1.9	4.8
1970	16.3	25.2	12.3	2.0	10.3	24.7	2.0	5.6
1978	16.8	15.5	12.2	1.9	10.4	24.6	2.0	5.8

* The Republic of Serbia encompasses the two autonomous regions of Vojvodina and Kosovo, but in this and following tables, data for Serbia excludes both these autonomous regions, which are represented separately.

Source: B. Pleskovič & M. Dolenc, 'Regional Development in a Socialist Developing and Multinational Country: The Case of Yugoslavia' International Regional Science Review Vol.7 No.1 (1982)

tion, which was indeed stated as one of the major aims in the Yugoslav constitution of 1974.[2] At the same time, however, population distribution has changed slightly in favour of the less developed republics and autonomous regions - Macedonia, Kosovo and Bosnia and Hercegovina (Table 6.4). Neverthe-

Table 6.4   Percentage changes in population by Republics and Autonomous Regions, 1947-1978

Year	Share of total population							
	Slo-venia	Cro-atia	Bosnia & Her-cegovina	Monte-negro	Vojvo-dina	Ser-bia	Kosovo	Mace-donia
1947	9.1	24.0	16.1	2.4	10.5	26.1	4.6	7.2
1960	8.6	22.5	17.6	2.5	10.0	26.1	5.1	7.6
1978	8.2	20.8	18.8	2.6	9.1	25.1	6.9	8.4

Source: B. Pleskovič & M. Dolenc, 'Regional Development in a Socialist Developing and Mutinational Country: the Case of Yugoslavia' International Regional Science Review Vol.7 No.1 (1982)

less these regions were amongst the major 'losers' of population in 1971 (Figure 6.1), and the percent-

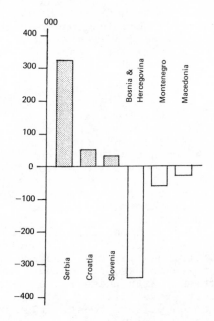

Figure 6.1 Inter-Regional Migration, 1971. Source: Savet za čovjekovu Sredinu i prostorno uredjenje, SIV i V Republika i pokrajina, Čovekova sredina i prostorno uredjenje u Jugoslaviji (Beograd, 1979).

age of total population living in urban areas increased from 19.8% to 46% over the period 1948-1979, causing a sharp increase in housing demand in the major cities.

The Main Stages in the Development of Post-War Housing
There were four main stages in the development of the planning and construction of housing in post-war Yugoslavia, which are closely related to the different stages of Yugoslav economic development as a whole. These four stages are discussed in turn below.

The Immediate Post-War Period (1945-1952). In the period up to 1952, relatively little was done to ease the massive post-war housing deficit, as reconstruction focused on the resurrection of the war-ruined Yugoslav economy as a whole. In 1947, the first Five Year Development Plan was approved; this stressed the development of basic industries and electrification of the country as the two top recon-struction priorities. Housing construction, then, although desperately needed, was limited, with 5,000 new dwellings being built per year, on average, up to 1950.

The Period of Communal Housing Funds (1953-63). Two important socio-political events in the fifties led to a dramatic increase in housing construction in Yugoslavia. In 1953, the new Federal Constitution was issued, in which not only different Republics but the Communes themselves (local governments) were given the responsibility to confront the acute housing problems of the day. It was also at this time that the self-management of enterprises (with their workers' councils) spread to apartment blocks (with their residents' councils). The 1955 Housing Act (based on the 1953 Constitution) systematised the collection of financial contributions from every employed person, to be used at communal level for house construction. With these funds, over 25,000 new dwelling units were built per year in the period 1956-1960, although private construction still accounted for the majority of new houses built (Table 6.5). The financial contribution for such public housing was defined as 10%, and then in 1958 as 7%, of all net personal incomes. These funds were administered by Communal Housing Authorities, which became independent legal entities, acting as both housing promotion bodies and the buyers of essential new housing stock. They did not construct housing themselves, but operated through the publicly-owned construction companies.

In 1959 a new Housing Act introduced more stringent norms for public housing construction and correspondingly reduced the contribution for housing to 4% of personal incomes. At the same time, practically all remaining Federal Regulations con-cerning the use of housing funds were transferred to the republic level.

The results of this period of considerable public investment in housing construction were not as satisfying as had been hoped, with 45,000 public dwelling units per year (on average) being built in the period 1961-65 (Table 6.5). Private construction was handicapped by the low availability of personal

Table 6.5   Number of dwellings built per five years,
1956-1978 (in thousands)

Year	Total 100%	Public	%	Private	%
1956-60	279	126	46	153	54
1961-65	558	226	40	332	60
1966-70	634	225	35	409	65
1971-75	684	238	35	446	65
1976-78	428	163	36	265	64
TOTAL 1956-78	2583	978		1605	

Sources: Savet za čovekovu sredinu i prostorno
uredjenje SIV i IV republikai pokrajina,
Čovekova sredina i prostorno uredjenje u
Jugoslaviji (Belgrade, 1979); Sretan
Vujović, Problemi Rekonstrukcije nehigi
jenskih naselja u Beogradu, (Referat na
Poljsko-jugoslovanskem semi-narju,
Ljubljana, 1981)

savings for investment in housing, whilst the low
rents in the public sector generally did not corres-
pond to the real quality of housing provided by the
Communal Housing Authorities. Rents were insufficient to cover even basic maintenance costs, let
alone providing finance for new investment in
housing.

The period of Market Regulations (1963-72). In the
sixties, further socio-political change took place
which again had a decisive influence on housing construction. In 1963, the Yugoslav Constitution was
amended to allow for certain market forces to act in
the functioning of the economy, together with a
further decentralisation of the means of production.
Two years later there followed two important pieces
of legislation. Personal tax contributions for
housing construction were slightly reduced and
housing construction was freed from many of the
administrative restrictions and interferences from
which it had suffered. A system of market
functioning was introduced that permitted the future
users (or buyers) of dwellings more freedom to
decide on the size and type of apartment they wished
to buy or construct. The intention was to stimulate
housing construction through a loosening of regulations and restrictions concerning both supply and

demand. The quality and the quantity of housing
were seen as central components in the nation's overall standard of living.

At this point the responsibility for resolving
the housing problems of their workers was entirely
transferred to workers' organisations and the Communal Housing Authorities were abolished. The commercial banks started to play an important role in
the credit system of housing construction and in
stimulating the purchasing power of potential buyers.
Further changes were introduced in the sphere of
housing rents, so that they became more on a par
with the monthly credit repayments of new dwelling
unit owners. Special enterprises for housing maintenance and reproduction were created as Communal
Enterprises.

All these measures attempted to create a
favourable situation, where industrial production of
housing could effectively operate within a market
system of demand and supply. In this period the
initiative for construction of individual housing,
as opposed to apartment blocks, also began to grow;
fewer apartments for rent were built, and private
sector dominance in overall housing construction
figures increased (Table 6.5). Yearly average construction in this period (1964-72) was 130,000
dwellings of which 35% were publicly built and 65%
were privately promoted; and illegal housing also
emerged as a significant form of habitat. In spite
of the quantitative rise in housing construction
during this period, supply never adequately satis-
fied demand. It became evident that certain social
categories - those with the lowest incomes - would
hardly ever be able to afford adequate housing, even
with loans from their enterprises or from the commercial banks.

The functioning of the market system in housing
construction was hampered by the failure of supply
to adequately match demand, the ever greater mono-
poly of construction firms and the inflationary rise
of prices. Private house ownership could not
adequately plug the gaps not filled by the public
sector. According to the results of the 1971 census
there was then a deficit of 507,000 dwellings in
Yugoslavian urban centres.

The Establishment of Self-managing Interest Groups
(1973 to present). The 1972 Resolution concerning
the further development of the housing economy
marked the beginning of a new period in the evolution

of Yugoslav housing policy. 'Self-managing interest
groups' were created at the Communal level, with
responsibilities for different aspects of Communal
management and administration. (Although very
individualised, this is somewhat akin to the Council
Committee system, although a broad cross-section of
society are incorporated. In a housing self-
management interest group, for example, members
would include representatives of the communal
assembly, residents, public construction companies
etc.)
        Thus each Commune would have a number of self-
managing interest groups, -- one for housing, one for
education, one for research etc. - all answerable to
the Communal Assembly. This reorganisation was continued when, in 1974, the existing system of
deputies was replaced by one of delegations. This
meant that each self-managing organisation could
elect from among themselves by direct, secret ballot
a specified number of people to constitute their
delegation. During their term in office the dele-
gates do not leave their jobs but act as a sort of
collective representative of the self-managing
organisation in question.
        These changes in socio-political life brought
with them important changes in house production and
management. Like the Communal Housing Authorities
before them, the Self-managing Housing Interest
Groups operated on a communal basis, and the
communal assemblies defined the percentage of contributions from personal net incomes to be used for
housing construction. Part of this was used as a
down payment in commercial banks for special loans
for house construction and part was used for the
creation of a 'Solidarity Housing Fund' in each
commune. This new Fund was to be used to tackle the
specific housing problems of the under-privileged
and young families. This period saw a general
improvement in the quality of residential environments, with the addition of service infrastructure,
often neglected in previous periods because of the
emphasis on quantitative rather than qualitative
production. At the same time the Solidarity Housing
Fund dwelling construction helped ameliorate the
critical social problems of the time, and many
'shanty' dwellings were cleared and their occupants
rehoused. Later a quantitative decline of housing
construction was evident, partly because of
increased societal control over construction costs,
and restrictions on prices in collective housing
construction. Unifamiliar housing - especially those

built by co-operatives (see below) - again became
important, and private sector dwellings continued to
account for over 60% of total construction (Table
6.5).

On the whole, the new system of housing finance
and construction ushered in in the early seventies was
successful in resolving the housing problems of the
poorest social strata; but the housing problems of
the lower middle classes, who were not eligible for
Solidarity Housing,yet could not buy or build their
own apartment, was not satisfactorily resolved, and
housing demand remained greater than the supply of
new housing. Construction companies often preferred
to invest in the more profitable office and factory
construction, where there were no price controls.

Housing co-operatives were of particular significance in the period from 1972-1979. By law, co-
operatives were granted developable land without
competition, and this led some construction companies
to create 'open housing co-operatives', sometimes
only as a means of enabling the construction companies to possess the (always scarce) supplies of
serviced sites specially prepared for organised
individual housing construction.

Another important aspect of housing dating from
this period is the formal introduction of urban
renewal. Renewal came about because rents in older
apartments failed to provide sufficient financial
return to cover the costs of regular maintenance,
let alone improvements and repairs. Within the city
centre Communes, where the percentage of older
housing is greatest, a part of the personal tax
contribution for housing (6% of personal income) was
put aside for the renewal of small designated areas.
The main objective of these schemes was to replace
apartments with apartments, without changing the
functional use of affected buildings through the
introduction of offices or commercial uses. Although
of interest, the number of new apartments built in
these schemes did not make a significant contribution
to the overall house construction figures.

Housing, Planning and the Urban Growth Process
Housing construction since the war has resulted in
the large scale additions of new housing areas in
many of the country's main towns, creating completely
new urban areas such as New Belgrade,[3] Split III[4]
and South Zagreb. These have generally taken the
form of high rise buildings with high population
densities, where industrialised building technologies

have been used. These constructions were seen as the most feasible alternative to unplanned urban sprawl and the spread of illegal housing.

In New Belgrade (Figures 6.2 and 6.3), a new

Figure 6.2   New Belgrade (built 1972): Typical housing towers and blocks.

city of 250,000 population was built in an area of 588 hectares between the existing Belgrade and Zemun cities, thereby creating a new conurbation of 1.4 million people (1979). On a somewhat smaller scale, Split III was built with a planned 50,000 population alongside the existing city of Split (Figures 6.4 and 6.5).

Although there have been several such large additions to existing centres, there have been very few attempts to bring about radical decentralisation through the construction of new towns. In some instances, new large housing areas have been built, such as at Titovo Velenje, following the discovery of new coal seams. Similarly, in Skopje, the capital of Macedonia, the city was rebuilt after the earthquake of 1963 had destroyed 42% of dwellings and partly destroyed a further 36%, leaving 150,000 home-

165

Figure 6.3 <u>New Belgrade (built 1972): children's playground within housing super-block.</u>

less. The dimensions and speed of construction in
Skopje were unique in Yugoslavia, and supported by
national as well as international finance,
channelled through the United Nations.[5]
    New housing areas were typically divided into
neighbourhoods of 5-10,000 inhabitants, each with
their own collective service infrastructure - kinder-
gartens, primary schools, markets and local community
centres. City structure has come to consist of three
main elements:- the city centre (where most office
and commercial activities are located), the industrial zones, and the housing areas (divided into a
number of neighbourhoods). The architectural form of
housing has changed over the years. The influence of
Le Corbusier and CIAM, and the Ville Radieuse, was
considerable in Yugoslavia, and sequences of housing
blocks up to 30 storeys high appeared in the sixties
with densities up to 600 persons per hectare. Such
new construction has since been seen as undesirable,
mainly for technical and safety reasons, and nine
floors is now the general maximum height (Figure

Figure 6.4   Split III (built 1975): Pedestrian
access ways.

6.7). At the same time, however, the social and
personal tensions caused by such high density living
in flats which are often no more than 50 m^2 floorspace have been increasingly evident. This has
reinforced a move back towards lower densities with
buildings of 3 or 4 storeys only and more variety in
typology (Figures 6.8, 6.9, 6.10, 6.11 and 6.12).
    Another housing type common to almost all the
larger urban centres is illegal development, known
as 'black housing'. It has recently been estimated[6]
that this constitutes up to 30% of all unfamiliar
dwellings in Yugoslavia. Such dwellings are
generally built by their inhabitants without building
permits, and located in the city peripheries on land
not necessarily zoned for residential development in

Figure 6.5 <u>Split III (built 1973): Housing blocks with differentiated heights.</u>

These dwelling units enjoy a south-west orientation with the panoramic view of the Adriatic Sea.

Development Plans, where land has not been nationalised and prices are lower. These dwellings represent an unplanned and spontaneous contribution to alleviating housing shortages and have sometimes been made necessary by the lack of co-ordination in the planning and development of new residential/ industrial centres. At the same time, they helped answer the demands for unfamiliar housing and were sometimes preferred to the high rise minimal dimension apartment blocks which were sometimes the only alternative.

With the transition from the market oriented housing construction of the sixties to the self-managing organisational system in the seventies,

Figure 6.6 Skopje: Central high-rise apartment
blocks forming the 'wall' around the
city centre.

The reconstruction and subsequent expansion of
Skopje was unparalleled elsewhere in Yugoslavia.
Prefabricated low-density housing outside the city
centre 'wall' has remained, and subsequently been
incorporated into the city's Development Plan.

qualitative changes were expected. In this latter
period, housing construction obtained a special
societal status and was seen as being 'socially
directed'. In practice this 'direction' was to
bring a closer integration of future users (inhabitants) into the overall process of housing
construction, starting with collaboration in the
planning and design phases. Such collaboration, it
was thought, would change the existing trends in city
growth, which could be described as an addition of
housing neighbourhoods along traffic networks. A
more complex 'socio-economic and spatially oriented
planning process' would see 'the construction of

169

Figure 6.7   Ljubljana: Neighbourhood 'Nove Dravlje II' built in 1978.

The ground level is for pedestrians only and motor traffic and free parking is underground (one parking lot per apartment). It was an attempt to segregate traffic and pedestrian flows, mainly for safety reasons.

cities as real synthesised entities'.[7] Yugoslav societal complexity was to derive from the plurality of self-managing interests: i.e. the basic organisations of associated labour (BOALs), local communities, self-managing interest groups, socio-political communities (communes, autonomous regions, republics and federation). In reality, however, too much emphasis is still given to individual families' interests, and the satisfaction of needs at the local community level in the cities is very often neglected.
        The zoning plan regulations and the consequent segregation of housing, working, and central areas have greatly influenced the pattern and quality of everyday life. Individual transportation was

Figure 6.8   <u>Ljubljana: Neighbourhood 'Nove Stozice',</u>
<u>built in 1974.</u>

Note the combination of lower blocks (4 floors) and
high rise buildings (foreground); in the background
is the 'Ruski Car' neighbourhood with pedestrianised
streets and underground parking.

favoured and the public transport system now fails
to adequately serve the journey-to-work and to-
recreation requirements of the inhabitants of
housing areas. This space segregation, together
with the increasing development of TV programmes, is
keeping more and more people isolated at home in
housing neighbourhoods, while the central areas
remain largely empty in the evening hours and on
holidays. The effective satisfaction of local community needs requires the devolution of power from
the upper-tier administrative and technical bodies
in the decision making process down to the level of
every inhabitant in the local community, or worker
in the basic organisations of associated labour.[8]

Figure 6.9   Belgrade: Neighbourhood 'Cerak 2'
              built in 1982 - recent tendencies in the
              design of housing and environment on a
              humane scale.

Concluding Remarks
An analysis of the four decades of housing construction in Yugoslavia since the war shows that none of
the systems applied has functioned perfectly, partly
because of changes in national-economic priorities.
Housing shortages still exist in the major urban
centres, whilst in the rural areas there is now a
surplus of housing. Although rural-urban migration
is now slowing, particularly in the more developed
regions of the country, the demand for new housing
still persists as qualitative expectations are continually rising, and average household size is
getting smaller.
     During the period 1951-76, 2.3 million
dwellings were added to Yugoslavia's housing stock
(Table 6.6), of which 35-40% were publicly built
(Table 6.7), largely through the communal housing
organisations. Although this is a considerable
achievement in numerical terms, the provision of
amenities remained relatively poor, with less than
20% of dwellings having central heating and only 40%

Figure 6.10   <u>Ljubljana: Neighbourhood Draveljska
gmajna built in 1982</u> - combination of
smaller apartment blocks (4 floors)
and low-density clusters of patio
houses.

having running water in 1976.
      The organisational and economic structure of
the public construction companies does not adequately
provide for the construction of different types of
dwelling, and special emphasis and stimulation to
housing co-operatives is now being given.   Other
issues of particular significance for the future
include land acquisition policy and procedure, the
whole question of procuring adequate funds to
finance housing construction, and the need to move
towards economically based apartment rents.   Only
then will the adequate and prolonged maintenance and
reproduction of the housing stock be possible.

Figure 6.11   Ljubljana: Neighbourhood 'Draveljska
gmajna' built in 1976 - pedestrian
pathway in low-density clusters of
patio houses.

Table 6.6   Number of Dwellings in Existence 1951-76.

Year	Slo-venia	Cro-atia	Bosnia & Her-cego-vina	Monte-negro	Vojvo-dina	Ser-bia	Koso-vo	Mace-donia	Yugo-slavia
				(Thousands)					
1951	368	882	491	85	460	876	114	214	3490
1961	390	1014	610	93	460	1138	142	234	4082
1971	471	1189	795	112	582	1391	181	322	5043
1976	539	1360	972	128	634	1582	217	364	5797

Source: Savet za Čovekovu sredinu i prostorno
uredjenje, SIV i IV republika i pokrajina;
Čovekova sredina i prostorno uredjenje u
Jugoslaviji; (Beograd, 1979).

Figure 6.12   Ljubljana: Neighbourhood 'Murgle'
built in 1977 - well organised low-
density housing with privacy of patio
gardens.

Table 6.7   Housing Production 1953-79 (selected
statistics)

	1953	1960	1965	1970	1976	1979
Dwellings completed (thousands)	38.2	75.7	122.0	128.8	149.9	145.7
Dwellings per 1,000 population	2.2	4.1	6.3	6.3	7.0	6.6
Type of promotor (percentage of total)						
Public	23.8	42.1	36.5	34.5	40.6	38.1
Private	76.2	52.9	63.5	65.5	59.4	61.9

Source: Annual Bulletins of Housing and Building
Statistics for Europe (ECE/UN, New York).

NOTES AND REFERENCES

1. Martin Schrenk et al., Yugoslavia, Self-management Socialism - Challenges of Development, (International Bank, Washington, 1979).
2. "In order to provide the material foundations for the equality of the nations and nationalities of Yugoslavia, to equalise the material conditions of the social life and work of working people and to achieve the most harmonious possible development of the economy as a whole, in the SFR Yugoslavia special attention shall, in the common interest, be paid to the faster development of productive force in economically underdeveloped republics and autonomous provinces, and to this end the necessary resources shall be ensured and other measures taken." Yugoslav Constitution, 1974.
3. Urbanistički zavod grada Beograda, Generalni urbanistički plan Beograda, (Beograd, 1973).
4. Braco Mušič and Marjan Bežan 'Urbanizam Splita 3 - od osnova k realizaciji' Čovjek i prostor, No.242 (1973); Slavko Jelinek, 'Split 3 u relacijama naše stambeno komunalne izgradnje' Čovjek i prostor, No.244 (1973).
5. United Nations Development Programme, Skopje Resurgent (New York, 1970).
6. Savet za čovekovu sredinu i prostorno uredjenje, Neka pitanje politike i razvoja gradskih i seoskih naselja (Beograd, 1981).
7. Delalle Radovan, Tepeš Ivan, Iay Vladimir, Bilič Tomislav, Kritovac Fedor, Usmerjena gradogradnja u socialističkom samoupravnon drustvu (referat na simpoziju v Novem Sadu, 1980).
8. Stipe Suvar, Društvenost u urbanom prostoru (referat na simpoziju Novi Sad, 1980).
9. Savet za čovekovu sredinu i prostorno uredjenje, SIV i IV republika i pokrajina, Čovekova sredina i prostorno uredjenje u Jugoslaviji, (Beograd, 1979).

ADDITIONAL BIBLIOGRAPHY

Černigoj Andrej, Public vs. Self-managed housing (the case of post WWII Yugoslavia), (Los Angeles, 1979).
Čovjek i prostor, 'Stanovanje, stanogradnja u SR Hrvatskoj', Prilog prikazu stanja, No.344 (Zagreb, 1981).
Fakulteta za sociologijo, politične vede in novinarstvo Univerze v Ljubljani, Ključni problemi razvoja in predlogi socioloških

raziskav (Ljubljana, 1981).
Kranjec Marko, Jože Kavčič, Aleš Vahčič, Finančni
    sistem stanovanjske gradnje (Ljubljana, 1980).
Krstic Branislav, Izgradnja naselja - dio razvoja
    socijalističkog društva (Beograd, 1980).
Mandelkar, D. 'Planning and Housing in the Yugoslav
    Republic of Slovenia' Urban Law and Policy, No.
    4 (1981) pp.357-372.
Mlinar Zdravko et al., Društvene vrednosti i
    stambena politika u Jugoslaviji, Savetovanje:
    "Osnove dugoročnije politike stanovanja u
    Jugoslaviji", (Beograd, 1969).
Pozenel Dare, Zadruga kot temeljna enota
    stanovanjske samouprave, (Ljubljana, 1982).
Stambeno preduzece Sarajevo, Prijedlog programa
    izgradnje i prostornog razvoja grada Sarajeva
    za period 1971-1985, (Sarajevo, 1971).
Stefanovic Dušan, Urbanizacija, (Beograd, 1973).
United Nations, Economic Commission for Europe,
    Kompleksan pristup planiranju i izgradnji novih
    stambenih naselja, (Beograd, 1974).

PHOTOS

Figures 6.7, 6.8, 6.10, 6.11 and 6.12 by Peter
Bassin.
Figures 6.2, 6.3, 6.9: courtesy of Janez Vovk.
Figures 6.4 and 6.5: courtesy of CIP.

7. DENMARK

by Ian Haywood

Introduction

The Making of Modern Denmark. Although Denmark is
one of the smallest European countries, both in
terms of area and population,[1] the 5.1 million Danes
enjoy one of the highest standards of living in the
industrial world.[2] But modern Denmark, consisting
of the peninsula of Jutland, the main islands of
Sjaelland and Fyn and some 481 lesser islands, is
only a little more than a hundred years old. In the
16th century Denmark formed a much larger part of
Scandinavia but 400 years of political and military
defeat, culminating in the loss of Southern Jutland
in 1860, resulted in Denmark contracting to almost
half its original size. The land that was left was
largely a flat land of poor sandy soil and peat bogs
with few forests and practically no mineral
resources. Yet from this unpromising start has
developed one of the most prosperous European countries, serving not only as a bridge between
Scandinavia and the rest of Europe but also as an
economic and political model for other countries and
a source of inspiration for European design in
general and housing in particular.
     Three key reforms were instrumental in effec-
ting this progress. The most important was the
reaction, from the beginning of the 19th century,
against the classical model of education with its
egocentric emphasis on individual accomplishment and
the perpetuation of an elite. This reaction was
formulated in a movement which came to be known as
the Folk High School[3] system (Folkehöjskoler) which
was concerned more with the development of the
person, through the acquisition of knowledge and
experience, than formal accomplishment. Denmark was

178

still in a feudal state at the time of their development, and students attending the schools were
mainly agricultural peasants in their twenties. It
is estimated that some 30% of the population benefited from such education. A parallel development
was a system of vocational agricultural schools aimed
directly at raising the technical skills of the
farming communities.

The early development of a broadly based educational system contributed to the second major area
of change. From the middle of the 19th century a
process of constitutional reform started to erode
the power of the monarch and was widely supported by
an educated proletariate as the franchise of the
people was extended and new political parties were
formed. The result was the eventual creation of a
parliamentary system which was both democratic and
radical.

The third main area of reform was on the land,
where agrarian change was effected during the second
half of the 19th century through the dismantling of
the great feudal estates and the transference of
freeholds to the peasant farmers. Agrarian reform
was supported by the widespread development of agricultural co-operatives offering new services and
markets to the farmers.

By the beginning of the 20th century the basis
was established for a modern social democratic state
founded on agricultural prosperity. Although agriculture served to develop the Danish economy, since
the 1950s it has been displaced by industry as the
main economic activity. The lack of mineral
resources meant that industrialisation occurred much
later in Denmark than in other countries. When it
did take place there was little development of heavy
industry and the main growth was in manufacturing.
As a result Denmark largely escaped the social and
economic traumas experienced by other countries as a
part of the industrialisation process.

The small size of the country, the small population and relatively low density, the early
emphasis on the development of the rural peasant,
the role of co-operatives, the creation of a
parliamentary democracy and the founding of economic
growth on agricultural development all contributed
to the development of modern Denmark. It is a
society which is largely homogeneous and prosperous,
mixing a high degree of self-reliance with a strong
sense of traditional values but, at the same time,
accepting a high degree of state control and
bureaucratisation in daily life.

The Pre-war Housing Situation. The democratic
nature of Danish society and the experience of agricultural co-operatives led naturally to the development of a collective solution to housing problems,
through housing associations working on a self-help
basis for specific sectors of society. The first
co-operative housing associations were formed in the
1860s, and were amalgamated into a National
Federation of Non-Profit Housing Associations in 1919
(Boligselskabernes Landsforening). They took their
place alongside the growing middle classes -
building their single family houses - and the
individual builder-developer - often building high
rise developments to let - as a part of the embryonic
housing system developing to meet the problems of
rural-urban migration and increasing population
growth which Denmark had faced since the turn of the
century.
     Although Denmark was neutral, the First World
War seriously aggravated the housing problem through
the reduction of housing development with the result
that in the 1920s a critical housing shortage had
developed. The government intervened by granting
subsidies to housing co-operatives, of up to 70% of
the construction cost, in an effort to increase
housing supply. The resultant development of inter-
war housing took two main forms. The first was the
democratisation of the single family house, partly
as a result of the influence of the English garden
city movement, with new low density residential suburbs being created around the main urban settlements
to accommodate the new urban migrants. The second
aspect was the increased building of multi-storey
flat developments within urban areas to replace the
older housing stock.
     The new impetus for housing development was
accompanied by significant changes in attitudes towards the general problems of housing design. Until
the 1920s, architecture and town planning had been
much influenced by the neo-classical traditions
which had spread up through Europe. After the war
these traditions came increasingly under the
influence of the concepts of functionalism, developing through the modern movement and the Bauhaus in
Germany.[4] This new emphasis was allied to the concepts of social and health ideals which had
developed through the English garden city movement
and proved to be a liberating influence on housing
design. Greater attention was now paid to aspects
of siting and orientation and the general environment. The provision of open spaces, or balconies in

the case of flats, became standard, and greater concern was shown for the provision of communal facilities. At the same time new structural methods and
the development of new materials contributed to the
development of better buildings, which were more
carefully designed and better planned with a higher
standard of services and facilities.

The world depression of the 1930s led to high
unemployment in Denmark and the reduction in house
building gave rise to a new act, in 1933, which
authorised the government to loan money for housing
erected by non-profit housing associations and
limited profit joint-stock companies. Safeguards
against speculation and the abuse of these provisions were provided for by the requirement that such
organisations had to be approved by the Ministry of
Home Affairs who enforced conditions to control
rents and ensure that profits were re-invested in
further housing development.

The War-time Period. In 1940 Denmark was invaded by
Germany and after 24 hours of resistance capitulated
and remained occupied until liberated by the Allies
in 1945. The result was that Denmark did not suffer
the physical destruction that so many other
European cities endured, although the economy and
development were largely paralysed. Before the end
of the war it was recognised that new energies
would need to be directed to solving the problems of
the accumulating housing needs of the country.

The effectiveness of the partnership between
non-profit housing associations, responsible for the
actual development of housing, and the government,
responsible for financing the associations, had
already been demonstrated. However private landlords were increasingly reluctant to invest in
housing, both because of the wartime conditions and
because rent control had been introduced by the 1933
act and, in 1939, the government had frozen all
rents and granted security of tenure to tenants. The
government therefore accepted that given the
economic situation and the limited resources available, the most effective role they could play in
increasing housing output would be to strengthen the
housing association sector.

In 1941, the Federation of Non-profit Housing
Associations, in collaboration with some of the
trades unions, set up a new organisation called
Workers' Housing (Arbejderbo) to assist in establishing new housing associations where they were

needed. To meet the particular needs of Copenhagen,
the KAB (<u>Kobenhavns Almindelige Boligselskab</u>) housing
association was set up to work throughout the metropolitan area of the city. The KAB had originally
been formed in the 1920s as a limited profit joint-
stock company and, having mainly operated as a
housing contractor, brought a great deal of
experience to bear on the development of housing
solutions.

The Post-war Period

<u>The Immediate Post-war Period.</u> The changed inter-
national post-war economic scene meant that the
Danish economy came under increasing pressure to
adapt to new markets and new opportunities. Efforts
to increase further the efficiency of the agricultural sector had already led to the amalgamation of
farms into larger units. The reduction in the
number of farms led to increased migration to urban
centres and provided a further stimulus to the development and diversification of the industrial sector
of the economy particularly into manufacturing. But
the weak state of the economy and the shortage of
materials made it clear that if the post-war housing
problems were to be solved, not only would there
have to be major changes in the national economy but
also new legislation and institutions would be
required. A number of measures were therefore taken
in the immediate post-war period to help make better
use of the housing stock, increase housing provision
and develop new administrative institutions.[5]
    In 1945 legislation was passed which enabled
the government to requisition empty property built
before 1939. The purpose of these measures was to
make sure that empty houses were quickly brought
back into use and that they could be allocated to
provide accommodation for families who, because of
size or circumstances, were most in need of housing.
In 1946 the government introduced the Building Subsidy Act, which made low cost government grants
available for all forms of housing irrespective of
cost or the income of tenant or landlord.
    In 1947, the government established a separate
Ministry of Housing and the State Building Institute
with responsibility for overseeing the provision of
housing and the development of appropriate fields of
research. A major initiative launched by these two
new organisations was the development of industrial-

ised housing construction techniques aimed at meeting the shortage of materials and speeding up the supply of houses (Figure 7.1).

Figure 7.1 Bellahøj, Copenhagen.
A typical early 1950 industrialised housing scheme. Site plan designed by Morgens Irming and Tage Nielsen. Buildings designed by various architects including Copenhagen City Architect's office.

Through making the granting of financial assistance conditional upon the use of industrialised building techniques, the government was able to ensure the development and adoption of such techniques on a wide scale. Smaller housing associations were encouraged to group together to form larger units which would be better able to take advantage of the economies of scale offered by industrialised techniques. Architects and engineers concentrated their efforts on the development of standardised building types and components.

As a result it is estimated that in the 1940s and 50s approximately 90% of all housing was erected with the assistance of government subsidies, with non-profit associations being responsible for the completion of about half the housing total. Although industrialised construction techniques were making an increasing contribution to housing provision, the development of schemes based on the individual small house were still being undertaken by many housing associations. In low density housing developments (Figure 7.2) the particular Danish concern for the

Figure 7.2   Typical example of low-density post-war private housing.

social aspects of housing drew inspiration from the neighbourhood concept being developed in England, but took it further by providing a range of community facilities aimed at increasing the mutual support basis of the communities created. In the higher density schemes there was a trend towards the development of collectives providing a range of services including restaurants, laundries, cleaning services, day care facilities for children and visitors' accommodation. An important ideological concern was seen as being the need to liberate women from the tasks which tied them to the home, by providing a wide range of collectively organised services.

The 1950s Onwards. The initiatives launched in the late 1940s and early 50s had been based on state intervention aimed at increasing housing provision and ensuring some match between need and supply. From the 1950s onwards a change of emphasis developed as the government became aware of the real costs of housing and the very high costs of its own intervention policies. As a result the accepted involvement of government in housing came under increasing scrutiny.

The results were seen in a number of moves. In 1954 the low interest government loans were superceded by a form of mortgage linked to the prevailing interest rates. From 1955 onwards restrictions enforcing rent control and the compulsory allocation of housing, which had been extended in 1951 to property built after 1939, were eased in an effort to introduce an element of market forces into the situation. Rent increases were permitted for some properties and new rental property built without government subsidy was freed of all rent control.

In 1958 the government withdrew completely from the direct mortgage market and instead established mortgage credit institutions operating through the private capital market. These changes enabled private house builders to borrow up to 75% of the construction costs, which could be increased to a maximum of 80-85% through insurance guarantee arrangements. Although these mortgages were more expensive and the person building his single family house was no longer eligible for a direct government subsidy, he was still entitled to substantial tax allowances by setting a portion of his housing costs against his income tax liability.

To aid non-profit housing associations the government introduced a system of guaranteed mortgages which could raise the loan for non-profit rental housing up to a maximum of 94% of the construction costs. Interest was payable at market rates but to reduce the initial effect of interest charges the government offered flat rate subsidies, for a period of six years, related to the floor area of the dwelling. The flat rate subsidy was available for all new rental property whether built by non-profit associations or private investors.

In the late 1950s the government, in an effort to regulate the housing market and reduce its own expenditure, limited its level of support for the non-profit housing sector to a maximum of 10,000 housing units a year. At the same time there was an upsurge in the private house building sector with the result that, whilst house completions which had averaged about 22,000 a year in the 1950s rose to some 28,000 in 1960, the number completed by the non-profit associations dropped from nearly 8,000 a year to a little over 6,000 a year. The Federation of Non-Profit Housing Associations protested successfully about this trend and in the early 60s the proportion of non-profit housing started to rise again.

However, in the early 60s interest rates started to climb and, coupled with the lack of control of land prices or construction costs, resulted in very substantial increases in housing costs. The end result was that by 1964 construction costs had increased so much faster than incomes that many non-profit associations and private landlords found it difficult to let their properties.

Housing Policies in the 60s. Although housing completions had risen steadily during the 50s and averaged some 38,000 a year during the 60s, the ruling Social Democrats recognised that there was an urgent need to develop comprehensive housing policies which would ensure a closer match between housing provision and need. Because the parliamentary system in Denmark is based on a form of proportional representation, with some 10-12 parties being represented in parliament, the Social Democrats had to obtain the support of the three main non-socialist parties for any new housing policies they wanted to adopt.

The ensuing discussions produced a pact in 1966 between the four main parties in the form of a series of proposals for the 8 year period up to 1974. These proposals were intended to achieve during this transitional period an uncontrolled and

unsubsidised housing market freed from government
intervention. In particular it was hoped that the
introduction of market forces would reduce the disparities between rents in the private and non-profit
sectors. The proposals contained five main elements.
Firstly, it was intended to move to the equalisa-
tion of rents by increasing rents in older properties
and reducing rents in newer properties. Secondly, it
was proposed to reduce the imbalance between subsidies received by the private sector and those
received by non-profit housing by reducing the tax
benefits the owner occupier received. Thirdly, the
initial rents in non-profit housing would be reduced
by the introduction of a new subsidy which would
cover any portion of interest charges exceeding 6%
per annum for a period of six years from completion
of the dwelling. Fourthly, a system of graded rent
subsidies would be introduced which would be related
to the householder's income, composition of his
family and the rent paid. Lastly, an effort would
be made to keep down building costs through establishing fixed prices and specific deadlines for any
housing scheme receiving public subsidies.

As a result of these measures rents in older
private properties increased by about 40% above the
1965 level and those in non-profit housing rose by
about 20% with comparable increases in the tax
burden of owner-occupiers. However the overall
success of the proposed measures depended upon a
drop in interest rates and a slowing down in the
rate of increase of land and development costs.
Neither of these necessary preconditions occurred
and, as costs and interest rates continued to rise,
the gap between rents in the different sectors and
between older and newer properties widened further.
The situation was further exacerbated by the
developing energy crisis and world recession in the
early 70s which caused increasing balance of payments
problems for Denmark.

In an effort to reduce its spending and divert
resources into exports or import substitution industries, the government introduced a number of cutbacks
in the building sector. In 1972 sharp reductions
were ordered in both the quality and quantity of
non-profit housing receiving government subsidy. As
a consequence the annual quota of non-profit housing
eligible for government subsidy was reduced from
some 13,000 dwellings to 7,000 and the average size
of units was reduced from 100 m² to 85 m². In 1973
private unsubsidised house building was limited to a
maximum of 31,000 units a year. The overall result

was that housing completions which had averaged
51,000 dwellings a year during the early 70s dropped
from 1975 to around 36,000 units a year.

In addition, the government introduced a freeze
on all public building between October 1973 and
October 1974. In a further effort to stabilise output and promote better use of the building industry,
the government set in hand the promotion of five
year rolling programmes to provide for the construction of a maximum of 7,000 dwellings a year by non-
profit associations using industrialised building
techniques.

The Last Decade

New Proposals for Reform. Housing policies in
Denmark are formulated in the context of five year
perspective plans derived from the recurring national
census of population and housing. These plans
attempt to predict likely changes in the housing
situation on the basis of current trends. Both the
1970 and the 1974 perspective plans had drawn attention to the housing sectors growing share of the
national resources and the effects of the direct and
indirect housing subsidies. These subsidies were
generally considered to be inflationary both because
they tended to push up wages and prices and, because
of the limited requirement for down payments, they
reduced the incentive to save and money was invested
directly in building.

As the 1966 pact neared the end of its life it
was therefore clear that it had failed to achieve
its overall objectives and a revision of policies
would be necessary. Further discussions were
started by the government which resulted in a new
pact being agreed in 1974 between the six main political parties. The general objectives of this pact
still adhered to the intention to eliminate subsidies
in the long term and develop a more carefully regulated housing market.

One of the major problems in developing new
policies was the need to reduce the discrepancies
between the level of direct subsidy to tenants and
indirect subsidies to owner occupiers through the tax
system. It was estimated that the total subsidy to
owner occupiers was twice that received by tenants.
However the pact did not address itself specifically
to these issues beyond agreeing that a committee
should be established to develop proposals for the

reduction of tax based subsidies. Proposals were
included to increase subsidies, under the graded
rent scheme, by providing for annual increases to
reflect rises in wages and salaries. Rent control
was further reduced by applying it in the future
only to local government areas with populations ot
more than 20,000 people. The principle of economic
rents was strengthened by their adoption for older
properties and tenants in large developments were
given a higher degree of autonomy including the
right to transfer tenancies. In an effort to limit
its expenditure and regulate the housing supply, the
government limited the subsidies it would give to
non-profit housing to a maximum of 8,000 dwellings a
year.
    In addition to the effects of the economic
recession, two other factors started to have an
increasing influence on housing policies. The first
was the wider concern being expressed in general for
environmental issues and the need to respect the
natural environment. The second was the increasing
public reaction against much modern development and
the desire for a more human environment with particular emphasis on policies of conservation.

Planning Reforms. The increasing government recognition of the importance of environmental issues
resulted in the creation of the Ministry of the
Environment in 1973. This new ministry took over
planning functions from the Ministry of Housing and,
for the first time, brought together a concern for
physical planning with a wide range of responsibilities for the environment. The ministry consists of
a main co-ordinating department and five agencies:
National Agency for the Protection of Nature, Monu-
ments and Sites, National Agency for Environmental
Protection, National Agency for Physical Planning,
the National Forest Service and the National Food
Institute.
    In 1969 the government had set in motion the
process of reforming the planning legislation which
was followed in 1970 by a major reform of the local
government system.[6] This reduced the number of
administrative units from over 1,400 to less than
300 in a two tier local government system of county
councils and districts. The Ministry of the Environment carried forward these planning reforms by
introducing four major planning acts which either
consolidated existing legislation or provided new
powers.

During the immediate post war period it had been recognised that changes in the national economy were generating an imbalance of development in the various regions of the country. In 1958 the Regional Development Act had been passed which gave the government power to provide financial incentives to encourage investment in the less developed regions. To provide a sound planning basis for national and regional development, parliament approved in June 1973 the Act on National and Regional Planning.[7] This act, which had been prepared in the Ministry of Housing during the time when it still had responsibility for physical planning, sets out the planning responsibilities for the newly reformed local government system. Denmark had been divided into 12 county councils and 275 districts excluding Copenhagen. The county councils were charged with the responsibility for preparing regional plans aimed at ensuring the uniform development of the county which would reflect the best interests of the community. In particular the plans had to set out the guidelines for the future distribution of urban development and the extent and situation of summer cottage areas.

Copenhagen was specifically excluded from the provisions of this act and was made the subject of separate simultaneous legislation by means of the Act on Regional Planning for the Metropolitan Area of Greater Copenhagen.[8] The separate treatment of Copenhagen reflects its importance as the largest urban agglomeration containing more than 30% of the total of the Danish population.[9] A metropolitan council was established to undertake mandatory planning for the Greater Copenhagen area with provisions similar to those of the national legislation.

The second important piece of planning legislation was the Municipal Planning Act of 1975[10] which defined the planning functions of the district councils. These required the district councils to prepare municipal structure plans for the whole of their area, setting out the main areas of land use and defining areas where development was likely to take place and detailed local plans would need to be prepared. The act requires that a local plan shall be produced and approved before the subdivision of larger areas or major building and investment works are carried out. Such plans have to conform to the requirements of the local structure plan and the regional plan for the area.

The first Urban and Rural Zones Act had been approved by parliament in 1969 but was subsequently modified in 1972 and 1975.[11] This act divides the

whole of Denmark into urban zones, rural zones and
summer house districts. Its general provisions are
to restrict all development to urban areas by
ensuring that an adequate supply of land is always
available for development in defined urban areas.
The general objective is to preserve the rural areas
from any further encroachment by development including summer houses.

The creation of the Ministry of Environment
provided a new focus for the concern with regard to
re-development policies and the growing emphasis on
rehabilitation and renewal as viable alternatives.
The Housing (Slum Clearance) Act of 1969 had given
local authorities power to order demolition or
improvement of dwellings they considered inadequate.
Provision was also made for grants to be made available to assist conversion, improvement or renovation.
These provisions were consolidated and extended by
the Urban Renewal and Housing Renovation Act of 1980.
This act extended the system of interest free
guarantees, given to non-profit associations for new
development, by applying them to rehabilitation and
renewal schemes.

The provisions of these four major acts dealing
with national and regional planning, municipal
planning, urban and rural land uses, and urban
renewal and renovation have set the planning framework for the development of current housing policies
in Denmark. But alongside the development of
planning legislation the government was implementing
positive policies aimed at more efficient house
building through, firstly, the development and adoption of industrialised techniques and, secondly,
through the use of energy saving techniques.

The Development of Industrialised Building Techniques.
The immediate post-war need for more houses and other
building types, coupled with the lack of building
materials and the limited capacity of the building
industry, were all factors which led to consideration of the need to develop a rationalised and
industrialised building industry. In a move to
assist this process the government established the
State Building Institute (Statens Byggeforskningsinstitut) in 1947.

The State Building Institute proved to be an
important force in the modernisation of the building
industry. Its efforts to improve the productivity
of the industry included the development of national
building regulations, which were adopted for the

191

whole country in 1961,[12] and the development of modular co-ordination of building design, through provisions in the building acts which require all buildings containing two or more dwellings to be designed on a modular basis. This provision ensures that where conditions are appropriate, industrialised techniques can be employed but do not have to be used.[13]

The government supported these provisions by encouraging smaller housing associations to group together to form larger units more able to take advantage of the economies of scale offered by industrialised techniques. Through the subsidy system the government was also able to require all grant aided schemes to be designed on the basis of being suitable for construction using industrialised techniques. In conjunction with the non-profit associations the government was able to draw up its five year housing plans aimed at achieving a degree of consistency and continuity in the building industry's planning of its own output.

Early efforts to rationalise the building industry concentrated on the development of industrialised systems which would transfer as much as possible of the building process from the building site to the factory floor. The impact was felt all through the building industry as the new techniques were developed and building component factories established. Changes in the building process meant a demand for new skills as well as new procedural and contracting systems. The greatest impact however was on the built environment as the new industrialised techniques appeared as multi-storey prefabricated buildings. The spread was so rapid that it was estimated that during the 1970s some 80-90% of all high rise development in Copenhagen and 60-70% elsewhere, was built using industrialised techniques.

Although the initial emphasis was on the development of large scale multi-storey developments, the further development of an industrialised approach resulted in the production of a range of modular co-ordinated prefabricated elements applicable to all forms of development, including low rise housing. This 'open system' of industrialised techniques provides a range of different components which can be used in a variety of situations but enable greater freedom of planning and design to be achieved, whilst benefiting from the economies of standardised industrial production on a large scale.

DENMARK

Investment in the house building industry has
seen substantial fluctuations over the last decade
but has averaged about 5% of the Gross National
Product. Industrialisation and standardisation have
however helped treble production in the building
industry from the mid 60s to mid 70s, with a labour
force which has remained virtually constant in size.
The modernisation of the building industry has been
the product of close co-operation between government
and industry but four main factors can be seen to
have especially contributed to the development of
industrialised techniques.

Firstly, the nationally applicable system of
building legislation has encouraged the use of
industrialised techniques across the country.
Secondly, the national building regulations have
been developed on the basis of performance specifications rather than specific design requirements and
have not inhibited innovation or the development of
new materials and techniques. Thirdly, national
requirements for the adoption of modular design
principles have resulted in the standardisation of
many building components facilitating their production and use. Lastly, government's efforts to
develop long term housing supply plans have helped
ensure some continuity and stability in the building
industry's production systems.

Energy Policy and Housing. The rise in energy costs
in the early 1970s emphasised the importance for
Denmark of saving on imported fuel. As a part of
overall energy saving measures, the government introduced from 1975 a number of measures aimed at energy
saving in housing through the development of higher
insulation standards, more energy conscious designs
and improved planning layouts.[14]

In 1975 grants were provided to meet some of
the costs of improving the thermal efficiency of
existing houses. The scheme was revised in 1978 and,
under the new provisions, owner occupiers are
allowed to deduct from their taxable income 50% of
their outlay on energy saving measures. In blocks
of flats grants are made available to cover 30% of
such costs for each unit. In each case the
proposed measures have to comply with general energy
saving requirements the government has established
and are subject to maximum financial limits.

A new Ministry of Energy was established in 1979
with specific responsibility for developing comprehensive energy policies and a series of further

measures were introduced to save energy in houses.
The building regulations were revised to increase
the requirements for thermal insulation in new
buildings. The annual inspection of small oil fired
boilers, which had been made compulsory in 1978, was
strengthened by requiring annual cleaning of oil-
fired installations and their compulsory adjustment
if necessary. Other legislation made it compulsory
for housing in certain areas to be connected to
district heating schemes aimed at utilising waste
heat from power stations and industrial plants. In
these areas other forms of heating were forbidden.
     Consideration has also been given to the role
density and housing layout and planning may have to
play in reducing energy demands. Theoretical studies
have indicated that heat consumption can be reduced
by up to 25% through using more compact higher density forms of housing layout. Further energy savings
can be made by giving greater consideration to the
relationship between different land uses and reducing
transportation movements. At the more detailed level
the Ministry of Energy commissioned a series of
prototype houses to explore different approaches to
energy saving through housing design and construc-
tion.15
     Between 1975 and 1981, the budget for state
financed energy research was more than trebled and
the positive steps taken to conserve energy were
reinforced by increased government taxes on fuel oil,
petrol, gas and electricity. The overall impact of
these policies has been difficult to assess. Energy
consumption for space heating declined at around 1%
per annum, despite a continuing increase in the
number of buildings. The tax allowance scheme for
owner occupiers is not attractive enough to generate
wide participation and the grant scheme does not
offer sufficient real economies to building owners.
However the grant scheme for the utilisation of
renewable energy resources has received a very
favourable response. Poor public support for energy
conservation measures was emphasised by the antipathy
generated by the compulsory inspection procedures
introduced for heating installations.
     Despite the limited experience gained so far, it
is clear that energy conservation measures are likely
to play an increasingly important role in affecting
future housing layout and design. These considerations will apply not only at the detailed level of
housing design and the use of materials, but also at
the wider level of housing layout and the planning
of settlements.

DENMARK

Current Housing Policies

The General Situation. At present Denmark has a
housing stock of some two million dwellings of which
about 60% are private owner occupied homes; 23.5%
privately rented dwellings, mainly in older apartment blocks; and some 16.5% are rental properties
belonging to non-profit housing associations. In
the early 1980s Denmark was building around 31,000
dwellings a year of which about 80% were private
owner occupied homes; 18.5% are being built by non-
profit housing associations and the remaining 1.5%
are being built for private rent or government use.[16]
   The current housing policies in Denmark are the
result of a long interplay between the social, economic and political forces which have formed Danish
society. The prosperity of the country has given
substance to the average Dane's desire for the ideal
of an individual detached family house in a low
density suburb as the typical form of housing development. The emphasis on self-reliance and the
development of co-operatives has meant that the
government plays a negligible role in the direct
construction of housing and, instead, affects the
housing market through legislation and direct and
indirect subsidies. The social role of assisting
those with some housing need has largely been taken
over by the non-profit associations who provide
housing not only for families but also for the elderly
or handicapped who require special housing. The
private rented sector now provides an extremely small
amount of new building but still maintains a large
stock of older properties.
   More recently growing concern for wider environmental issues and energy costs, as well as a general
reaction against the anonymity of much development,
has given a new impetus to more dense and neighbourly
forms of development including the trend towards
urban renewal and rehabilitation. At the same time
the growing middle classes have intensified their
search for a weekend or holiday second home and have
put even more pressure on the rural and coastal
areas.

The Private House. Most private houses in Denmark
are built on an individual basis with the private
owner buying a serviced plot of land and then having
a standard house of his choice erected on the site.
Serviced plots are mainly provided by local authori-

ties who buy suitable land, sub-divide it, put in
roads and services and then sell the plots individually. In some instances the local authority may
operate a co-ordinating design role by establishing
design guidelines or providing architectural and
landscape design services for the provision of open
spaces, communal areas and general landscaping.
Planning regulations and covenants are used to
ensure that schemes conform to the required design
criteria, both at the initial development stage and
in the later life of the scheme when changes and
further development may take place. Design criteria
would commonly cover such aspects as building height
and form, use of materials, building lines, plot
ratio, parking provisions and general landscaping
and planting requirements. Private developers
provide sites in a similar manner to local authorities but only account for some 10% of the private
house market. In addition to carrying out the sub-
division scheme they would normally erect a standard
house and sell the plot and house complete.

A typical housing scheme, whether developed by
a local authority or a private developer, would have
average plot sizes of some 900 m^2 with between 30-
35% of the total development area being devoted to
open space, roads and communal areas giving a gross
density of some 8 houses per hectare. A typical
house would be detached, single storey with three
bedrooms and a gross area of about 140 m^2 giving a
plot ratio of about 15%.

The house would have been selected from one of
some 400 different house manufacturers who each
produce a standard range of house types.[17] The
relative small size of the country and the adoption
of modulor construction techniques mean that a
housing manufacturer can offer a standard service
throughout Denmark with completion of a finished
house often taking not more than two months. Houses
can be completed to various stages so that the owner
can undertake some finishing work himself and thus
reduce the overall cost.

Seventeen of the larger standard house manufacturers have joined together to form an Association
of Standard House Builders (Typehusforeningen) to
regulate standards in the industry and improve
protection for the consumer. The association
produces detailed descriptions and specifications
for all its members' houses and regulates prices in
accordance with an official building cost index. It
has also produced standard conditions of sale and
delivery and provides an after sales guarantee

against faults and defects for a period of five years
after completion of the house. Provision is made for
independent arbitration in case of disputes. The
association has not only been an important force in
establishing the standard house but it has also,
through the Ministry of Housing, been closely
involved in the development of building legislation
and, in addition, performs a training function for
administrators and supervisors in the house building
industry.
     Most housing development schemes come under the
provisions of the Municipal Planning Act which
requires a statutory local plan to be prepared for
all large developments or developments where the
proposed plot sizes are less than 700 m^2 or the plot
ratio is more than 25%. In certain circumstances,
where the proposals are being undertaken by a
private developer, provisions are made for the developer to assist in the preparation of the local plan.

Finance for Private Housing. Approximately 80% of
all housing completions are accounted for by private
houses and about 90% of them are developed by individual owner occupiers. Private house development
is financed in two stages. Firstly, the prospective
owner must raise a short term loan to cover the cost
of buying the land and building the house. Normally
such loans are arranged through commercial and
savings banks. Secondly, he has to secure long term
finance to cover the costs of his development which
is generally arranged through building mortgage
societies. These societies will provide loans in
the form of bonds equivalent to a maximum of 80% of
the value of the development with the owner having
to provide the remaining 20%, either from savings or
secondary finance. The mortgage society bonds are
then sold on the open market at current interest
rates as a form of investment for other private
individuals, companies and private and public investment organisations. The bonds are repayable over a
period of 20-30 years and repayments are made in the
form of a series of equal installments reflecting
repayment of capital and interest. Interest rates
are set at the outset and therefore the real value
of the repayments will tend to diminish as incomes
rise.
     In the past mortgages were available from
different societies in the form of first, second and
third mortgages each covering a portion of the
building cost. More recently the mortgage societies

amalgamated to form four main national bodies which
offer one single loan to meet the borrower's requirements. These mortgage loans are now increasingly
issued as cash advances with the mortgage society
taking responsibility for selling the bonds on behalf
of the borrower and paying him the proceeds. Mortgage
loans can also be offered as provisional advance
loans, before construction work starts on the house,
to enable the owner to be clear what his future
financial commitments will be once the house is completed and his repayments start. A further innovation has been index linked bonds where the initial
repayment charges are low but increase in time as
incomes increase.
      Although land and building costs reflect
inflationary trends and mortgage loans are based on
market rates of interest, the owner occupier is able
to reduce his actual housing costs through being
able to deduct some of his housing expenses from his
tax liability. The local authority calculates a
theoretical rental value for each house based on a
percentage of the actual sale value. The owner can
claim against his tax liability the difference between the theoretical rental value and his outgoings
on mortgage interest, maintenance costs and local
property taxes. The theoretical rental values are
reviewed every four years and in 1980 were computed
as 1.7% of the assessed market value plus 35%.
Maintenance cost deductions are subject to a maximum
limit and are generally taken as 1% of the assessed
value of the house. Local property taxes are
calculated as a percentage of land values.
      Since standard income tax rates in Denmark
exceed 50% there can be substantial savings for the
private house owner and, since the tax system is
progressive, the relative advantages increase as
income levels increase. In addition to these tax
allowances the owner occupier makes substantial
capital gains through the appreciating value of his
house and these gains are not subject to tax.

Non-Profit Housing Associations. Non-profit housing
has a long history in Denmark going back to the
1860s, when the first non-profit association was
formed, but its modern history really dates from
1919 when the Federation of Non-Profit Housing Associations (Boligselskabernes Landsforening) was
formed. At present there are over 650 non-profit
associations in Denmark owning some 340,000 dwellings. Most of the associations are however small and

the majority own less than a thousand dwellings each.
Approximately 70% of all non-profit associations
belong to the federation which accounts for about 90%
of all non-profit housing, of which about 80% is in
multi-storey blocks of flats. During the 1950s the
non-profit associations were extremely active and
were responsible for some 40-50% of all dwellings
completed during this period. As the Danish society
became more affluent, there was an upsurge in private
house building and the completions by non-profit
associations dropped in the 60s and 70s to between
25-30% and is now less than 20%.

The federation was originally formed to safe-
guard the interests of non-profit associations and
maintain their essential role of providing housing
for lower income groups, by acting as a political
influence on the formation of housing policy. The
federation was instrumental in forming the Copenhagen
Housing Association in 1920 (Københavns Almindelige
Boligselskab) to work specifically on the housing
problems of Copenhagen. This association has subsequently developed into the largest non-profit association in Denmark and is responsible for more than
30,000 dwellings.18 In 1941 the federation formed
the Workers' Housing Association (Arbejderbo) to
promote housing associations in areas where it is
considered there is a need. The association provides
an advisory service to assist groups of people who
want to form their own association. It can also
directly promote new associations if it considers it
desirable.

The original non-profit associations were formed
by groups of people who came together to solve their
housing problems on a collective basis. In time the
concept has changed to include the general provision
of housing for the public at large on a non-profit
basis. The principle however remains the same of
providing housing at a modest cost for middle and
low income groups with any profits going back into
the association to provide further housing. All such
schemes provide a range of dwellings for families
and single people and are generally planned to
function as communities with a high degree of self
sufficiency, through the provision of a range of
communal facilities which might include some form of
central management services, house cleaning and
laundry services, restaurants, libraries, sports
facilities, games and hobbies rooms, workshops,
shops and visitors' accommodation. Kindergarten and
child care centres may be provided but are often
leased out to private institutions or the local

authority. Special housing may also be included for
the elderly or handicapped.
     All schemes built by non-profit associations
are obliged to include a minimum of communal facilities as a condition of receiving government financial
assistance. The range of facilities provided above
the minimum level will depend upon the size and
character of the association. Some function as co-
operatives and provide fully serviced dwellings with
a wide range of communal facilities including
restaurants, which tenants are expected to support
through buying a minimum number of meal tickets each
month. Other associations have formed separate companies to run their own shops and bus services and
produce news magazines. Some organise a wide range
of collective activities including communal holidays.
Other associations are much looser and are simply the
product of peoples' desire to solve their own housing
problem at modest cost.

Financing Non-Profit Housing. Non-profit housing is
financed through a mixture of funds from central
government, the local authority and the private
sector. 74% of the construction cost is normally
raised through the ordinary bond system operated by
mortgage societies with central government
guaranteeing any part of the loan exceeding 65% of
the construction costs. A further 23% of the cost
is met through a non-returnable grant, comprising 6%
from local government and 17% from central government. The tenant is normally expected to pay the
remaining 3% as a deposit but in certain circumstances
may be eligible for a government grant to meet this
charge. If or when a tenant leaves the association,
he receives back his deposit which is adjusted to
reflect increases in price in accordance with the
consumer price index. He is not entitled to any of
the capital appreciation of the development beyond
the adjustment of his original deposit. An incoming
tenant will pay the same adjusted level of deposit.
     The basic rents members of the association pay
are calculated as economic rents which should cover
capital and interest repayments and operating costs.
The initial rents of new development are reduced by a
government subsidy which covers any portion of
interest charges which exceed 6% per annum for a
period of four years after completion of the development. This subsidy is then phased out at a rate
which ensures that the tenant's share of interest
charges will not exceed 75% of the wages and prices

increases in the previous year. The purpose of this
scheme is to reduce the effect of the cost of development on initial rents, but to phase out the
assistance as increased living standards reduce the
real cost of rents. It has been estimated that this
scheme reduces the rents by up to 40% during the
period of its operation. Other subsidies specially
directed at operating costs are available for associations which find that the high initial costs make
it difficult to find suitable tenants. Some tenants
may also be eligible for rent subsidies under a
separate government scheme.

Associations can also reduce rents by trans-
ferring contributions from older properties, where
the loan has been paid off, to newer and more
expensive developments. Rents are not normally
reduced after the capital costs have been paid off
but instead are maintained at their original level
to generate income for the association's building
fund to finance further development. Legislation
also provides for rents to be increased in step with
inflation and for a part of the proceeds to be paid
into a National Building Fund. This fund was set up
in 1963 for the purpose of contributing to the
financing of new development but, during the early
80s, it is intended that the fund's role in financing new development will be absorbed by the government and the fund will instead concentrate on the
funding of the rehabilitation of older properties.

As a part of its overall housing strategy, the
government applies an annual quota for the amount of
support it will offer non-profit housing associations.
The total number of units which can be built with the
subsidy varies but has steadily declined from around
13,000 in the 60s to 10,000 in the 70s and some 8,000
in the early 80s. Over the last few years non-profit
associations have been completing less than 6,000
dwellings a year.

Housing for Special Groups. Rural-urban migration
and changing economic conditions have resulted in
changes in the social structure of Danish society
which have had a substantial impact on housing needs
and, to a lesser extent, the housing stock. The concept of the house as a home for several generations
has given way to the need for a variety of housing
types to meet the requirements of different sectors
of society including the elderly, the disabled and
the young single person (Figure 7.3).

Figure 7.3 Møllegarden, Gladsaxe.
An example of sheltered housing built in
the late 1970s. Architects: Erik Ejler
and Henning Graversen.

DENMARK

Improved health care has brought new hope to
the elderly and disabled and the consequent reduction in death rates, coupled with a declining birth
rate, are leading to an increasingly aged population.
It is estimated that some 15% of the population is
in receipt of some form of pension through either
normal retirement, premature retirement because of
health reasons or disability. Approximately two
thirds of these people require some form of special
housing. Whilst social policy is aimed at providing
support services to enable the elderly or disabled
to continue to live in their own homes, government
housing policies have also been directed at the provision of specialised accommodation in the form of
collective, sheltered and full care housing.[19]

Collective housing is intended for people who
can still live independently but may require some
support services and need help in an emergency. Such
housing is either built by voluntary associations or
non-profit societies specially formed for this purpose, or as special units in the normal housing
programme of a non-profit association. Where the
housing is eligible for government subsidy the gross
floorspace for each dwelling should not exceed 60 m^2
and costs have to be kept within an index linked
limit.

Schemes built by voluntary organisations can
receive up to 80% of the cost as a loan through the
normal mortgage society system, with the local authority granting either a loan or standing guarantee
for the remaining 20%. Where collective houses are
built as a part of a non-profit association's normal
programme, they are financed in the same manner as
other dwellings and are eligible for the same range
of grants. Additional loans may be available from
the government where special provisions have to be
made for the severely disabled.

Sheltered housing is intended for residents who
require a higher level of assistance and it is normally developed in relationship with a nursing home
or day-care centre where expert assistance is always
available to provide nursing care, meals, laundry
and similar services. Individual units consist of
one or two rooms, each of about 15 m^2, with an
individual kitchen and bathroom. Common rooms are
provided close to the dwelling so that residents
have opportunities for social contact and recreation
with other people. Sheltered housing is sometimes
incorporated in standard housing schemes to increase
the possible range of social contact.

Although it is the responsibility of the local
authority to provide sheltered housing it is often
undertaken by voluntary organisations. Financing is
available through mortgage society loans for up to
80% of the cost with the rest being met either by
the promoting organisation or, in the case of voluntary organisations, through further loans guaranteed
by the local authority. The operating costs are
shared equally between central and local government.
People who can no longer live independently and
require constant nursing care are accommodated in
full care housing. This normally consists of a bed
sitting room, of about 15 m^2, with its own toilet
and shower facilities and sometimes a small kitchen.
The dwellings are provided with a wide range of
central services including a dining room, lounges
and recreation rooms. The local authority is again
responsible for providing full care housing but may
do so in co-operation with a voluntary organisation.
The same financial provisions apply as for sheltered
housing.
Some elderly people still live in special
pensioner flats which were built before the last war
for elderly people of moderate means. They were not
subjected to any specific standards or requirements
concerning size or construction and have largely
been superceded as a form of housing for the elderly
by specially designed units. Where the elderly or
disabled are still able to live in their own homes
special local government grants are available to
assist in the cost of carrying out any modifications
which may be necessary.
In 1979 a new form of tax free housing benefit
was introduced for all social welfare pensioners,
including those receiving old age pensions, widows'
benefits or disabled pensions. The housing benefit
amounts to the differences between the actual rental
cost and a calculated 'own payment value' related to
income, size of household and size of dwelling. Own
payment value varies between 15-35% of income
depending on the particular circumstances. Maximum
limits are set for this housing benefit but they are
index linked and are paid to all social welfare
pensioners, irrespective of whether they own or rent
their home, except those living in pensioners' flats
and people living in special housing. The rents in
pensioners' flats are controlled and the tenant
normally pays a maximum of 15% of his income as rent.
In collective and sheltered housing tenants pay a
rental charge assessed at 25% of income. In full
care housing the residents waive their rights to a

pension and receive instead an index linked allowance, with the balance going to meet the rent costs.

As conditions within society change an
increasing problem has been the need to provide
accommodation for the young single person.   Non-
profit housing associations provide one room flats
for single people under the normal subsidy system.
Government subsidies are available for up to 45% of
the cost of special halls of residence or hostels
for the single young.   However land and construction
costs have resulted in rents being too high, even
with subsidy, and there has been a consequent
decline in the provision of this form of accommodation in recent years.

Slum Clearance and Housing Improvement.   Widening
public concern for environmental issues in general
and the particular reaction against much post-war
development, coupled with the energy crisis of the
early 70s, gave a fresh impetus to the need to
develop urban policies which offered a wider range
of social benefits.   The new Ministry of the
Environment helped focus some of this concern and in
1980 a new Urban Renewal and Housing Act was approved
which consolidated and extended earlier legislation
and provides a new basis for the development of
urban housing policies.

In addition to the general social benefits of
improving urban housing and its related facilities,
urban renewal schemes are seen as providing additional employment and having reduced energy demands
during construction, compared to new development,
whilst generally reducing the need for imported
building materials.   Slum clearance and housing
improvement is therefore seen as a part of a wider
effort by government to develop housing strategies
which are commensurate with the economic conditions
of the country and, at the same time, respond to
changing social needs.

The general principle adopted for such schemes
is that the poorest housing will be demolished and
housing which is retained will be improved to modern
day standards, including the creation of better
environmental conditions through demolishing infill
and rear development to provide communal open spaces.
The legislation specifies requirements for public
participation in the preparation and approval of
proposals including the need to establish information
centres in the areas being affected and rights of
objection.   Efforts are made to integrate renewal

and new development policies by making provision for
people from demolished housing to be allocated new
housing, commensurate with their family structure
and financial circumstances, close to their old
homes. There is a general requirement that 20% of
the units in new non-profit housing schemes should
be made available for such re-housing purposes.

Housing renewal schemes may be undertaken by
local government, building owners, societies formed
specially for the purpose or a combination of all
three. To ensure a consistent overall level of
improvement in any renewal scheme, legal powers are
available to compel a private building owner to
improve his building to the standards and guidelines
laid down by the proposals. The local authority
also has powers to acquire property by compulsory
purchase if it is unable to acquire by agreement.
Government grants can be made available to private
landlords, development companies and special societies for the conversion, improvement or renovation
of existing properties provided they form part of an
approved overall improvement plan. In addition to
internal improvements, grants can cover the cost of
external improvements including the clearing and
converting of areas to provide outdoor communal
facilities. Housing improvement schemes must be
approved by the local authority and central government and people who are affected by the proposals
have a six week period to lodge objections, which
must be considered by the local authority before
they approve the scheme.

Schemes which are undertaken privately are
eligible for a government loan of 60% of the cost of
renovation to be repaid over a period of twenty years
at an interest rate of 6.5% per annum. The balance
of the costs would be met by the owner out of his own
funds or through a private loan. If the renovation
is undertaken by a non-profit housing association,
the same general financing provisions apply as for
new development. Where the local authority is
responsible for the scheme the costs are shared
equally between the authority and central government.
If the proposals are in an area of particular architectural or historic interest provision is made for
the state's share of the costs to be increased to 75%.

Renovation schemes which do not form a part of
an approved overall improvement plan and are undertaken by a private building owner or society would be
financed through the normal open market or from funds
provided by the Property Owners' Investment Fund.
This fund is financed through the profits of its

members and is intended to assist them undertake
improvement and renewal schemes. Similar provisions
apply to such schemes undertaken by non-profit
associations except that they have access to a separate National Building Fund set up by the Federation
of Non-Profit Housing Associations and used to
finance member's renovation schemes.

Rents in rehabilitated dwellings are set at
levels comparable to rents in modern non-profit
housing in the area. A system of limited subsidy
operates to compensate the building owner for any
difference between the actual rent received and the
economic rent represented by the amortised capital
value of the scheme. Such a subsidy is only intended
to reduce the initial impact of improvement costs and
is phased out during a period of 5-10 years. Special
rent subsidies and loans are available for people who
are obliged to leave slum properties being demolished
or improved and are intended to assist in meeting the
costs of transference and possible rent increases.

Copenhagen, as the largest conurbation in
Denmark, has been a centre for slum clearance and
improvement schemes for many years (Figure 7.4). In
1970 the Council of Copenhagen brought together
various housing associations and the Society of Rate-
payers Associations to create a new Town Renewal and
Rehabilitation Society (Det Københavnske
Byfornyelses-og Saneringsselskab) to carry out slum
clearance and improvement schemes. Co-operation between these different bodies has made it possible to
undertake renewal schemes on a more comprehensive
basis throughout Copenhagen, as well as generating a
considerable body of expertise.

The Private Rented Sector. Although some 20% of the
housing stock is in the private rented sector, the
rise in land values and construction costs together
with the lack of direct government subsidy, have
meant that the private building of accommodation to
rent now only makes a very small contribution to
housing supply. Rent control in the private sector
has been almost entirely removed, with the exception
of urban areas with populations of more than 20,000
people, but the increasing gap between economic rents
and market rents means that new schemes are seldom
likely to be economically viable. Where such schemes
are built they are financed through the normal mortgage society with loans of up to 80% of the cost
repayable over 30-40 years at market rates of
interest.

Figure 7.4   Vesterbro, Copenhagen.
A housing improvement scheme from the
1980s carried out by the Københavnske
Byfornyelses-og Saneringsselskab.

Many of the older properties are being improved,
either as a part of overall improvement plans or on
an individual basis. Since 1966 the government has
permitted the sub-division of private rented property to provide flats for sale. Legislation in 1976
obliged building owners to offer converted properties
to the tenants for purchase on a co-operative basis.
Further legislation in 1977 strengthened building
standards for conversions and introduced a property
conversion tax, assessed as a percentage of the
building value. Since 1979 there has been a restriction on rented properties built before 1966 being
converted for sale.

Graded Rents. In 1966 the government introduced the
Graded Rents Act, which established a subsidy system
aimed at giving large low income families a better
opportunity to rent housing suited to their needs.

Later legislation has modified the original provisions but in general it applies to private rented and non-profit association tenants where the rented accommodation complies with a set of basic housing standards.

The subsidy represents 75% of the difference between the actual rent paid and a theoretical rent which is calculated in relationship to the family income and structure. The subsidy is subjected to a maximum income level and, in general, the lower the family income the higher the theoretical level will be and the smaller the portion of income they will have to pay in rent. It is estimated that about 25% of the people in rented accommodation benefit from this subsidy and roughly half are old age pensioners who receive a larger subsidy equivalent to the full rental difference. Legislation provides for the subsidy to be increased to reflect salary increases and for the full rental allowance to be paid to low income families which the local authority deems to be in need of special assistance.

Second Homes. The holiday home has a long tradition in Denmark going back at least to the 19th century when it was fashionable for the rich middle classes to have a summer house on the coast. The more recent growth of urbanisation and the desire to maintain an attachment to the land, resulted in the development of small allotments and gardens on the perimeter of urban settlements. These plots were provided with small cabins and served not only for recreational purposes but also as a source of produce for the urban dweller. Increased leisure time and improved living standards and mobility have strengthened the desire of urban dwellers to have a second home in the country. The pressures have come not only from within Denmark but also from Germany, where its limited coastline has induced people to look northwards for holiday homes. The results have been seen in the demand for small farms and cottages, vacated as agricultural patterns have changed, and the growth of purpose built second homes.

In an effort to control the development of holiday and weekend homes the government introduced in 1972 a number of restrictions in addition to the normal planning and zoning controls. One piece of the legislation stipulates that any purchaser of a farm of more than five hectares must live permanently on the holding and have farming as his principle occupation. Other legislation aims to control the development of holiday villages, camp sites and the use of ordinary houses for holiday uses by making the commercial letting of holiday accommodation dependent upon the granting of a licence by the Ministry of Housing. Commercial letting is defined as being two or more units and licences are not generally issued. Additional powers have made it possible to acquire compulsorily land which is required for recreational facilities.

Sub-division schemes for holiday homes have mainly been developed along the coastline of Jutland. Much of the development is undertaken on the same basis as other housing with house manufacturers erecting standard holiday homes on serviced sites to meet the individual client's needs. The standard of construction and space standards are generally comparable to first homes and provide similar standards of comfort. In an effort to prevent such developments turning into permanent settlements, with a consequent demand for services and facilities, some local authorities have introduced restrictions concerning the length of occupation permitted in any one year.

It is estimated that about 10% of all households in Denmark have a second home. However the resultant 200,000 or so holiday houses and cottages are largely the product of a growing affluent middle class and it has been increasingly questionned whether so much land and resources should be allocated to houses which are perhaps only used for a month or so a year. Efforts to widen access to holiday accommodation and ensure a higher degree of usage have been made both by private developers building holiday hotels and non-profit associations building holiday centres.

One of the oldest non-profit holiday associations is the Danish National Holiday Association (Dansk Folkeferie) established in 1938. The earliest developments were designed to provide simple accommodation with shared restaurants and community rooms and were intended to enable working class urban dwellers to enjoy a rural holiday. More recent developments have improved the quality and design of the dwellings to provide all the year round accommodation. An even more recent innovation has been the development abroad of holiday accommodation for Danes who want to holiday in the sun.

Review of Progress

The Influence of the Past. Current housing policy
reflects the broad values of society which are themselves a product of the forces which have formed
modern Denmark over the last three hundred years or
so. The early loss of her territories meant that
Denmark never became a great international power and,
as a consequence, developed a more introspective
society concerned with its own problems. This spirit
of self reliance helped evolve the educational,
social and parliamentary reforms which generated the
broadly based co-operative and agricultural movements
necessary to create a modern economy and a democratic
society.
    The lack of mineral resources has meant that
agriculture had to develop to provide the basis for
growth and when industrialisation did take place, not
only was it much later than in other European
countries, but it was largely based on the development of the manufacturing sector and consequently
meshed in smoothly with the modernisation of agriculture. The small scale of the county, the emphasis
on agricultural development and the assimilation of
industrialisation without great economic and social
upheavals, have helped maintain the continuity and
homogeneity of a set of values based on rural traditions and skills.
    This combination of self-reliance and a strong
sense of traditional values is allied with a very
high standard of living in a strongly bureaucratised
society. In the resultant unique housing system the
state has wide legal powers but plays little role in
the direct provision of housing. High quality private housing emerges as the main component of housing
policy with the social housing functions being taken
over by the voluntary sector through the non-profit
associations.

Post-war changes. Although the roles of the state,
the private sector and the non-profit associations
were established in the 1930s, as the main actors in
the development of housing policy, their relationship
has undergone and is undergoing continual change.
    Constant themes in the development of housing
policy have been the need to balance the demands of
the owner occupier with those of the rental tenant
and the desire of government to withdraw from the
housing market. In a situation where some 60% of the

population are private house owners, it has obviously
been politically very difficult for a government
dependent upon the support of minority parties to
implement policies aimed at reducing substantially
the tax benefits of the owner occupier. Whilst some
adjustment has been made, by increasing theoretical
rent levels and marginally reducing tax benefits,
the main emphasis has been on increasing the benefits
to tenants through such schemes as the Graded Rent
Scheme. As a result the rate of subsidy to the private house owner is still estimated to be twice as
much as tenants receive overall and, during the last
decade, the amount of rental housing being built by
non-profit associations has decreased by some 40%.

At the same time poor economic performance over
the last decade has necessitated continuing government intervention in subsidising the housing market
and regulating the building industry to mitigate the
effects of inflation. As a result the overall
objective of opening the housing market to the play
of market forces has largely been defeated.

A further complicating factor has been changes
in the social structure of Denmark which have been
reflected in demographic change over the last twenty
years or so. The mid-sixties were a period of relative demographic stability but since then the birth
rate has dropped further resulting in an overall
decline in the population growth rate from 0.7% to
0.4%. During the same period divorce rates have
doubled and formal marriages have declined by about
30% whilst the proportion of married women working
has increased from about 50% to 80%.[20] The overall
pattern of an almost stable but ageing population
with an increasing number of single person households,
set in the context of continuing national economic
decline, means that further re-assessment will be
necessary of a housing policy which is mainly
directed at the typical middle class family and is
increasingly failing to meet the real needs of the
country.

Housing Design. With the exception of farms, the
traditional Danish house was a terraced form of
dwelling providing individual houses in rural areas
and houses or flats in urban centres. It was not
until the 1850s, when the affluent middle class
started to move out of the towns, principally Copenhagen, that the single family detached house started
to appear as the villa. After the first world war
the influence of the English garden city movement

DENMARK

started to be felt and large areas were devoted to
the development of single family houses. During
this time the non-profit associations were still
mainly concentrating on the traditional forms of
terraced development but for a wider sector of the
population.

From the 1930s onwards there was a change of
emphasis and, whilst the popularity of the single
family house continued to grow and provide homes for
the middle class moving out of urban centres, the
non-profit associations were increasingly building
three or more storey blocks of flats, in addition to
the terraced forms of development, to provide housing
for the rural migrant. These divergent trends were
further strengthened by the development of industrialised and pre-fabricated building techniques, from
the 1940s onwards, with the resultant emphasis on
large scale multi-storey forms of development
providing 1,000 to 2,000 dwellings at a time. Up
until the 1940s the annual production of single
family houses and dwellings in multi-storey flats was
about the same. From the 1950s increasing affluence
brought the single family house within reach of a
wider section of society and development of the type
house overtook the building of flats.[21]

Public Reaction. During the 1960s and 1970s criticisms of the effects of this polarisation of housing
policy increased. Criticism was directed not only at
the scale and monotony of much high rise industrialised development but also at the single family house
with its high consumption of land and services and
lack of any feeling of community.

From the early 1970s the trend in housing design
changed again. The previous emphasis by non-profit
associations on large scale high rise developments
has given way to smaller low rise high density
schemes with much greater concern being given to the
needs of the user (Figure 7.5). Although economic
necessity forced the reduction in area of the average
unit, provision is now more often made for some
flexibility in layout to meet individual preferences
and the changing needs of families, and tenants are
encouraged to play a major role in the management of
schemes as a means of promoting the growth of communities.

More recently criticism has focused on the rigid
separation of land uses, which has been a characteristic of much post-war planning, and the resultant
high energy costs of commuter and movement patterns.

213

Figure 7.5   <u>Frederiksberg, Copenhagen.</u>
A late 1970s low rise housing scheme with
a high provision of community buildings.
Architects: Faellestegnestuen - Jørn Ole
Sørensen, Viggo Møller-Jensen and Tyge
Arnfred.

This particular concern derives not only from economic considerations but also from the wider perspective of the need for communities to live in more
ecologically balanced forms of development consuming
less resources.   Two reactions have resulted.
Firstly, new efforts are being made to develop more
compact house types and layouts for the private
sector[22] which will be both more economical to construct, through requiring less land and services, and
more economical to operate through being more energy
conscious.   Secondly, there has been a general shift
of emphasis from new development to renewal and
rehabilitation as being both economically more
attractive and socially more desirable.
     Despite these shifts of emphasis and adjustments
to policy, there has been little response to the

fundamental criticism that Danish housing policy
lacks diversity and does not provide access to
reasonable housing for the socially disadvantaged or
less well off. The policies are largely aimed at
those who already have the initiative or resources
to participate in solving their own housing problem.

Concluding Remarks. No housing policy is ever right
in that it tends to be reactive and is often
responding to economic conditions which will themselves preclude the development of a satisfactory
policy. Building activity accounts for about 11% of
the Gross National Product in Denmark with a little
less than a half of all building activity being concentrated on new housing. Over the last few decades
however, investment in new housing starts has
fluctuated severely as the national economic conditions have changed. Currently new dwellings are
being built at the rate of about 31,000 a year,
equivalent to approximately 6 dwellings per thousand
people. This represents a steady decline after the
post-war build up from around 22,000 units a year in
the 1950s to 38,000 a year in the 1960s and a peak
of 52,000 a year in the early 1970s. It is estimated
that about 9,000 dwellings a year disappear through
demolition or conversion and that current demand is
between 50 to 55,000 dwellings a year.
     Of the existing housing stock about 25% or some
500,000 dwellings, are considered to be below current
building standards and nearly half the total housing
stock is in the form of high rise developments, of
which about 30% was built before 1920; 20% dates
from the 1920s to 1930s; a further 20% is from the
1940s to 1960s and the remaining 30% has been built
since 1960. However, despite the heritage of problems and the economic difficulties of the 1970s,
Denmark has consistently managed to improve its
housing stock measured in terms of the increase in
the number of dwellings compared to the increase in
population and declining occupancy rates.
     The relative success of these housing policies
can be attributed to the inherent flexibility of
limiting government intervention to financing and
approval systems and relying upon the voluntary
sector to respond to housing need and provide housing
for particular social groups. The operation of this
system has been further strengthened by the role
played by institutions, such as the Federation of
Non-Profit Housing Associations, the State Building
Institute and the Association of Standard House

Builders, who have all been important in developing
new administrative mechanisms and legislation and
liaising between the Ministry and the housing industry.

However the flexibility of the system has been
within constraints of what has been considered
socially desirable and politically acceptable. At
the perimeter of housing policy there has been the
development of squatter groups and communes as
evidence of the inability of some social groups to
be accommodated within official housing policy. Urban
renewal schemes have been the scene of much public
protest and demonstration against a housing policy
which has tended to define solutions in terms of
applied standards and criteria rather than as
assessed need. It is now clear that what was a
limited and poorly articulated response to particular
circumstances may be given increasing significance as
economic conditions change so much as to effect the
whole basis on which housing policy has been developed.

It is normal that an affluent society in a time
of inflation should invest in land and housing. The
rapid growth in the development of one family houses
has reflected that trend but changes in economic
circumstances, and particularly the effects of
increased energy costs, have meant that a form of
development which was a sound investment increasingly
appears as an individual and social liability. At
the same time the low density developments of individual houses can be seen as a drain on resources
which will need to be spent on upgrading some of the
obsolescent housing stock, particularly the earlier
high rise developments built by the non-profit
associations, and providing new housing to meet the
needs resulting from demographic and social change.

The strength of a democratic society is that it
is resilient and responsive. Some aspects of the
trends described above have already been anticipated
and policy changes effected: the efforts by the
State Building Institute to encourage both greater
innovation in housing design and more economical
layouts; the trend towards low rise developments
with greater user participation; the emphasis on
urban renewal and rehabilitation, are all encouraging
examples of the ability of the housing system to
respond to change and develop new policies.

Denmark is a small country with a small population but one of the highest standards of living in
the industrial world. The government has therefore
had less need than other European countries to employ

interventionist housing strategies based on considerations of equity and wealth generation. However
changes in the condition of the Danish economy have
indicated that the adoption of policies largely
effecting control through subsidies, which allowed
the demise of the private rented sector, the diminu-
tion of the role played by non-profit associations
and the domination of housing supply by the private
sector, has not resulted in an ideal solution to
housing problems nor the best use of resources
either in economic or social terms. The process of
policy adjustment continues.

NOTES AND REFERENCES

1. Although Greenland and the Faroe Islands
form a part of the kingdom of Denmark, they have
evolved separately and are therefore excluded from
consideration in this chapter.
2. For an interesting view of both modern
Denmark and how the Danes see themselves, see: Anders
Georg, (Ed) Denmark Today - The World of the Danes,
(Ministry of Foreign Affairs, Copenhagen, 1979).(In
English).
3. The influence of the Folk High School system
on the development of Denmark is traced in Olive
Dame Campbell, The Danish Folk High School. Its
Influence in the Life of Denmark and the North,
(Macmillan, New York, 1928).
4. For an illustrated review of the development
of Danish architecture see: Danish Architecture 1879-
1979, (Arkitektens Forlag, Copenhagen, 1979).(English
Summary).
5. The development of post-war housing policies
is further elaborated in Housing in Denmark,
(Ministry of Housing, Copenhagen, 1974) (In English).
6. For a general description of the development
of Danish planning and its legislation see: Byplan -
Special Issue 1973, (Arkitektens Forlag, Copenhagen,
1973).(In English).
7. Act on National and Regional Planning. (Act
No.375), (Ministry of Housing, Copenhagen, 1973).(In
English).
8. Act on Regional Planning for Metropolitan
Area of Greater Copenhagen. (Act No.376), (Ministry
of Environment, Copenhagen, 1973). (In English).
9. For a description of the development of
planning for Copenhagen see: Regional Planning in
the Greater Copenhagen Region 1945-1975,
(Hovedstadsrådet, Copenhagen, 1976). (In English);
and Kai Lemberg, Planning in Greater Copenhagen,

(General Planning Department, City of Copenhagen, 1970). (In English).

10. Municipal Planning Act, (Act No.287), (Ministry of the Environment, Copenhagen, 1976).(In English).

11. Urban and Rural Zones Act, (Act No.315 amended by Act 340, 100 and 288), (Ministry of the Environment, Copenhagen, 1976). (In English).

12. Building Regulations 1977, (National Building Agency, Ministry of Housing, Copenhagen, 1978). (In English).

13. For a fuller description of the development of industrialised housing see: Marius Kjeldsen, Industrialised Housing in Denmark, (Danish Building Centre, Copenhagen, 1976). (In English).

14. For further details see: Denmark's Energy Conservation Policy, (Ministry of Housing, Copenhagen, 1980). (In English).

15. For an illustrated report on six houses see: Six Low Energy Houses at Hjortekaer, (Thermal Insulation Laboratory, Report No.83, Technical University of Denmark, Lyngby, 1979). (In English).

16. A review of housing progress is normally published annually as Current Trends and Policies in the Field of Housing, Building and Planning, (Ministry of Housing and the Ministry of the Environment, Copenhagen). (In English).

17. Typical house plans of manufacturers are published by various organisations. A typical example containing plans for 125 permanent homes and 60 holiday homes is Typehus Revyen -80, (Bo Bedre, Copenhagen, 1980). (In Danish).

18. For an illustrated review of the Copenhagen Housing Associations work see: Bygge-og Boligvirksomhed 1965-70, (Københavns Almindelige Boligselskab, Copenhagen, 1970). (In Danish but extensively illustrated).

19. For further details see: Institutions and Housing for the Elderly and the Handicapped in Denmark, (Housing Committee for the Handicapped, Ministry of Housing, Copenhagen, 1979). (In English).

20. Demographic data are published by Danmarks Statistik in the form of monthly or quarterly newsletters (Statistiske Efterretninger) and a statistical yearbook (Statistisk Arbog) in Danish. A recent summary in English appeared as Factsheet Denmark - The Demographic Situation, (Ministry of Foreign Affairs, Copenhagen, 1981).

21. A review of the development of Danish housing is given in Preben Hansen and Flemming André Larsen (Eds), How the Danes Live, (Ministry of Foreign

Affairs, Copenhagen, 1981). A wider review of
Danish architecture is contained in Tobias Faber,
Danish Architecture, (Det Danske Selskab,
Copenhagen, 1978). (In English).
    22. In 1977 the State Building Institute
issued a design guide aimed at improving the layout
of estates for individual houses. For details see:
Parcelhuset som taet-lav, (SBI Byplanlaegning 32,
Statens Byggeforskningsinstitut, Copenhagen, 1977).
(In Danish).

All photographs by courtesy of the Royal Danish
Ministry of Foreign Affairs.

8. EAST GERMANY (THE GERMAN DEMOCRATIC REPUBLIC)

by Gerlind Staemmler

Examination of housing policy in an Eastern Bloc
country requires a basic understanding of political
and economic conditions quite alien to Western
Europe, which have produced policies and products
which might appear unthinkable in economies oriented
to free enterprise. If one disregards the foreign
political and economic dependencies of the German
Democratic Republic (GDR), which are certainly considerable, then three key aspects of the overall
planning system within which the house construction
industry operates are characteristic: central economic planning, state housing management, and de facto
state control of all real estate. It is within this
social-political-economic framework then, that
housing policy has been formulated, and house construction and occupation taken place on the ground.
    The chapter is divided into two major sections,
each of which, in turn, is subdivided into several
subsections. In the first section, the origins and
evolution of housing policy in the post-war are discussed, from the early first reconstruction phase,
through the second phase from the mid-fifties onwards,
when industrialised building techniques were used on
a large scale, through to the National Housing Programme of the seventies and eighties. Then, in a
second section, some key aspects of present housing
and housing management in the GDR are discussed - the
nature of the housing stock, different ownership
types, their relative importance and different
functions, and the lot of the tenant; and in a brief
final section, some concluding remarks are made, which
attempt to highlight certain major issues discussed
in the chapter as a whole.

EAST GERMANY

An Overview of Housing Policy 1945-1982

The General Situation in the Immediate Post-War. At
the end of the Second World War, the Soviet-occupied
zone (which became the GDR in 1949) faced great hard-
ships. The war had cost an enormous number of lives,
and the production capacity of the country had been
largely destroyed. Reparation payments weakened the
economy further, and the division of Germany cut this
part of the country off from most of the coal and
iron ore resources and steel production plants, which
until then had provided the basis for its manufacturing industry.
    Reconstruction in the Soviet occupied zone began
with a land reform programme involving a restructuring of both property boundaries and property ownership. Major industrial firms were nationalised,
commercial co-operatives were encouraged and private
retailing was bound to state or co-operative trade
organisations by means of contracts.1
    Somewhat later the construction of a planned
economic system began. The planning and control of
the economy (which had at first been carried out by
the Soviet Military Administration in Germany, together with the economic planning authorities of the
Soviet-occupied zone) were transferred to the German
Economic Commission (Deutsche Wirtschaftskommission)
in 1948 and then to the National Planning Commission
(Staatliche plankommission or SPK) in 1950, which had
been founded to carry out this function. The first
two-year economic plan was drawn up in 1949-1950 to
rebuild the economy in the Soviet-occupied zone; the
first five-year plan quickly followed, covering the
period 1951-1955. Since then, strictly centralised
national economic planning has been conducted by
means of five-year plans closely linked to more
detailed yearly economic plans. The political guidelines and economic strategy for each 5 year plan are
determined at the party congress of the United
Socialist Party of Germany (Sozialistische Einheits-
partei Deutschlands - SED); and in addition the
ideological, political and economic actions of the
GDR are decisively influenced by its membership in
the Warsaw Pact and the Council for Mutual Economic
Assistance.
    Despite the dire consequences of the war and the
widespread devastation suffered especially by the
major cities,2 the housing deficit in the immediate
post-war was less acute in the GDR than in the
Federal Republic of Germany (FRG). Population densi-

ties were traditionally lower in the GDR, and the new state did not experience the rapid increase in population that occurred in the FRG in the post-war; further, the degree of destruction suffered in the war had been less in the GDR (10% of all houses had been destroyed in the GDR, compared with 18% in the FRG). By 1950, the accommodation figures for the GDR showed an average 3.6 persons per dwelling, compared with 4.9 persons per dwelling in the FRG.[3]

Planning and Reconstruction 1949-1956. The post-war reconstruction period in the GDR lasted from the late forties through till the mid-fifties.[4] At the outset, two major goals were established which were to have a major impact on house construction. First, new industrial complexes were to be built and old ones reorganised, based on the iron and steel, metallurgical, power and chemical industries. In this connection, a number of new cities were founded, or old ones enlarged, to accommodate the new or increased work force. Parts of Calbe, Merseburg, Lauchhammer, Eisenhüttenstadt, Hoyerswerda, Aue and Sangerhausen, for example, were built during this period, as industrial installations were rebuilt or enlarged and new industries established, with new housing areas and cultural centres not far away. Secondly, in the destroyed areas of the old major industrial centres, measures for instigating new house-building were introduced, and 'reconstruction cities' (Aufbaustädte[5]) were declared. These inner city new construction measures were usually carried out along the main streets, for example in East Berlin along Stalinallee, in Dresden along Thälmannstrasse, in Rostock along Lange Strasse and in Magdeburg along Wilhelm-Pieck-Allee.

In 1950, the national government issued sixteen city planning principles that were used as architectural and ideological guidelines in the reconstruction of the country's major settlements. The city was recognised as 'the most economical and culturally rich settlement form'[6] and industrial development, the municipal authorities and cultural centres were identified as the key factors in ensuring successful urban development. The most important political, administrative and cultural functions were to be located in the city centre - the kernel and political heart of the city; the city centre would, therefore, comprise the most important and monumental buildings. The artistic style of cities is today determined by the nature of squares, major roads and dominant

central buildings. Each residential district was to
have its own centre where cultural, social and community service buildings were to be located. Residential complexes, however, were smaller units,
providing public services for the day to day needs of
residents (including child care centres and schools)
and containing a series of housing blocks, the next
planning unit down the scale. Multi-storey
buildings were to be favoured in large cities for
economic reasons; city architecture should be
'democratic in content and national in form',[7] providing every city with its own unique, characteristic
appearance.
    A little later the same year, in September 1950,
the National Reconstruction Act[8] was passed, providing new administrative and legal frameworks within
which the reconstruction process could take place.
Planning authorities and their administrative
boundaries were established, and provision was made
for state acquisition of private real estate; and
the Ministry of Reconstruction was given overall
responsibility for city planning matters. A four-
tiered hierarchy of plans was established for city
planning - Metropolitan Land-Use Plan
(Flächennutzungsplan), Urban Development Plan
(Stadtbebauungsplan), Building Project Plan (Aufbau-
plan) and Partial Development Plans (Teilbebauungs-
pläne) - with the Ministry retaining strict control
over the two uppermost levels, thereby permitting
regional (district) city and community councils only
limited responsibilities in the planning field. (The
GDR is divided into 14 Regions or 'Districts'.) The
Central Government were given powers to declare
'Development Areas', with the consequence that in
those areas 'a claim on built-up and empty plots of
land for developmental purposes'[9] could be made, and
expropriation with obligatory compensation could then
follow. In general, however, in urban areas, old
property boundaries and ownership patterns have
largely been respected, and expropriation has only
taken place in order to start new building projects
(and at first particularly in city centres). As
early as 1951, for example, the central districts of
Dresden, Leipzig, Chemnitz (now Karl-Marx-Stadt),
Magdeburg, Dessau, Rostock-Warnemünde, Wismar and
Nordhausen were declared Development Areas, and it
was in these that many of the 200,000 new dwellings
built between 1951 and 1955 were located. Development Areas were also declared in most of the other
important cities in the 1950s.

In accordance with the sixteen planning principles outlined above, this first phase of reconstruction saw the creation of expansive roads and squares, and the general architectural tendency was towards classical design. In order to create a unique, individual appearance for each city, regional traditions were emphasised - classical architecture in East Berlin, baroque in Dresden, 'backstein gothic' in Rostock. The political demand that the poor should live in palaces was expressed in the complicated and expensive way housing was built. In the design of new housing estates, there were vehement ideological and political disagreements which ended the professional careers of some architects and saw others leave for the West. The SED leadership rejected modern architecture as influenced by imperialism, and favoured instead the Russian style. The conflict was particularly fierce in East Berlin, where, after several proposals and false starts, Stalinallee (today Karl-Marx-Alle) was built according to Hermann Henselmann's revised design,[10] in the style of Russian-socialist realism and along the lines of Karl Friedrich Schinkel's architecture.[11] And in order to justify the new architectural direction, a series of attacks was made on constructivism and functionalism and the later influence of the Bauhaus School under Hannes Meyer.[12] These have since been retracted.

The existence of two political systems in Germany and the city of Berlin made any comprehensive city planning unlikely, although a number of plans for Berlin as a whole were drawn up by planning groups and institutions in both West and East Berlin.[13] In addition, a few design competitions were open to entrants from both the East and the West in the early fifties, although these came to an abrupt end[14] in 1957, when the Federal Government attempted to hold a competition for the redevelopment of the old Berlin city centre, through which the border between East and West runs; the GDR government forbade participation from East Berliners, and attempts at co-operation between the two sides in planning matters ended there, to be replaced by one of professional rivalry and political tit-for-tat. With the construction of the Stalinallee residential complex in East Berlin, city planners in the west countered with the Interbau scheme in 1957 and the resultant construction of the Hansa quarter.[15]

The Second Phase of Reconstruction 1956-71. In the
mid-fifties, the GDR Government initiated the
industrialisation of building production, for economic and ideological reasons. Traditional building
practices were slow, costly and inefficient -
providing only 1.9 new dwellings per year per 1,000
inhabitants in the mid-fifties (Table 8.1), whilst
at the same time 'destalinization' (following the
lead of the USSR) brought with it a move away from
prestige building. The proportion of industrialised
building units in total new house construction was
first mentioned in official GDR statistics in 1958
as 12%, rising to 90% by 1965.[16] A storey-height
wall panel system was used for flat construction,
with each region at first developing its own particular system. The impact on house production figures
was dramatic, with annual completions almost trebling
over the period 1956-61 (Table 8.1).

In this second, industrialised, phase of reconstruction, new residential areas, mainly consisting
of linear, four or five storey blocks,[17] were built
in the city suburbs, with city centres largely
unaffected. The standard settlement unit became the
residential complex (defined in the 1950 'planning
principles'), comprising about 1,000-1,500 dwelling
units housing up to 5,000 inhabitants, with all the
necessary schools, shops and day-to-day facilities.

Architectural opinions were changing, as illustrated by the changing assessment of the architectural design of Stalinallee. Its official, positive
evaluation only held for a few years 'until the time
when - supported by experiences in the USSR -
construction was industrialised, but also when
modern architectural conceptions managed to spread
widely due to a growing criticism of economically
unjustifiable superfluities and of a one-sided
orientation of architecture to the past and its
national traditions'.[18] A move back towards modern
architecture with rational and functional components,
which only a few years before had been rejected as
imperialistically influenced, was evident around
1960. A few years later, parallels in city structure
between the GDR and Western European countries began
to become clearly visible.

From the mid-sixties onwards, new housing areas
tended to increase in size in accordance with
advances in industrialized building technology and
associated economies of scale. Layout and structure
became increasingly a function of traffic circulation
and infrastructure provision, with ever higher
building densities (up to 11-20 storeys), which were

225

Table 8.1 Population Change and House Production in
the GDR, 1949-80

Year	Population (thousands)	Housing Units completed (New Dwellings, Modernizations and Rebuilding)	Housing Unit Completions per 1,000 inhabitants
1949	18,892	29,800	1.6
1950	18,388	31,000	1.7
1951	18,351	61,000	3.3
1952	18,328	47,600	2.6
1953	18,178	32,300	1.8
1954	18,059	34,700	1.9
1955	17,944	32,800	1.8
1956	17,716	32,800	1.9
1957	17,517	61,100	3.5
1958	17,355	63,500	3.6
1959	17,298	80,000	4.6
1960	17,241	80,500	4.7
1961	17,125	92,000	5.4
1962	17,102	87,200	5.1
1963	17,155	76,000	4.4
1964	16,983	76,600	4.5
1965	17,020	68,200	4.0
1966	17,058	65,300	3.8
1967	17,082	76,300	4.5
1968	17,084	76,000	4.4
1969	17,076	70,300	4.1
1970	17,058	76,100	4.5
1971	17,061	86,777	5.1
1972	17,043	117,026	6.9
1973	16,980	125,769	7.4
1974	16,925	138,301	8.2
1975	16,850	140,793	8.4
1976	16,786	150,617	9.0
1977	16,765	162,745	9.7
1978	16,756	167,799	10.0
1979	16,740	162,743	9.7
1980	16,740	169,223	10.1
TOTAL 1949-1980		2,772,893	162.2

Sources: M. Hoffmann Wohnungspolitik der DDR. Das
Leistungs-und Interessenproblem, (Düsseldorf, 1972),
p.197; the Statistisches Jahrbuch der DDR 1981
(Annual Statistics of the GDR, 1981), pp.1 & 149;
and author's calculations from disparate sources.

held to be the most economical. The traditional methods of construction were almost completely discontinued, except in the quantitively insignificant unifamiliar and rural construction sectors.

In 1963, economic planning in the GDR underwent major revision with the introduction of the 'New Economic System of Planning and Control' (Neues ökonomisches System der Planung und Leitung or NOS[19]). General powers and jurisdictions were decentralized, and individual cities and townships were given powers to plan and execute their own house construction programmes. In 1970, however, after an initial improvement in the economy after 1963, but little improvement in house construction figures (Table 8.1) the NOS was abandoned. Since the housing deficit had grown considerably in the meantime and the condition of the older housing stock had rapidly become worse, the decrease in building activity was not a result of planned economic measures, but rather, it signified the non-fulfillment of the plans that had been made.

The National Housing Programme 1976-90. At the 8th Party Congress of the SED, a radical change in housing policy was approved, coinciding with the succession of new party leader Honecker. House construction became 'the most important social-political task of the present and future'[20] and was given an elevated position in the economy as a whole.[21] This should be viewed not only as a direct response to the growing housing deficit, but also as an attempt to placate an increasingly dissatisfied population who had witnessed internal upheavals in neighbouring Czechoslovakia (in 1968) and Poland (in 1970). By 1973 a 15 year National Housing Programme, in 3 five-year phases, had been drawn up, which aimed at 'solving the housing problem' by 1990.[22] Between 1976 and 1990, it was planned to build or modernise 2.8-3 million dwellings, with an investment of more than 200 milliard marks, and short-term construction objectives for the period 1971-75 were also set (Table 8.2). In the longer term it was hoped that the proportion of new build to improvements and modernisations would gradually be reversed to a ratio of 1:2. Until then, new house construction had assumed the dominant role.

During the past decade the sub-goals for new house construction have been more than attained, with industrialised building construction accounting for 85% of all new-build dwellings and pre-fabricated building producing 100,000 flats annually.[23]

Table 8.2 Housing Construction Targets established
in the Five Years Plans in accordance
with the 1973 National Housing Programme.

HOUSING TARGETS				
Period	New Housing Units	Dwellings Improved	Total	Houses Built or Improved in respective period
1971-75	385,000	115,000	500,000	608,666
1976-80	550,000	200,000	750,000	813,127
1981-85	600,000	330-350,000	930-950,000	

Sources: 'Gesetz über den Fünfjahrplan für die
Entwicklung der Volkswirtschaft der DDR 1971-1975
vom 20. Dezember 1971', (GBl. I, p.175); 'Gesetz
über den Fünfjahrplan für die Entwicklung der Volkswirtschaft der DDR 1976-1980 vom 15. Dezember 1976'
(GBl. I, p.519); and 'Direktive des X. Parteitages
der SED zum Fünfjahrplan für die Entwicklung der
Volkswirtschaft der DDR in den Jahren 1981-1985' in
Neues Deutschland, April 15, 1981, pp.3-8.

The regional variations in finished-parts systems
are gradually being phased out, and replaced by a
single unified system, the industrialised building
series 70 (Wohnungsbauserie 70 or WBS 70), the main
component of which is a single storey high building
slab. The logistical and technical requirements of
using this system have had a direct influence on the
location of new housing areas, which tend to be built
in the city peripheries, on open undeveloped land,
where slabs can be readily unloaded, stored and then
fitted as construction progresses. In this way,
huge satellite cities have been, and are being,
built, above all in the peripheries of the large
industrial conurbations. For example, Marzahn
(Figure 8.1) in East Berlin and Grünau in Leipzig,
will have 35,000 new dwellings each by 1985, and
10,000 were built at Prohlis, an outer district of
Dresden, in the late 70s. Such housing construction
was undertaken because the worst deficits existed in
these cities, and accommodation was needed for the
workforce attracted there by newly installed industrial plant. Indeed, a study[24] of the General Urban
Development Plans of nine major cities in 1975-6
revealed that 69% of all planned house construction
was located in the outer peripheries of these cities.

Figure 8.1 <u>The satellite city of Marzahn, East Berlin.</u> Photo by G. Staemmler

Since 1980, however, significant changes in the optimum size and preferred location of planned housing areas have been forced upon planners and politicians. Until recently, it had been assumed that the overall cost per housing unit was lowest in the city periphery,[25] because of the abundance of virgin land, general proximity to industrial places of work, and absence of compensatory and demolition expenditure. In the last few years, however, with sharp increases in the GDR's foreign trade debts, rigorous economic measures have been necessary to enable the Housing Programme to continue. These economies primarily affect energy consumption, which, for the purposes of heating buildings, is to be lowered by 30% by 1985. At the same time, construction costs are to be reduced by 15% and construction time (especially for industrial and scientific projects) by 30-50%,[26] over the same period.

A review of location planning has revealed the significance of infrastructural and related costs in the overall costing of new peripherally located housing areas, and the consequent recommendation has been for a new emphasis on smaller infill housing

developments within the existing built-up area,
where service infrastructure already exists, whilst
the construction of large new residential estates
outside the existing centres is to be phased out,[27]
although it is not yet clear whether approved
projects and those already under construction will
be affected. In summary, then, this change in house
construction planning, which has seen the rejection
of large building sites on the city peripheries in
favour of smaller inner city developments, has
resulted from the need to make urgent economies, and
has not been a product of architectural, city
planning or urban sociological considerations.

Until the 1960s, very little investment was
made in the repair and improvement of the building
stock, and it was largely ignored in government
housing policy. In the mid-sixties, the problems of
rehabilitation in the old urban residential and
'mixed' industrial/residential areas were discussed
theoretically for the first time, and a card cata-
logue of the building condition of older housing was
compiled between 1965 and 1967.[28] Not until after
the 8th SED Party Congress in 1971, however, were
particular goals for the improvement and modernisation of buildings set,[29] to be formally expressed in
the 1973 National Housing Programme (Table 8.2).
According to 1971 figures,[30] 53% of existing dwelling
units in the GDR were built before 1919, of which the
largest part are the so-called Gründerzeit quarters,
built in the major cities between 1870 and 1918. By
the early 70s, it was becoming clear that these
buildings were in imminent danger of decay beyond
repair, representing a great economic loss. Moreover,
it was realised that the housing deficit was such
that there would be no chance of achieving the 1990
objective of solving the housing problem, unless the
older dwellings were retained as part of the housing
stock.

Improvement and modernisation policy has had
the objective of restoring as many dwellings as
possible using minimum materials, finance and time.
Improvement has taken place on both a house-to-house,
and area basis. Quantitatively, the former is still
more important, but the latter has been favoured for
propaganda reasons, and been used to try out more
modern renovation techniques. Until recently, the
possibility of urban renewal and functional change
in older residential areas had been disregarded.
Even now, however, housing improvement is relatively
small - some 50,000 dwellings a year are currently
being improved - although Complex Reconstruction

Areas (CRAs), as they are called, are to be found in nearly every large city, usually in the <u>Gründerzeit</u> areas dating from around the turn of the century (Figures 8.2 and 8.3). CRAs may include as few as

Figure 8.2   <u>Langestrasse, in the Glaucha CRA in Halle.</u>

100 dwellings, whilst the largest - Arnimplatz in East Berlin - encompasses some 8,000 dwellings in multi-storey blocks (characteristically 4-6 floors).
     Running parallel with the house improvement movement has been city centre restoration which has been completed in most large and medium-sized towns, and is now being undertaken on a step-by-step basis in smaller settlements. Emphasis has been laid on the restoration of culturally and historically valuable buildings (although older dwellings are rarely included) and <u>ensembles</u>, and on the establishment of pedestrianised areas (Figure 8.4).
     The failure and discontinuation of the NÖS in 1971 was followed by a recentralisation of economic planning and control under the new party leadership of Honecker. The jurisdiction and powers of middle administrative levels were again limited, and state control was strengthened by means of a number of new laws, regulations and guidelines.[31]   In the

Figure 8.3   <u>Torstrasse in the Glaucha CRA, Halle.</u>
             <u>Photo by G. Staemmler</u>

housing and planning field, the National Planning
Commission and the Ministry of Construction introduced a series of 'Central Plan Regulations' to
guide quantitative and territorial aspects of house
construction and improvement, which were to be
implemented by authorities at the regional, sub-
regional and settlement levels. These regulations
are based solely on economic criteria, and guiding
standards relating to city planning or architectural
considerations do not exist. In official and semi-
official publications, identification with the new
residential areas is made only by euphorically
emphasising quantitative results, whilst, with the
recent moves towards inner city rebuilding and
improvement, a certain attractiveness of the
<u>Gründerzeit</u> quarters has now been officially con-
firmed.[32]

Figure 8.4   Pedestrianised Zone in Klement-Gottwald-
              Strasse, Potsdam.
              Photo by G. Staemmler

Housing and Housing Management Today

The Housing Stock in GDR. Despite the large scale
construction undertaken in the 70s within the framework of the National Housing Programme, the housing
stock remains relatively old, with the average
dwelling age being 58 years, and 47% of the stock
pre-dating 1919 in 1978 (cf. 25% in the FRG, for
example). Table 8.3 shows how, even by the late 70s,
50% of the total stock were without bath or shower,
and similarly only 50% had an interior WC; and this
is despite the fact that all dwellings constructed
since 1965 have had a bath or shower (Figure 8.5).
Similarly, although nearly all new houses built in
the 70s had central heating fitted (Figure 8.5), in
1979 22% of total housing stock had this facility.
This can be explained not only by the high percentage of old dwellings in the total stock, but also by
the poor level of service provision in dwellings
built in the 50s and 60s. There are also considerable regional differences in housing provision. Two

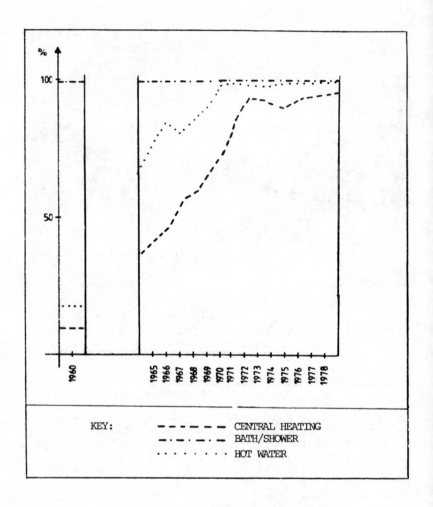

Figure 8.5 <u>Basic Amenities Installed in New
Dwellings, 1960 and 1965-78.</u>

Source: G. Staemmler <u>Rekonstruktion innerstädtischer
Wohngebiete in der DDR</u> (IWOS-Bericht zur Stadt-
forschung 7, Institute of Housing and Urban District
Planning, Technical University of West Berlin, W.
Berlin, 1981), p.19.

trends overlap: in the larger communities are the
better provided dwellings, whilst there is a large

Table 8.3 Basic Amenities in Housing Stock in the
GDR, 1961, 1971 and 1979.

Amenity	1961	1971	1979
	(% of total housing stock)		
Running water	66.0	82.2	89.0
Interior WC	33.0	41.8	50.0
Bath or Shower	22.4	38.7	50.0
Central Heating	2.5	10.6	22.0

Source: G. Staemmler, Rekonstruktion innerstädtischer
Wohngebiete in der DDR (IWOS-Bericht zur Stadt-
forschung 7, Institute of Housing and Urban District
Planning,Technical University of West Berlin, West
Berlin, 1981), p.19.

gap between housing provision in important cities,
and in less important ones.

Bleak living conditions resulting from poor
service provision have been made worse by minimum
sized rooms and low overall floorspace. The average
flat size in the GDR today is as low as 58m^2 floorspace, and even new dwellings built in 1979 only
averaged 61m^2 floorspace each (cf. 100m^2 in the FRG,
for example).

The Organisation of Housing Investment and Development. The programming and planning of house construction is undertaken at a series of strictly
defined, hierarchicalised levels of decision-making,
firmly related to, and controlled by, central plan
objectives. The owner thus has little say in
decision-making relating to the designation of construction and improvement projects, which are,
rather, an aspect of national economic planning.

In 1973, regulations for the drawing-up and
approval of 'Housing Programmes' (Komplexer
Wohnungsbau) were established to cover all new construction and improvement and repair projects in all
types of house ownership.[33] These are drawn-up by
the central authorities for each region of the
country, but actual sites have to be confirmed and
approved by the local authorities, based on central
plan guidelines and taking into account the content
of General Urban Development and General Urban
Transportation Plans; and local representatives also
have direct control over the co-ordination and
implementation of housing projects, in accordance
with established norms and procedures.

Investment planning for house construction takes place in three main phases of decision making. There is the long term planning for a period of 15 years by the Regional (District) Councils, which is continually adjusted and updated. Then, the location of housing projects is settled, and finally specific investments are allocated. These decision-making phases apply to all state and co-operative housing projects. The local representatives and councils have to control the preparation and execution of housing projects as a whole, but implementation on the ground lies in the hands of special institutions. Owners of the housing to be built or modernised do not carry out the work themselves, but have to make an economic contract[34] with a so-called main developer (Hauptauftraggeber or HAG), who carries out the project for the owner. Then, there is a so-called general or main contractor (General-oder-Hauptauftragnehmer - GAN or HAN), who is responsible for carrying out concrete construction works bound by contract to the main developer.

These decision-making structures and responsibilities apply to all new construction projects as well as CRAs with more than 100 housing units. There are no special laws for improvement procedure as exist in many other countries; rather the laws and guidelines pertaining to new construction have been modified accordingly as some of the old stock have been improved.

State, Co-operative and Private Housing. There are three different ownership types for housing in the GDR - state (officially called 'People's Own'), co-operative and private. In the immediate post war, at the time of the creation of the GDR, the great majority of dwellings were privately owned, and even in 1950 private house construction accounted for 61% of total houses constructed that year. By 1957, however, with industrialised building well established, the balance was more than reversed with state housing accounting for 79% of construction, private housing only 8%, and co-operative housing 13%. Since then, private house construction has remained relatively insignificant at levels of up to 10% of total construction, whilst the share of state and co-operative housing has varied considerably (e.g. 1961: 35% to 59%; 1971: 80% to 15%).[35] Whilst census statistics[36] in 1971 showed that 62.5% of all dwellings were still privately owned, the National Housing Programme of 1973 provides for a 45% state,

45% co-operative and 10% private split in house
production in the 1970s and 80s.

Rents are exceedingly low, about 48-54 marks
per month for a new 60m² flat in the provinces and
somewhat more, 60-75 marks, for a similar property
in East Berlin. In addition up to 25 marks a month
may also be paid for central heating. In older
properties, rents are lower still, having remained
at the same real level since a rent freeze in 1936.
These rents are 'only a partial economic compensation for the use of a flat'[37] and SED leader
Honecker has publicly stated that a citizen pays
only one third of the State's running costs for the
maintenance and management of his State dwelling.[38]
It is also interesting to note that 1979 statistics
show the average gross income per household to be
1,642 marks per month with an average 3.7% of that
income (61 marks) being spent on rent, electricity
and gas.[39]

State housing stock is administered by the
Community Housing Administration (Kommunale
Wohnungsverwaltung or KWV). New construction is
financed from the budgets of local authorities,
which in their turn, are part of the national
budget.[40]

Co-operative housing schemes were set-up and
run by non-profit and other co-operative building
societies founded before the war, which were
reorganised by decree in 1957.[41] In 1954, the AWGs
(workers' co-operative building societies) were
first formed, and it was these that were to finance
the bulk of co-operative house construction thereafter. In a period of low capital availability in
the national budget, it was an initiative on behalf
of the GDR leadership aimed at finding a new source
of capital to finance house construction, rather
than turn to the ideologically inacceptable option
of allowing the expansion of private home ownership.
Members joining an AWG were guaranteed accommodation
within a fixed period, a considerable attraction in
an era of acute housing shortage. AWGs can be
established in factories and other institutions of
work where you must be employed if you want to
become an AWG member. In order to receive a co-
operative flat, members have to make obligatory contributions which become co-operative property and
obtain a certain number of shares in the co-
operative.[42] In contrast to co-operative schemes in
some other countries, the co-operative retains
exclusive ownership of all its housing, partly
because the AWGs remain financially very much depen-

dent on local authorities, who provide up to 85% of construction costs in the form of interest free loans.[43] Co-operative house construction also comes within government planning, which establishes the location of, and level of investment in, such dwellings.

Private house construction since the end of the war has been limited to one-family and duplex houses, which are owner-occupied. The ideological stance of the State towards private housing has fluctuated somewhat, but since the 8th Party Congress in 1971 private housing has been increasingly tolerated and its importance has thereby been enhanced. Substantial financial benefits (e.g. low interest loans) are available to owner-occupiers, especially in small and medium sized towns, in villages, and on the periphery of the large cities,[44] i.e. in those areas where it is unlikely that large state or co-operative projects will be located in the future. A 1973 study revealed that 47% of owner-occupiers were in medium and small-sized towns, 42% in villages, and only 11% in the large cities.[45] But private house construction in the GDR, which presently comprises a good 10% of all housing construction in the country, plays a much less important role than in Western European countries.

The State does, in fact, exert certain controls over the private house construction sector. Private house builders have to observe construction regulations[46] which are aimed at minimising construction costs. And, because of the very low, state regulated rents, the letting of privately owned flat-houses is often more of a financial burden than a source of income. Most of these houses are old buildings, often in bad condition; repair work is a financial burden for the owners that is not covered entirely by the rents. Neither State nor local authorities are usually interested in obtaining such properties, particularly when tenants may then demand that long-overdue repairs be undertaken. Similarly a sale to a private individual is unlikely, because old flat-houses have little attraction. It is in fact, possible to apply for a permit to relinquish ownership of property to the State, although this can be refused. Hoffman's study of this subject[47] suggests that this has been a popular practice amongst flat owners, because of excessive repair maintenance and running costs compared with low level rents.

If the land on which owner-occupied or AWG dwellings are to be built is State property, the State may grant the right of usufruct to the future

building owners (private or AWGs) for an unlimited
period.[48] If an owner-occupied house is sold to
another citizen (and this is only possible if the
latter does not yet have his own house), the right
of usufruct is transferred also, and similar transfer may be made through inheritance. Citizens have
to make a compensation payment to the State for the
right of usufruct, but according to Jenkis[49] this
is very low, on average about 20-30 marks per month
for a 500m^2 plot. Pre-existing private and co-
operative real estate is not subject to the grant
of usufruct rights. In these cases, the unified
ownership of house and land remains intact, although
the State retains the right to expropriate land and
property for development or improvement purposes if
need be.[50] For example, if a 'reconstruction area'
is declared, private house owners cannot prevent the
modernization or improvement of their dwellings,
even though they cannot be forced to finance the
operation. If they agree to the planned measures,
they remain owners and have to participate financially in their implementation. If they do not,
owners lose ownership rights to their real estate,
which the State either buys or, if no agreement is
reached, expropriations with obligatory compensation.

The Tentant's Lot. In the GDR, all living space is
subject to State housing control. To be assigned a
flat, families or single persons must place an
application at one of the institutions responsible
for housing control. Applications are decided upon
according to the principle of just distribution. The
exchange of dwellings, for example because of an
addition to the family or the need to move to
another city, is also controlled by the said
institutions. If a dwelling is too large for the
number of tenants living there, then part of it can
be assigned by the controlling institutions to
another person or family.
     The tenant's situation in large cities may be
superficially compared to that in Western European
countries in terms of 'housing shortage', but its
causes and the obstacles to acquisition of a dwelling are markedly different in the GDR. The 'average
tenant' in the GDR has to wait many years before
being assigned a flat (six years, according to one
GDR commentator[51]), after applying to the respective
housing institution. Such delays are in part the
result of the relatively low construction levels,
compounded by the closing of older decaying flats by

the supervisory Boards and the long and inflexible
bureaucratic procedures involved. The possibilities
of moving, once a flat is acquired, are generally
limited because of the difficulties of agreeing an
exchange with other tenants and their owning agencies, which is often hard to come by. The allocation of living space is carried out strictly
according to family size, and experiments in non-
familial living or the leasing of rooms for
community activities run counter to the SED's ideological conceptions, which dictate that social
activities take place within the framework of
official, state run organisations.

There is practically no published urban sociological data in the GDR and so the housing desires
of inhabitants are largely unknown. This is
particularly so because systematic enquiries conducted by persons not authorised by the government are
generally forbidden. However, an analysis by the
author[52] of flat exchange advertisements placed by
tenants in East Berlin, Dresden and Leipzig news-
papers suggests that their prime objective is
acquisition of a larger flat, with comfort and
location being very much secondary considerations.
At the same time, the desire to rent a unifamiliar
dwelling continues to be conspicuous, even though
the availability of such houses is low.

A further characteristic of the tenants' lot is
the lack of consultation and participation in the
house construction and improvement process. Tenants
are not consulted on the design of new settlement
areas, nor are they given the opportunity to express
their preferences regarding the nature of rehabilitation in CRAs. Indeed, tenants in CRAs cannot even
be sure they will be permitted to return to their
flat once the improvements have been implemented.
The ruling SED and its national authorities allow no
room for a collective, emancipated representation of
tenants' interests,[53] and construction planning and
implementation are technologically and organisation-
ally structured in such a way that planning authorities would consider participation by affected
residents to be a disturbance or delay. Independent
initiatives from tenants, members of co-operative
societies and private home owners are only accepted
and supported if they involve additional work and
effort that goes beyond that planned for by the
State. In addition, the State initiates and
organizes competitions for citizens to participate
in the construction of community facilities. But
again, individual effort is strictly controlled and

channelled by the State, and initiatives that go
outside these formalised structures are likely to be
prohibited.

Concluding Remarks

The evolution of housing policy in the GDR in the
post-war has been orientated towards the reconstruction of war damaged cities and an attempt to meet
the acute national housing deficit by the construction of increasingly large estates, characteristically located in the city peripheries. Flats, rather
than houses, have been the order of the day, with
minimal room dimensions, constructed using
industrialised building techniques.

The typical East German city today has a recon-
structed and/or restored historical city centre,
contrasting markedly with the old housing stock
surrounding it. A number of parallels with the
appearance of Western European cities are to be
found, although the political - ideological and
economic - organisational starting points are very
different. Traditional commercial and service
locations have often become pedestrianized shopping
zones, but the process of commercial concentration
in the centre is far less marked than in the west,
with little attempt having been made to replace the
old inner city housing zones (Gründerzeit) with
tertiary service buildings.

The older housing areas surrounding the city
centres are rapidly decaying and in desperate need
of repair and improvement, but despite the emphasis
put on rehabilitation and modernization in the
National Housing Programme since the seventies, new
build continues to dominate the housing industry. A
systematic rehabilitation of this older housing is
unlikely because the construction industry is geared
to panel and wall system technology, and comprehensive rehabilitation would be too costly in terms of
materials and labour. It is thus difficult to see
how the planned quantitative increase in improvement
schemes can occur.

New housing construction in the form of vast
satellite settlements is resulting in a radiocentric
sprawl of the country's major cities. Dormitory
suburbs of 100,000 residents, exceedingly monotonous
in their design and layout, are still being planned
and built, although recent cost reassessments,
particularly in the light of increased building
costs and energy problems, suggest that future construction may take place largely within the existing

built-up area.

Housing policy and construction are, of course, firmly dependent upon the finance available from within the National budget, and as the GDR's foreign debts mount, so the prospects of 'solving the housing problem' by 1990 diminish. It remains to be seen whether the State can continue to provide the same level of resources for house construction, let alone the increased allocation planned for in the National Housing Programme; and also what political, domestic, importance the SED attaches to achieving its targets. Overall, however, the large stock of old decaying housing, the massive estates of minimal dimension rooms and of questionable material standards, and the inadequacy of existing economic and administrative measures to effect the required improvements, suggest that the current stock alone will pose serious management problems for the housing authorities in future years.

NOTES AND REFERENCES

1. See DDR-Wirtschaft. Eine Bestandsaufnahme, Deutsches Institut für Wirtschaftsforschung, (ed.) (Frankfurt am Main, 1974), pp.23-25.

2. See G. Krenz 'Zu einigen Grundtendenzen der Stadtebaupolitik in der DDR, Teil I', Kunsterziehung, No.5, (1977) pp.5-9.

3. See DDR-Handbuch, 2nd revision and enlarged edition from the Bundesministerium für innerdeutsche Beziehungen (Cologne, 1979), pp.136-143.

4. See Städtebau. Grundsätze Methoden Beispiele Richtwerte, Bauakademie der DDR, Institut für Städtebau und Architektur, (ed.)(East Berlin, 1979), p.42.

5. Ibid; and also 'Gesetz über den Aufbau der Städte in der Deutschen Demokratischen Republik und der Hauptstadt Deutschlands, Berlin (Aufbaugesetz) vom. 6, September 1950' (GBl.* No.104, p.965) article 2.

6. 'Grundsätze des Städtebaues', Ministerialblatt der DDR No.25 (1950).

7. Ibid.

8. See 'Gesetz über den Aufbau der Städte in der Deutschen Demokratischen Republik und der Hauptstadt Deutschlands, Berlin (Aufbaugesetz) vom. 6, Sept. 1950' (GBl. No.104, p.965).

9. 'Gesetz über den Aufbau der Städte in der Deutschen Demokratischen Republik und der Hauptstadt

* GBl is the State Bulletin of Legislation

Deutschlands, Berlin (Aufbaugesetz), vom. 6,
September 1950'. (GBl. No.104, p.965) article 14.
    10. Karola Bloch writes about how this design
came about: 'The designer of Stalin-Allee Hermann
Henselmann, told me with tears in his eyes, how he
was forced to design this hollow magnificence. He
showed me his own designs, which really were very
different and much better, but had been rejected'.
K. Bloch, Aus meinem Leben (Pfullingen, 1981) p.208.
    11. See B. Flierl, 'Hermann Henselmann,
Architekt und Architektur in der DDR', in the intro-
duction to H. Henselmann, Gedanken Ideen Bauten
Projekte (East Berlin, 1978), pp.26-52; and H.
Heckmann, 'Architektur kritisch. Stalinallee -
Traum oder Irrtum', Der Architekt, 3 (1980), pp.149-
154.
    12. See H. Henselmann, 'Der reaktionäre
Charakter des Konstruktivismus' in Henselmann
Gedanken Projekte, pp.78-80.
    13. See F. Werner, Stadtplanung Berlin 1900-
1950 (Berlin, 1969).
    14. See F. Werner, 'Der Städtebau in Berlin
(Ost) und Berlin (West)', in Zwischen Rostock und
Saarbrücken. Städtebau und Raumordnung in beiden
deutschen Staaten, (Rev. by H. Isenberg),
(Düsseldorf, 1973), pp.135-156.
    15. The Interbau was the name given to a
building exhibition held in West Berlin in 1957,
where in a special area called the Hansa Quarter,
many well-known architects designed houses and flats
for lower income groups. It was a response to the
construction of Stalinallee in East Berlin.
    16. See Statistisches Jahrbuch der Deutschen
Demokratischen Republik 1979 Staatliche Zentralverwaltung für Statistik (East Berlin, Staatsverlage
der DDR), p.31.
    17. See Städtebau. Grundsätze Methoden
Beispiele Richtwerte, Bauakademie der DDR, Institut
für Städtebau und Architektur, (Ed.)(East Berlin,
1979), p.44.
    18. B. Flierl, 'Hermann Henselmann...' p.30.
    19. See DDR-Wirtschaft. Eine Bestandsaufnahme,
pp.64 f.
    20. According to W. Junker, The Minister of
Construction at the time. W. Junker, Das Wohnungsbauprogramm der Deutschen Demokratischen Republik
für die Jahre 1976 bis 1990. 10. Tagung des ZK der
SED, 2. Okt. 1973 (East Berlin, 1973), p.6.
    21. See the 'Direktive des VIII. Parteitages
der SED zum Fünfjahrplan für die Entwicklung der
Volkswirtschaft der DDR in den Jahren 1971-1975', in

Dokumente des VIII. Parteitages der SED (East Berlin, 1973), pp.42-152.

22. See W. Junker, *Das Wohnungsbauprogramm der Deutschen Demokratischen Republik für die Jahre 1976 bis 1990. 10. Tagung des ZK der SED, 2 Okt. 1973* (East Berlin, 1973).

23. See G. Staemmler, *Rekonstruktion innerstädtischer Wohngebiete in der DDR* (IWOS-Bericht zur Stadtforschung 7, Institut für Wohnungsbau und Stadtteilplanung, Technische Universität Berlin, West Berlin, 1981), p.53, Table 6.

24. See J. Schattel, 'Für eine höhere Qualität der Generalbebauungsplanung', *Architektur der DDR*, 7 (1977), pp.389-392.

25. After reviewing 10 General Development Plans, J. Schattel concluded in 1975 that the expense per living unit (including primary maintenance) was about 36 percent higher in the centre of the city, and about 7 percent higher in the inner-city area than on the edges of the city. See J. Schattel, 'Einfluss der Standortwahl auf die Höhe der Investitionen für den Wohnungsbau', in *Architektur der DDR*, 11 (1975), pp.646-647.

26. See '7. Baukonferenz. Aus dem Referat des Ministers für Bauwesen, Wolfgang Junker: Das Bauen hat in unserem Land eine klare Perspektive', in *Architektur der DDR*, 8 (1980), pp.452-3.

27. See J. Schattel, 'Einfluss der Standortgrösse auf den Investitionsaufwand', in *Architektur der DDR*, 11 (1980), pp.644-5.

28. See 'Beschluss über die Vorbereitung und Durchführung der Ermittlung des Bauzustandes der Wohngebäude in der Deutschen Demokratischen Republik vom 19. August 1965' (*GBl.* II, p.651); and 'Ordnung über die Vorbereitung und Durchführung der Ermittlung des Bauzustandes der Wohngebäude in der Deutschen Demokratischen Republik vom 23. August 1965' (*GBl.* II, p.652).

29. See 'Gesetz über den Volkswirtschaftsplan 1972 vom 20. Dezember 1971' (*GBl.* I, p.191).

30. See 'BDA der DDR - Zentrale Fachgruppe Wohn - und gesellschaftliche Bauten: Kurzfassung zur Wohnungsanalyse', in *Komplexer Wohnungsbau - Aufgaben der Architekten* (Schriftenreihen der Bauforschung, Reihe Wohn - und Gesellschaftsbauten, Heft 17 from the Bauakademie der DDR; East Berlin, 1973), pp.9-10.

31. See *DDR-Wirtscahft. Eine Bestandsaufnahme*, p.69; and W. Klein, 'Wirtschaftspolitische Aspekte der Rezentralisierung in der DDR', in *Deutschland Archiv*, 1 (1978), pp.36-51.

32. See, for example, K. Rasche, 'Gedanken zur Gründerzeitarchitektur', in Architektur der DDR, 11 (1979), p.701.

33. See 'Durchführungsbestimmung zur Verwirklichung der Grundsätze für die Planung und Leitung des Prozesses der Reproduktion der Grundfonds auf dem Gebiet des komplexen Wohnungsbaues vom 30. June 1972' (GBl. II, p.499), including appendix 1.

34. The basis of such a contract is outlined in the following ordinance: 'Achte Durchführungsverordnung zum Vertragsgesetz - Wirtschaftsverträge im Rahmen der Reproduktion der Grundfonds - vom 12. Januar 1972' (GBl. II, p.33).

35. All figures taken from H.W. Jenkis, Wohnungswirtschaft und Wohnungspolitik in beiden deutschen Staaten, 2nd. revised edition (Hamburg, 1976), p.29.

36. See 'BDA der DDR: Kurzfassung zur Wohnungsanalyse', in Komplexer Wohnungsbau, pp.9-10.

37. M. Muhlmann, 'Miete', Grundriss Zivilrecht, 4 (East Berlin, 1977), p.30.

38. E. Honecker, 'Zur Durchführung der Parteiwahlen 1975/76', in 15 Tagung des ZK der SED (East Berlin, 1975), p.21.

39. See the Statistisches Jahrbuch der Deutschen Demokratischen Republik 1980, Staatliche Zentralverwaltung für Statistik (East Berlin, Staatsverlage der DDR), pp.272-3.

40. See M. Hoffmann, Wohnungspolitik der DDR. Das Leistungsund Interessenproblem (Düsseldorf, 1972), pp.41-2.

41. See 'Verordnung über die Umbildung gemeinnütziger und sonstiger Wohnungsbaugenossenschaften vom 14. März 1957' (GBl. 1, p.200).

42. In general, to gain allocation of a one roomed flat, a co-operative member must hold 3-4 shares costing 300 marks each. A 1½-roomed flat would require 6 such shares, and larger accommodation requires a correspondingly greater number.

43. See 'Verordnung vom 21. November 1963 über die Arbeiterwohnungsbaugenossenschaften' (GBl. II, 1964, p.17) Appendix, Section III, Finanzierung.

44. See 'Gemeinsamer Beschluss des Sekretariats des ZK der SED und des Ministerrates der DDR über Massnahmen zur Förderung der Initiative der Werktätigen im individuellen Wohnungsbau vom 6. Juni 1972' (GBl. II, p.395).

45. See R. Linke, Eigenheimgebiete - Probleme der städtebaulichen Einordnung (Reihe Städtebau und Architektur, Heft 57 from the Bauakademie der DDR;

East Berlin, 1974), pp.6-7.
   46. See 'Verordnung über die Förderung des
Baues von Eigenheimen vom 24. November 1971' (<u>GBl</u>.
II, p.709), article 5.
   47. See M. Hoffmann, 'Lösung der Wohnungs-
frage' bis 1990. Zur Wohnungs - under Bodenpolitik
in der DDR', in <u>Bauwelt</u>, 5 (1975), pp.118-135
   48. See 'Gesetz über die Verleihung von
Nutzungsrechten an volkseigenen Grundstücken vom 14.
Dezember 1970' (<u>GBl</u>. I), p.372 i.d.f. des Gesetzes
über den Verkamf Volkseigener Eigenheime,
Miteigentumsanteile und Gebäude für Erholungszwecke
vom 19. Dezember 1973' (<u>GBl</u>. I, p.578).
   49. See Jenkis, <u>Wohnungswirtschaft</u>, pp.111-112.
   50. See J. Klinkert, E. Oehler, G. Rohde,
'Eigentumsrecht, Nutzung von Grundstücken und
Gebäuden zum Wohnen und zur Erholung', <u>Grundri</u>
<u>Zivilrecht</u>, 2 (East Berlin, 1979), p.71; and G.
Rohde, <u>Die Bereitstellung von Boden für</u>
<u>Investitionen und andere bauliche Massnahmen</u>, (East
Berlin, 1974), p.179.
   51. See 'Sechs Jahre warten für eine Wohnung'
in <u>Parlamentarisch Politischer Pressedienst</u>, Aug.
21, 1978 (Bonn), p.3.
   52. See G. Staemmler, <u>Rekonstruktion</u>, part IV,
pp.269-322.
   53. See W. Gramann, <u>Nationale Front und</u>
<u>Bürgerinitiative</u> (from the Akademie für Staats - und
Rechtswissenschaft der DDR, Potsdam-Babelsberg; East
Berlin, 1973), p.61.

The translations of all quotations are not
authorised.

9.   ITALY

by Liliana Padovani

Introductory Remarks
In Italy today there are 86.6 million rooms for 56.2
million inhabitants.[1] In theory, then, each person
should have on average one and a half rooms each,
within a dwelling. Although this figure is just an
average and has little real significance, it does
give an idea of how much has been accomplished in
housebuilding in Italy since the war. The 1951
census reported 37.3 million rooms for a population
that exceeded 47 million, at a time when dwellings
were overcrowded and often lacked the basic amenities. Only 40% were equipped with internal lava-
tories and only 10% had bathrooms. From this
situation of serious crisis, the country, after a
period of rapid economic growth and expansion in the
building industry during the 1950s and 60s, has now
reached a point that surpasses the standards that
are generally considered optimum with respect to the
overall housing stock.[2]
     The housing problem takes on a different aspect,
however, when it is analysed from a point of view
which does not examine only the evolution of the
general conditions of the overall housing stock.
Indeed, the picture is not so bright if the analysis
also takes into account differences in housing conditions between the social classes, and variations
in different parts of the country: urban areas,
rural areas and areas of emigration. The complexity
of the situation becomes even greater if we examine
the evolution that has taken place in the use of
residential resources during this period.
     An assessment of the above considerations
brings out a whole series of problems and shortages
of great importance that must be dealt with in order
to satisfy the pressing need for housing. Part of
the population is still living in overcrowded condi-

247

tions, and the incidence of <u>housing sharing</u> persists
and is, in fact, on the increase.[3] Furthermore, the
number of families on the waiting list for public
housing is very high, and contrasts markedly with
the available supply;[4] and lastly, conditions of
<u>unfitness and disrepair</u> are extremely widespread.
Recent estimates have indicated that in order to
eliminate overcrowding it would be necessary to
rehouse - either through housebuilding or rehabilitation - a quarter to a fifth of the total number
of families in Italy.

The major housing needs are concentrated in the
large urban areas: 41% of the estimated deficit
comes from the eleven major metropolitan areas
(Milan, Turin, Genoa, Venice, Bologna, Florence,
Rome, Naples, Bari, Palermo and Catanis), where 28%
of the population live. As regards physical deterioration and lack of basic amenities in the housing
stock, a 1976 survey[6] showed that more than 7 million
dwellings - a little less than half the total stock -
were in a state of disrepair, and half of these
suffered from <u>serious</u> disrepair. This disrepair is
not confined to areas of emigration or rural areas,
but can be found in the major urban centres. In
1979, a second survey[7] taken only in cities with
more than 500,000 inhabitants confirmed these
trends, and actually reported a slight increase in
the percentages of the housing in a state of disrepair or unfit for habitation.

This brief description sums up the current
situation, which is far from satisfactory and is the
result of a long period of intensive activity in new
housebuilding. This reached its highest levels
during the 1950s and 1960s, and has continued in the
last ten years at lower levels and with different
characteristics (Tables 9.1 and 9.2). Between 1951
and 1981, whilst there was an 8.7 million population
increase, the number of rooms increased by 49
million, an increase of more than five times that of
the population. During this same period, there was
a 6.7 million increase in dwellings. Even over the
last 10 years, in a period of supposed crisis in the
house building industry, the increase in the number
of habitable rooms, - partly due to new housebuilding
and partly to rehabilitation, - has been ten times
greater than the increase in population, and more
than twice the increase in the number of families.

How can this apparent paradox be explained? The
more dwellings that are built, the greater are the
housing needs of that portion of the population who
still live in unfit dwellings, a portion that has

Table 9.1 Evolution of Housing Stock and Population 1951-1981

| | Housing | | | | | | Population | Households |
| | total | | occupied* | | non-occupied** | | | |
	rooms	dwellings	rooms	dwellings	rooms	dwellings		
1951	37,342,217	11,410,685	35,062,611	10,756,121	2,279,606	654,564	47,515,537	11,528,480
1961	47,527,666	14,213,667	43,423,845	13,031,618	4,103,821	1,182,049	50,695,211	13,562,289
1971	63,833,732	17,433,969	56,242,463	15,301,424	7,591,269	2,132,545	54,136,547	15,865,869
1981	86,570,148	21,852,717	71,465,194	17,509,054	15,104,954	4,343,659	56,243,935	18,536,570

*   dwellings occupied as first residence
** dwellings occupied temporarily for study, work or second homes;
    and unoccupied dwellings

Source: National Censi, 1951-81

ITALY

Table 9.2   Average Annual Increase in Housing Stock
            and Households 1951-81

	total dwellings	occupied dwellings*	non-occupied dwellings**	households
1951-61	280,298	227,550	52,748	203,381
1961-71	322,030	226,981	95,049	241,189
1971-81	441,875	220,763	221,111	255,539

*   dwellings occupied as first residence
**   dwellings temporarily occupied for study, work
     or second homes; and unoccupied dwellings

Source: National Censi, 1951-81

only slightly decreased since the Second World War.
How can it also be that the increase in rehabilitation activity over the last few years (Table 9.3)
does not seem to have curbed the deterioration in
the housing stock?

Table 9.3   Investments in New Housing and
            Rehabilitation, 1951-79

Period	Milliard lira, 1978 equivalents			Investment in Rehabilitation as % of Total
	New housing	Rehabilitation	Total	
1951-1960	5,099	702	5,801	12.1
1961-1970	9,603	2,416	12,019	20.1
1971-1975	8,845	3,790	12,636	30.0
1976	7,097	3,822	10,919	35.0
1977	6,815	4,231	11,046	38.3
1978	6,787	4,340	11,127	39.0
1979	6,700	5,000	11,700	42.7

Source: Economic and Social Research Centre for the
        Building Market (Cresme).

A first series of answers to these questions can
be found in the fact that, together with the substantial building of new dwellings, a certain amount of
underuse has occurred, especially in the older housing stock. Due consideration has not been given to
the far-reaching implications this might have. A
part of the older housing stock has been consistently underused due to the persistence of situations
that tend to curb the mobility of the population.
One such example is the freeze on rents and its

after-effects,[8] which made it more advantageous to
stay in a large dwelling with controlled rent rather
than look for a house more suitable to the size of
the family. At the same time, the tax system makes
real estate transfers burdensome and thus restricts
mobility within the house-ownership sub-market.[9]
     Some of the housing stock, particularly in the
older parts of the urban fabric, has been abandoned
in conditions of serious deterioration until it has
fallen completely into ruins. Even those parts
which were of great cultural value like the old city
centres, were not spared this fate. They were either
overlooked by the strongly dualistic approach to the
processes of urban growth pursued in the 1950s and
1960s, or else they were considered to be of little
value due to a misjudgement of the quality of life
offered by more modern residential units. This is
still happening in certain southern areas where
housebuilding is going on in newly developed areas,
while the old deteriorating city centres are neglected. Furthermore, there are functional changes
taking place that are bringing new uses for some
parts of the stock; from primary dwellings to vaca-
tion housing in tourist areas, and to short-term
residences or offices in urban areas. In this way,
the overall housing supply is being further eroded.
     A second series of reasons derives from the
existence and growth over the last few years of what
might be termed 'opulent consumption' in the housing
market, a characteristic of societies that have
arrived at a mature stage of development. Part of
the population can, in fact, afford to live in very
large dwellings and possibly own one or more other
dwellings as well. The number of second homes,
estimated at below 500,000 units in 1961, exceeded a
million in 1971 and is still on the increase. During
the three decades from 1951 to 1981, the increase in
the housing stock tended to include ever-growing
numbers of dwellings that were either used on a
temporary basis only (second houses, temporary residences) or else unoccupied altogether. Whilst the
primary housing stock increased an average of
approximately 200,000 dwellings per year during each
of these three decades, the number of unoccupied or
temporarily occupied dwellings increased fourfold,
from an average yearly increase of 50,000 units between 1951 and 1961 to more than 200,000 during the
last decade - half of the total increase of all
dwellings (Table 9.2).
     Another factor to bear in mind is the great
increase in the number of households in relation to

population growth, reflecting the complex social
phenomenon of the transformation of the traditional
family. Over the last decade, this process has
involved all parts of the country, urban as well as
rural, the North as well as the South. The nature
of rehabilitation also requires attention and
reassessment. Rehabilitation has been directed
either towards superficial patching up in emergency
situations, or towards improving the internal layout
of dwellings that are not in serious disrepair.
Little effort has been made to comprehensively solve
the problems of deterioration and decay.

The Main Periods in Housing Policy and Construction in the Post War

During the span of time from the end of the war to
the present it is possible to recognise a series of
periods characterised by striking differences, both
in the nature of housing problems and in the
criteria and the policies adopted for intervention.
The rate and nature of urban expansion and housebuilding differ from period to period, as does the
manner in which the problem is studied and the role
the building industry plays within the economic
policies pursued at the time. Consequently, each
period is characterised by striking differences in
the planning of public intervention and in housing
policies enacted by the Government, at different
territorial and sectoral levels of control. The
subdivision most commonly used in the literature,
and for the purposes of discussion, on housing in
Italy comprises four main periods and it is these
that are the subject of the following four sections.
Here, however, a brief introductory overview of each
period is provided.

Post-War Reconstruction (1945-50). By the end of
the War the housing problem in Italy had worsened
considerably. Over one million rooms has been
destroyed by bombing, and a further million had been
badly damaged. The building industry had been in
decline since the start of the war, with house construction figures falling from 98,000 dwellings in
1936 to 23,000 in 1942. By the end of the war the
industry was at a standstill, and came up against
the difficulties of starting up again.
     The political situation was uncertain and the
entire Government system, after the twenty year
fascist period, had to be completely rethought. This

period was characterised by high levels of public investment and of direct Government involvement in the building industry, and particularly in house-building. It is during these years that the main features of post-war public housing in Italy were determined.

Growth and Expansion (1951-63). Once the difficulties of the immediate post-war years were overcome, the recovery that has since been termed an 'economic miracle' began, and with it a boom in the construction industry started and continued right up to the recession of 1963-64. The country was affected by the intense processes of industrial expansion which, however, were limited to only part of the national territory, and in particular to the areas of the industrial triangle of Milan, Turin and Genoa in Northern Italy. Massive migration from rural farming areas took place, and there were large migratory movements from the south of Italy towards northern regions. Waves of people moved from the rural areas towards the urban centres, and during the 50s the provincial capital cities - the major urban centres - absorbed 90% of the demographic increase in the country as a whole; and the metro-politan systems, especially in northern Italy, experienced population growth rates that were far in excess of national demographic equivalents (Table 9.4). The country was subject to growth processes

Table 9.4   Population Increases in Metropolitan Areas, 1951-1971

| | (millions of inhabitants) | | | | | | |
| | 1951 | | 1961 | | 1971 | | 1951-61 | 1961-71 |
	Popn	% of Total	Popn	% of Total	Popn	% of Total	Increase in Popn	Increase in Popn
Metrop Areas								
North	8.4	17.7	11.8	23.4	16.8	31.0	3.4	4.9
South	6.3	13.4	8.0	15.8	9.9	18.3	1.6	2.0
Total	14.7	31.1	19.8	39.2	26.7	49.3	5.0	6.9
Italy	47.5	100.0	50.6	100.0	54.1	100.0	3.1	3.5

Source: National Censi

which were intense, but extremely imbalanced, with
the formation of urban areas that were characterised
by a marked growth whilst vast areas were being left
abandoned by the waves of emigration.
   Building activities and the production of
dwellings were at very high levels and in continuous
expansion, as was the size of investments and the
amount of resources that were poured into building.
In this context, the urban policy of the public
administration tended towards permissiveness and
laissez faire, whilst in the housing field government policy centred on providing maximum direct and
indirect support for private enterprise, particularly
for new housebuilding in the areas of expansion.

A Rethinking of Housing Policy (1963-75). This
period is characterised by a decrease in building
activity, especially in the parts of the country that
had witnessed maximum growth in the 1950s. Another
feature is the changes in the processes of housing
production that were taking shape (the form of
capital, building systems etc.), and the growing
interest in rehabilitation and redevelopment in the
older parts of the urban fabric. Negative effects -
on cost, congestion and resource use - associated
with the ongoing processes of urban development and
building expansion demanded a rethinking of urban
and housing policies. Greater control by public
authorities over the resources targetted for urban
development and over the nature of the urban growth
process were agitated for, as were investment programmes which aimed at a more rational use of
resources, to be more in accordance with the overall
needs of the country. The period is characterized
by the setting in motion of laborious and often contradictory reforms in town-planning and building
policies, as well as in the general housing strategy.

Further Legislative Reform (1976-82). During the
second half of the seventies, following political
and social debate of the problems evident in the
preceding period, a group of legislative measures
were approved which greatly changed the framework
for public sector intervention in housebuilding.
This legislation (The Land Regulation Act of 1977,
the Tenancy Agreement Regulation Act of 1978 and the
10-year Plan for Public Housebuilding of 1978)
widened the scope of the instruments available to
the public authorities for regulation, intervention

ITALY

and administration in both new-build housing projects
and those dealing with the existing housing stock.
The results, however, which will be discussed
later, have to date been rather unsatisfactory.

Post-War Reconstruction (1945-50)
The number of dwellings built in the immediate post-
war period was extremely low. The reasons that were
holding back the resumption of building were many
and diverse. It was partly due to the high building
costs and the low amount of private funds, and
partly to the inflationary processes and the limited
productive capability of the building industry; but
above all it was due to the economic and political
uncertainty of these years. There was a rent freeze
in force that continued until 1947,[10] and it was
unclear what the future regulatory framework would
be with respect to property rights on buildings and
on the land to be built upon. Not until 1948, after
the Prime Minister's trip to the United States and
the subsequent loan that followed, and the Christian
Democratic electoral victory, did the private sector
take part in building activities again. The first
centrist government was formed, with the consequent
exclusion of the parties of the left from the political administration of the country.
Reconstruction in the immediate post-war period
presented the first concrete opportunity after the
twenty year fascist period for a rethinking of the
procedures that would structure the relationships
between the various social, economic and political
groups in the processes of urban growth and housing
provision. The approach adopted as regards the interaction of public and the private sectors, and the
instruments introduced for regulating urban expansion
and the private sector, forged the basic characteristics of the territorial policy of the housing programme and of the public intervention in housing that
ensued. For this reason it will be helpful to
briefly outline a few of the major policy initiatives
of this period, which are of importance for their
direct and indirect effects on the housing problem.

Town-Planning Policy. Like in other European
countries at the end of the war, the Government had
to confront the problems of reconstruction of both
the housing stock and the network of infrastructure
that had been destroyed or damaged. The difference
between what happened in other countries, like Great

Britain or France, and what happened in Italy is
that reconstruction was not dealt with from within
an organic framework of town-planning, but rather
was conducted through the formula of special
emergency intervention.

Although the 1942 Town Planning Act[11] provided
instruments for regulating development at different
territorial levels, special 'reconstruction plans'
were used as the main planning instrument for <u>ad hoc</u>
intervention. This decision to by-pass statutory
planning procedure was justified because, on the
whole, very few regulatory plans had been approved,
and the time necessary for their prepation was long,
whereas the time scale for repair and reconstruction
had to be short. Reconstruction plans were mandatory for the damaged towns included in lists compiled by the Ministry of Public Works, and had to be
prepared within three months of the date of notifi-
cation. The financial burden for the plan's
preparation was covered by the Ministry, which could
also grant the local administration advances on the
sums necessary for the public works. These plans
were supposed to have guaranteed swift but planned
reconstruction in such a way as not to compromise
existing urban planning and growth, and provision
was made for their replacement by town plans within
two years. In practice, however, this whole process
became rather problematical.

The same bureaucratic sluggishness which affected the preparation of town plans slowed down the
adoption of the reconstruction plans. Meanwhile, the
private sector, stimulated into action by the fear
of stricter regulations on the density, location and
volume of development that might be imposed by
future town plans, rapidly redeveloped to the maximum density allowed by the laws in force. And so
the chance of utilizing the spaces produced by
bombing to improve the organization of some of the
most important urban areas in the country was missed.
In the following years, large areas of intense and
accelerated growth took place outside the framework
of town and territorial planning. Cities as
important as Milan and Rome were without town-
planning schemes until 1953 and 1964 respectively.

These first years of reconstruction are
important because they mark the passage from an
hypothesis of the programming and administration of
urban development and the housing policy in
existence at the end of the war, to a <u>laissez-faire</u>
policy towards private sector development and to an
increasing confidence in the benefits to the

country's economy generated by the expansion of the
building industry. This strategy characterised the
direction that building and housing policies would
take in the next two decades, and is responsible
for most of the negative effects - as regards congestion, pollution, and environmental quality -
connected with urban development.

The Organisation of Public Sector Housing. State
intervention in the two years immediately following
the war was mostly concerned with repairing damaged
buildings. The strategy followed was to concentrate
the scarce financial resources and available productive capabilities in repairing the damaged housing
stock rather than in reconstruction or new building.
In 1947, upon completion of emergency intervention,
the lifting of the restraints placed on new housebuilding by the private sector gave rise to a more
varied range of housing projects. At the same time,
public housing policy and the instruments for its
implementation were redefined as regards their basic
characteristics, and it is to this that we now turn.
There were certain basic investment strategies in
the public sector, set up in these years, which can
be summarised as follows:

Total Government Subsidy for Housebuilding. This
was first provided for in the 'Consolidation Act' of
1938 in the event of 'natural disasters' and was
used in the immediate post-war period for financing
dwellings for the homeless. It was later redefined
through specific acts aimed at solving the housing
problems of certain categories of the population: in
the second half of the 1940s, for veterans, refugees
and war invalids; and in 1954 for clearance of unfit
dwellings. Provision for this type of intervention
persists in the 1971 Housing Reform Act which
allocated a specific amount of the available funds
for this purpose. These completely state subsidized
dwellings are mostly let in accordance with established regulations. On the whole, this type of
housing (Figure 9.1) is intended to help cope with
problems originating from crisis situations.

Partial Government Subsidy for Housebuilding. The
most predominant system for financing public housing
was through annual government grants to agencies set
up specifically for public housebuilding purposes.

Figure 9.1 Public Housing dating from the late
1940s in Via Alcuino, in the Milan inner
area. Source: Studio Architetti B.B.P.R.

This means of financing housing was introduced in
the 'Consolidation Act' of 1938, and was also included in the 1949 Housing Act (law no.408), which
became the point of reference for successive measures.
The 1949 Act stated that the Government would
allocate annual grants for thirty-five years equal
to a certain percentage (initially 20% and success-
ively, 75% and, in some instances, up to 100%) of the
maximum authorised expenditure by public agencies and
developers certified to build public housing. In
short, the Government was committed to allocate the
proportion granted in thirty-five annual payments
while the agency was responsible for raising the
necessary resources in the way it saw most suitable,
often resorting to loans.
      Various Public Agencies and Statutory Agencies
are eligible for these annual resource grants, such
as the Autonomous Institute for Public Housing (IACP)

which plays a very significant role in housebuilding.
Certain private enterprises are also eligible including co-operatives, developers, and companies that
promote the building of dwellings for their own
employees. Following the 1971 Housing Reform Act,
which imposed greater restrictions, these grants
were allocated primarily to IACP. The statutory
provisions in force for the assessment of applicants,
the characteristics and the cost for this kind of
public housing were originally very inadequate,
being both imprecise and unrealistic. These dwellings could either be rented out or sold to the
future occupants.

The INA Casa Programme. Ina Casa was created in the
1949 Employment Act, and represented a totally new
approach to public housing provision. Its novelty
lay in the ways financial resources could be pro-
cured, the creation itself of an autonomous agency
for project programming (INA Casa), and in the
agency's objectives. The declared aims of the
strategy were, first, to build houses with controlled
rents as well as to increase blue collar employment,
and secondly, to set the course for the building
industry by direct control of a part of it, and,
lastly, to stimulate the industrialisation of the
sector. The last of these is in part contradictory
to the objective of achieving maximum employment
growth in the building industry. In general, however, these objectives had a wider scope than those
traditionally dealt with by public housing strategies.
     The sources of finance came mostly (75%) from
taxes paid by employees and employers, from Government grants and from proceeds from rents and mortgage payments.[12] It was through these channels that
continuous funding was made available. The first
plan covered a period of seven years from 1949 to
1956 and was followed by a second seven-year plan in
1956.[13] These plans were under the sole authority
of the Ina Casa Enactment Committee, which managed
the distribution and allocation of the financial
resources. Housebuilding could be commissioned by a
variety of agencies - INA itself, Government bodies,
IACP, works co-operatives and certain companies. All
workers could apply for INA Casa dwellings as long
as they had paid INA taxes on at least one month's
salary. There were various criteria for compiling
and classifying the applications received. As
regards the kind of occupancy, at first, half of the
dwellings (Figures 9.2 and 9.3) were rented and the

Figure 9.2   Layout of the INA-Casa estate Cesate,
               15 kms outside Milan.
               The 600 dwelling estate was built in the
               early fifties and houses 3,500 inhabi-
               tants.   Source: Studio Architetti B.B.P.R.

other half were owner-occupied. The latter proportion has since been increased to two thirds by the
successive restructuring acts. Altogether, through
these three kinds of subsidy, an average of 132
milliard lira per year was invested in housing from
1951 to 1965, equal to 10.6% of the overall housing
investment. The proportion of total public investment was higher in the early post-war years, equal
to 25% in 1951, and decreased in successive years,
reaching its lowest point ever during the 1971-75
period (see Table 9.5).
     In addition to these three kinds of public
investment (which are for public housing per se),
there is a fourth kind which consists of advance
grants for interest payments on loans taken out by
private sector agencies. These grants are meant to
cut the cost of borrowing necessary for house building and to facilitate the construction of cheap
private housing. In 1950, a Special Fund for
Building Development was set up in the Ministry of
Public Works to actually make low interest loans to
the private sector for house building, to be paid

Figure 9.3   Housing in the Cesate Esate, Milan.
             Source: Studio Architetti B.B.P.R.

back over 35 years. This form of state subsidy was
further developed and extended to encompass the
house purchaser in 1965. Grants were made available
to certain categories of both constructors and
buyers, to cover interest charges on loans secured
from the Credit Institutes.

Table 9.5 Investment in Housing 1951-78

(in milliards of lira, 1978 currency equivalents)

Date	Total Investment (a)	Private Sector (b)	Private Sector with Public Subsidy (c)	Public Sector (d)	Percentages of Total			
					(a)	(b)	(c)	(d)
1951-55	552.2	450.5	-	102	100	81.5	-	18.5
1956-60	1088.8	922.8	-	166	100	84.8	-	15.2
1961-65	1987.6	1861.6	-	126	100	93.7	-	6.3
1966-70	3047	2832.6	38.4	176	100	93.0	1.2	5.8
1971-75	5222.2	4831.8	121.2	219.2	100	93.5	2.3	4.2
1976	7964	6834	325	805	100	85.8	4.1	10.1
1977	9708	8258	650	800	100	85.0	6.7	8.3
1978	11127	9662	750	715	100	86.9	6.7	6.4

Source: Economic and Social Research Centre for the Building Market (CRESME)

Growth and Expansion (1951-63)

The fifties and early sixties was the period of maximum growth and expansion in the construction industry. The number of dwellings completed per year in
all Italy rose from 93,000 in 1951 to 313,000 in
1961 and reached a peak of 450,000 in 1964. Investment in housing during this period was also
substantial, reaching the highest levels from 1963-
64, when housing investment made up one third of the
total capital investments and equalled 6-7% of
Gross National Revenue (Table 9.6).

Table 9.6   Housing Investment, Total Investment and
             Gross National Revenue, 1951-76 (in
             milliards of lira)

Years	Values at 1976 currency equivalents				
	Gross National Revenue (GNR)	Total Investment (TI)	Investment in Housing	Investment in Housing	
				% of GNR	% of TI
1951..	10,748	1,894	352	3.3	18.6
1952..	11,591	2,210	442	3.8	20.0
1953..	12,826	2,480	523	4.1	21.1
1954..	13,656	2,735	647	4.7	23.6
1955..	15,050	3,093	797	5.3	25.8
1956..	16,394	3,371	907	5.6	26.9
1957..	17,622	3,808	1,056	6.0	27.7
1958..	18,923	3,888	1,088	5.7	28.0
1959..	20,113	4,185	1,172	5.8	28.0
1960..	21,828	4,804	1,221	5.6	25.4
1961..	24,289	5,514	1,376	5.7	24.9
1962..	27,303	6,331	1,711	6.3	27.0
1963..	31,261	7,360	2,087	6.7	28.3
1963..	34,179	7,402	2,453	7.2	33.1
1965..	36,818	6,904	2,311	6.3	33.5
1966..	39,829	7,283	2,303	5.8	31.6
1967..	43,804	8,323	2,516	5.7	30.2
1968..	47,280	9,322	2,901	6.1	31.1
1969..	51,951	10,695	3,630	7.0	33.1
1970..	58,181	12,327	3,939	6.8	32.0
1971..	63,319	12,793	3,729	5.9	29.1
1972..	69,323	13,624	3,948	5.7	29.0
1973..	82,700	17,156	4,832	5.8	28.2
1974..	100,728	22,831	6,586	6.5	28.8
1975..	113,670	23,753	6,945	6.1	29.2
1976..	141,482	28,810	8,179	5.8	28.4

The concentration of such a considerable amount of resources in the building sector, and in new housebuilding in particular, was brought about by the interaction of a series of factors. The ever-increasing demand for housing and space for urban activities exceeded supply during this entire period, whilst land and property prices escalated and family incomes rose steadily. Growth was concentrated in a limited number of areas, thus creating territorial imbalances and contributing to the large migrations of population from the South and the poorer economic areas of the country towards the industrialised centres. While in the areas of great exodus, the infrastructure went under-used and the housing stock lay in abandon, these industrialised areas experienced chronic disproportions between the demand and supply of urban space and housing.

The process of rapid growth in highly concentrated urban areas was accompanied by significant increases in land and property prices. This happened not only because the availability of development areas was insufficient to satisfy the demand, but also because, in a situation where the demand was ever-increasing and diversified, certain mechanisms of profit-seeking were triggered which tended to favour delay in putting land and buildings on the market. At the same time, factors connected with the pattern of growth and development contributed to the strong expansion and diversification of the demand for urban space. For example, the evolution of the methods of production (horizontal rather than vertical), the evolution of living standards (increased incomes changed the size and the characteristics of dwellings), the greater complexity of the organisation of the urban areas (transport systems, establishment of new services, etc.) all increased and qualitatively changed the use of urban space per inhabitant. In a situation where the demand exhibits such characteristics, prices of land and buildings tend to increase and, if this rate of increase is higher than the average interest rate, it may be considered more advantageous to artificially withdraw the property from the market, with the prospect of greater profits in the future. In this way supply starts to decline and prices increase, creating a self-feeding mechanism for such speculationary retention of land and property.

In the housing sector, rents also tended to go up, with the exception of those subject to the freeze. Immediately after the war, different kinds of incentives were offered to aid acquisition of new

dwellings by future owner-occupants and to create
employment opportunities. These included easy
credit terms and tax exemptions which were primarily
owner-oriented and worked against the private rented
sector, that became progressively smaller and
smaller. Houses that had previously been rented
became owner-occupied, and rents tended to increase
to levels just below corresponding mortgage repayments. The increase in rents, on the one hand, and
the increase in house prices on the other, drove
those who could afford it to become house-owners
themselves, thus contributing to the imbalance between demand and supply in this sector of the market,
for both owner-occupier and rented accommodation. As
can be seen, there were mechanisms and processes
going on that interacted and tended to corroborate
and strengthen one another. The condition necessary
for these processes to perpetuate one another was
that incomes continued to grow, and this is more or
less what happened. The period described is the so-
called Italian 'economic miracle'.

Public housing policy during this period was
one of substantial abstention from playing a guiding
role in either the production of dwellings or in
controlling the processes of expansion. This attitude, which characterised the strategies with which
the public authorities intervened in the housing
sector, from town-planning to the system of assigna-
tion of the dwellings, was present even at the level
of direct public intervention. In the period under
discussion, in fact, the role of the public housing
authorities, rather than trying to provide dwellings
to satisfy the demand for housing for the poorer
classes, was merely one of overseeing situations of
potential conflict[14] or giving access to owner-
occupation to a limited number of households.[15] As
a result, public intervention grew narrower and
represented a smaller proportion of the total
investments in housing, going from 25% in 1951 to 6%
from 1961 to 1965. On the other hand, however,
indirect public assistance in the form of tax relief
and low interest credit terms, in particular,
increased considerably, in support of the demand for
new-occupied housing.[16]

During these years, as seen above, both private
and public sectors were primarily concerned with new-
build and, as a result, the existing housing stock
tended to be neglected. Deterioration and abandonment or clearance and redevelopment were options
frequently pursued. Conditions of serious deterioration were to be found in the areas of exodus of the

population - such as the South, mountainous areas
and some agricultural areas. Activities were progressively abandoned, leaving the already deterior-
ated housing stock to fall into ruins.

Even in the medium-sized urban areas with
stable populations, there was no public investment
in older sections of the housing stock, which was
also left in abandon in conditions of increasing
deterioration. The strategy behind granting easy
credit terms and tax reductions only for newbuild,
and the cultural reference models that bestow
privileges on products of 'modern' technology,
ensured that available investments were earmarked
more for new building in the areas of growth, rather
than for rehabilitation and restoration of the housing stock in older town centres.

In the major metropolitan and urban areas,
different policies were adopted as regards the older
housing stock and the old town centres, depending on
the nature of demand for urban space at any given
time. If there was the necessary demand for high
income residential and commercial uses, then there
was a tendency to intervene in the older urban
fabric, which was usually centrally located, and
carry out those operations of transformation that
made those buildings available and appealing to the
categories of people and activities that could
afford to pay a price reflecting the value of the
location of these areas. This was the case with the
urban renewal, clearance and redevelopment schemes
undertaken in the centre of Milan during the fifties
and sixties (Figure 9.4). When the demand, however,
was from low-income users, then it was in the
interest of the owners to postpone any kind of
investment in the older part of the housing stock,
deferring any decision until the increase in the
value of the buildings reached what they thought
would be its highest level. This is how the formation of ghettos for the immigrants came about in
some sections of the old town centre in Turin, for
example.

A Rethinking of Housing Policy (1963-75)
The building crisis of 1963 brought the self-feeding
mechanism described above to an end. What caused
this to happen? The conditions necessary for
expanding building activities along the lines of the
preceding period were no longer present. With the
decline in the waves of migration towards the North,
the disproportion between the demand and the supply

Figure 9.4 <u>The Milan 'core', showing the results of
            late fifties and early sixties renewal.</u>
            Photo: Foto-Studio CASALL, Milan.

became less pronounced. The rhythm of increasing
land and property prices slowed, and the growth of
incomes also came to a standstill. There were significant instances of property going unsold, and
the reasons for speculationary property retention
were no longer valid.

Another interpretation of these changes provides a more complex explanation of the situation.
According to this line of thinking, the significant
amount of money that flowed into the building sector
from family savings and investments during the preceding years was not just in response to the need
for housing or urban space in the areas of greatest
density, but also because of the great possibilities
to accumulate large sums of money that the building
sector offered, especially on account of the
characteristics that it took on, such as the very
high increases in value of land and property. These
processes encompassed a large range of social groups,
who all felt that they had in some way or another
'benefitted' from the pattern and intensity of
building expansion during this period. This group
was made up of divergent social forces who were
united in their support for policies to promote
building expansion: from the large construction companies through the small businessmen in the old city
keen to sell up at great profit, to the small-time
savers who invested in dwellings to be let, or those
aspiring to become owner-occupiers.

During the sixties, partly due to the building
crisis itself, and partly as a consequence of the
strategy for the building sector that was followed
during the previous decade, the cohesion of this so-
called 'building coalition' started to fall apart.
The capital accumulated in this sector tended to be
reinvested in building operations rather than being
transferred to other kinds of enterprise, and
escalating house prices, congestion, and the chaotic
growth of urban areas that were exacerbated by
building speculation, came to have an effect on the
cost of industrial production. This gave rise to
potentially conflicting situations among the
different components of the building coalition,
there being particular tension between the building
sector and the industrial sector, who contended for
the allocation of available resources, which were,
moreover, scarcer than before since this was a
period of recession.

This brought about a change in the context
within which the public housing policy was to
operate. Until 1963-4, the intricate but coherent

network of inter-relationships in the 'building coalition' did not leave room for autonomous action on the part of the public authorities, except in the strict sense of an indiscriminate support for the new building industry. But after 1964, the potential conflicts in the 'building coalition' placed the public administration in a different situation where, if nothing else, it had to play the role of mediator among the conflicting interests.

Significant change also came out in the political arena. During the first half of the sixties, in the wake of a string of Centrist Governments, the first Centre-Left coalition took office. This marked the start of the complex process of reforms in town-planning and housing policy undertaken by the Centre-Left during the sixties. In 1962 the Public Housing Areas Act (law no.167) was passed, allowing municipal councils to acquire land for public housing schemes through expropriation. For the first time public housing programmes could be provided for in town plans, and the Act stipulated that municipal councils with more than 50,000 inhabitants had to include such schemes, worked out in accordance with ten-year estimates of public housing needs (Figures 9.5 and 9.6). In practice,

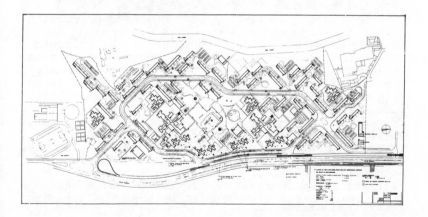

Figure 9.5   Layout of the Gratosoglio Public Housing Estate, built outside Milan in the late 1960s.
Source: Studio Architetti B.B.P.R.,Milan

Figure 9.6   10-storey Housing Blocks in the
             Gratosoglio Estate, 1969.   The estate as
             a whole houses 20,000 inhabitants.
             Source: Studio Architetti B.B.P.R.,Milan

however, the Act encountered considerable difficulties in the implementation stage, largely because no
machinery had been created to make available the
finance necessary for undertaking expropriation. In
1963, a national Ten-Year Plan (2) for the construction of public housing was approved. A new authority, GESCAL (Workers Housing Management) was
created to take the place of Ina Casa and direct the
ten-year programme. During this ten-year period,
however, only a small part of the allocated funds
was spent, and measures were introduced to transfer
the ownership of the public housing built in previous years.
    In 1967, the Town-Planning Reform Act (law no.
765) introduced significant new measures. Town
centres were to be safeguarded, and there was to be
greater control over development in the main areas
of urban expansion; but most importantly, the
responsibility for providing service infrastructure
in growth areas was to be borne by the developers
rather than the public authorities. The Act, however, did not come into effect until the year
following its approval, and once again the road was
opened up for rapid speculative development that
permanently changed certain parts of the country.
    The last step taken by the Centre-Left coali-
tion in the planning and housing field was the
adoption of the Housing Reform Act of 1971. The
importance of this Act lay in its relaunching of a
public housing policy and its serious attempt at
solving the housing problem.
    During the period of reform policies in the
sixties, public housing construction was, perhaps
ironically, at its lowest levels, and housing suitable for the less well-off categories of the population became scarcer and scarcer. In fact, a large
part of the public housing stock was sold off, no
new subsidised dwellings were built, and funds earmarked for the new formula of easy-credit building
(law no.1179 of 1965) were instead used to subsidise
the sale price of highly priced dwellings that had
gone unsold after the building crisis of 1963-4 (and
these certainly did not go to the low-income groups).
The financial burden imposed by the Town Planning
Reform Act on developers was shifted to the buyers,
and the areas destined for public house construction
went unused. However inefficient and contradictory
these measures might seem, they did, nevertheless,
constitute a significantly different legislative-
economic framework for housing construction, compared with the previous period.

This was certainly one reason for the shift in interest towards used buildings, especially at the beginning of this period. The series of legislative measures enacted through the sixties put heavier restraints and burdens on operations in areas of new expansion, which thus tended to favour intervention on existing buildings. At the same time, the building crisis of the early sixties made the speculationary retention of older properties less attractive, and older housing began to appear on the market again. Furthermore, in line with developments in other European countries, there was a growing awareness that a consistent part of public resources would be earmarked for intervention in the existing housing stock, in the main urban areas, rather than for new-build activities. A widespread belief in the need for intervention aimed at a more 'rational' and 'efficient' use of the existing housing stock emerged. There were, however, conflicting positions regarding how to intervene, what use the existing stock should be put to, who should benefit from the operations of rehabilitation and reutilization, and how to best combine renewal and rehabilitation activity (Figures 9.7 and 9.8).

Concerning housing in particular, there were two alternative rehabilitation strategies. The first advocated reutilization for 'social purposes', which would centre on a more rational and balanced use of the existing housing stock, through a range of interrelated programmes: public improvement projects, policies for income-based rents, minimal disruption of existing communities in improvement schemes, and special taxation on high price dwellings. The second strategy, favoured by construction interests, is aimed at using the oldest part of the housing stock, after its improvement, for upper-middle class housing. This view holds that it is the State who must provide for, with direct or indirect subsidies, the needs of groups who are penalised by this kind of approach. The most obvious consequences of this strategy are that the supply-demand ratio will stay the same or become worse, an upward spiralling of house prices will be triggered, and a new cycle of new-build development will start. Which of these two strategies prevail for the use of the existing housing stock is an important aspect of the present debate on housing policy. It goes without saying that in practice the processes are much more complex than outlined here, and there can be no absolute predominance of one or the other.

Figure 9.7   Rehabilitation of 112 dwellings, Via
              Scaldasole, Milan.
              This rehabilitation programme was under-
              taken by the Milan Council in the late
              1970s, and aimed at preserving the archi-
              tectural style and local community in an
              old part of central Milan.

Further Legislative Reform (1976-82)
In the years 1977-78, the Government passed three
acts which modified substantially the framework for
public control over urban development and construction activity. This legislation represents the most
recent episode in a series of contradictory half-
reforms in town planning and housing policies
approved in the sixties and seventies. It also set
up new machinery for central, regional and local
authorities to confront the housing problem anew.
The nature and scale of the housing problem had
changed somewhat since the fifties and sixties, with

273

Figure 9.8   Systematic Phased Renewal of old public
             housing in Via Forze Armate, Milan.
             Old public housing, dating from the fif-
             ties (foreground) is being replaced in
             phases by new multi-storey public
             dwellings (background).

the problems of allocation and optimal use of
existing stock being more important than overall
quantitative deficits. Between 1972 and 1975, an
average 660,000 households per year moved house, but
only a quarter of these went into newly-built
dwellings. Rehabilitation and re-use of existing
stock, and the shifts from one submarket to another,
had thus become of critical importance. The three
pieces of legislation approved in the late seventies
attempted to take account of these realities.
     The Land Regulation Act (law no.10) of 1977
introduced some important innovations in urban land
development control. It became more costly to
acquire a Building Licence, with the developer having
to pay a tax for the provision of social infrastructure and a further tax proportional to the building
cost. This latter tax could be substantially reduced
for public housing, for private low cost housing, and
for residential rehabilitation. In the planning
arena, local authorities were obliged to draw-up
three to five year Implementation Programmes to plan
and budget for the overall implementation of plans

(PRGs), an important tool in the management of urban and residential development or renewal.

The second act, the Ten Years Plan (law no.457) of 1978, was directly concerned with housing problems and in particular with public housing. The act established a set of norms for housing construction and finance, sweeping away certain inadequacies and contradictions inherent in the Housing Reform Act of 1971. The roles and responsibilities of new and existing authorities concerned with house programming and management were clearly defined. At the central government level, a special Committee for Housing was created within the Ministry of Public Works; this was to be responsible for the 4-yearly allocation of public housing funds to the regional level, and the determination of housing needs in different areas of the country. The Committee was additionally charged with the definition of technical norms at national level and the promotion of experimental building programmes and research. At the regional level, regional authorities were made responsible for drawing up 4-yearly regional housing programmes, and for the approval of local level programmes to determine local authority funding for new houses or rehabilitation, for public or subsidised housing. Local Authorities were in turn made responsible for land acquisition and infrastructure provision; and a set of norms to guide private and public rehabilitation activity was introduced.

The Housing Reform Act of 1971 had previously opened up the possibility of implementing public housing programmes for the rehabilitation of old unfit houses in urban areas. Local Authorities were empowered to acquire by compulsory purchase[17] portions of the old unfit stock in need of improvement. These programmes, generally harmful to land-owning interests, were strongly opposed by large sections of the building sector, and came up against all sorts of legal difficulties. The political and legal disputes over compulsory purchase in built-up areas held things up to such an extent that between 1971 and 1978, only modest results were achieved in terms of the number of dwellings repaired. The 1978 Act therefore attempted to rectify this situation by introducing a series of new measures. It was stipulated that a minimum percentage of public housing funds had to be allocated to rehabilitation programmes (at least 15% in each region), whilst special 'rehabilitation plans' could be drawn-up for public and private action; 'special agreements' could be made between local authorities and private developers

for rehabilitation purposes, and short-cut procedures
were introduced for short-term rehabilitation on a
house by house basis.

With the Fair Rent Act, approved in 1978, the
government attempted to put an end to the double
market for rented accommodation, i.e. the free
sector, including the most recently built houses,
and the sector subjected to a rent freeze. The act
also aimed to put an end to the distorted effects
induced by this double market in terms of misalloca-
tion of housing resources to households, of rent
increases in the 'free rented' sector, and of decay
of stock in the 'frozen rent' sector. The mechanisms
for rent control introduced in the act may be
summarised as follows: as regards tenancy, tenure
length was to be four years, and at the end of this
period could, at the landlord's discretion, be
renewed; as regards rent levels, they were to be
calculated at a set percentage (3.8%) of an estimated
dwelling value, determined on the basis of new house
construction (fixed by the Ministry of Public Works
every year), adjusted by coefficients taking account
of typology, age, location, size and fitness of the
house. Rents were also linked to cost of living
increases.

From this short examination of the principal
contents of the three acts, it is possible to develop
some considerations on their overall housing policy
goals, most of which stem from the government's mis-
trust of the free market to satisfactorily meet
housing needs. As regards new housing, the aim is to
achieve a shift of private building activity into the
area controlled by 'special agreements' between
private developers and the local authorities, through
offering appropriate incentives - land at low cost
(within areas acquired by compulsory purchase for
public housing), lower taxes on building licences,
mortgages at subsidised rates, promotion of industrialised building processes - and imposing constraints
on housing quality and costs. Regarding the existing
stock, the aim is to promote rehabilitation, especially in the owner-occupied sector and of older
dwellings, and to increase mobility within the rented
sector. Public housing construction figures will be
maintained at the low levels of recent years, and
directed towards meeting the most pressing housing
needs.

It remains to be seen just how effective these
new policies are in the long term. To date, it is
clear that the lack of dominance by any one group in
the political arena is holding up any firm applica-

tion of the new legislation. The supporters of a
reformist approach, which mobilises a range of public
controls and centres on direct action, are counter-
balanced by the supporters of free market mechanisms
as being more effective for the attainment of similar
goals. The political consequences of this presence
of opposing interests and proposals has been the
definition of a set of institutional solutions as in
the three acts examined above - which are rigidly
structured in normative and procedural terms, but
quite blurred in the statement of qualified general
goals (where political disagreement is highest).
This lack of clarity on certain issues has been
transferred to lower bureaucratical levels, and to
the formation of relationships between developers
and the public administration. An initial analysis
suggests that the results in terms of house production are unlikely to accord with the overall aims of
this legislation described above.

Summary

One of the main features of the housing problem in
Italy today is the coexistence of symptoms of severe
housing stress on the one hand and evidence of over-
consumption on the other. This has meant that the
steady growth of the housing stock has not substantially reduced the ratio of people living in bad
housing conditions. The overall housing situation
in the country has improved tremendously since the
end of the war, but still there remain a large number
of people inadequately housed.
     This situation is the end product of a number
of different policies in the housing and building
fields pursued in the post-war. In the years
following reconstruction and up to the mid-sixties,
steady urban and residential growth was concentrated
in limited areas, mainly in the North of Italy, and
housing policies offered the maximum direct and
indirect support to private sector building,
especially for new housing in newly developed urban
areas. Large amounts of public and private resources
were poured into the building sector, and into housing in particular. It was argued that if the public
sector promoted maximum new house construction, then
market mechanisms would ensure an improvement of the
overall housing situation. Only occasionally did
public housing policy concentrate on areas of specific need.
     This conception of housing and urban problems
resulted, in that particular phase of Italy's devel-

ment, in an anarchic process of urban growth characterised by high housing costs, poor standards in
both construction and the urban environment and
waste of natural resources in some parts of the
country, and neglect and emigration in others. The
older housing stock suffered disrepair, demolition
and transformation into slum areas. In the mid-
sixties, partly because of the economic crisis of
1963-4, but mainly because of the increasing awareness of the negative effects of existing policies,
large sectors of the social and political spectrum
pressed for greater public control over resources
targeted for urban development and housing. A number
of reforms followed in the housing field. Great
attention was paid to rehabilitation and public sector initiatives in improving older stock and
replanning urban areas. A further goal was to
achieve more effective <u>direct</u> public intervention in
housing construction: investment in public housing
totalled only 3% of total new housing investment in
the early seventies.

This reform process culminated in the approval
of three major new Acts in 1977-8 (Land Regulation
Act, Fair Rent Act and Ten-Year Plan), which greatly
changed the framework for state intervention and
involvement in housing construction. They widened
the scope and means available to public authorities
for the regulation, promotion and administration of
both new housing projects and those dealing with
existing stock. It is too early yet to evaluate the
success or otherwise of these new initiatives, which
are currently the focus of conflict between their
original supporters and the defenders and proponents
of freemarket mechanisms as the most effective way
of solving housing problems.

NOTES AND REFERENCES

1. National Housing Census, 1981.
2. The index for overcrowding decreased from
1.35 persons per room in 1951 to 0.79 in 1981. The
level of the basic amenities improved, and the percentages of dwellings equipped with sanitary fixtures
rose from 40% in 1951 to 83% in 1971, and went up to
92% in 1976.
3. Shared households comprised 14.4% of families in 1951, dropped noticeably to approximately 8%
in the 1961 and 1971 censuses, but went up again to
11.1% in the 1981 census.
4. It is estimated that the number of families
on the waiting list is near one million whereas the

public housing dwellings built per year are approximately 20,000 to 25,000.

5. The deficiency of dwellings due to overcrowding is calculated as the number of dwellings that it is necessary to build in order to provide all families with acceptable living space standards. The dwellings that would become free within the overcrowded housing stock are included in this calculation. See: Stime CRESME (Economic and Social Research Centre for the Building Market - Cresme - Rome, 1980).

6. Sample Survey, Economic and Social Research Centre for the Building Market (CRESME) Rome, 1976.

7. Sample Survey, Economic and Social Research Centre for the Building Market (CRESME) Rome, 1979.

8. In Italy freezes on rents were imposed on a sizeable portion of the housing stock during the post-war until the approval of the Fair Rent Act in 1978.

9. Measures are currently under discussion to change the structure of house purchase tax for owner-occupiers.

10. At the end of 1947, a new rent system was put into effect which excluded from the rent freeze new buildings and those left free by their occupants. This brought about a progressive liberalization of the market and offered new incentives for private investment.

11. For more detail on the functioning of the planning system in the post-war, see D. Calabi, 'Italy', in M. Wynn (Ed.) Planning and Urban Growth in Southern Europe, Mansells, 1983.

12. 0.6% of the employees' monthly salaries went into taxes, while the employers paid in an additional 1.2% of their employees' monthly salaries. The Government paid a share equal to 4.3% of the previous sum, as well as 3.2% of the cost of building each finished dwelling.

13. In 1963 Ina Casa was replaced by another Agency with similar characteristics and goals called the Workers' Housing Management (GesCal). GesCal was responsible for directing the Ten-Year Public Housing Programme. The housing stock of Ina Casa, its predecesssor, was sold off to its sitting tenants. The activity of GesCal came to an end with the 1971 Housing Reform Act. The funds earmarked for this kind of investment were then pooled with the Government's available financial resources for public housebuilding.

14. This was the case, for example, with the 1954 Act for the clearance of unfit dwellings.

15.   During the period from 1951 until the
Housing Reform Act of 1971, the proportion of public
dwellings sold to sitting tenants was very high.
Some estimates place this figure at from 700,000 to
800,000 units, equal to the entire public housing
stock in 1965.

16.   For more detail on the significance of tax
concessions, see C.A. Mortara, 'Twenty years of
public housing in Italy' Economia Publica, nos.2-3,
(1975).

17.   For the purposes of compulsory purchase,
the land value was estimated on the basis of the
rural land value multiplied by coefficients taking
account of the area location; building value was
estimated as the cost of new public housing less the
cost of any necessary repairs.

10. PORTUGAL

by J.R. Lewis and A.M. Williams*

Introduction

In the early hours of 25th April 1974, soldiers
opposed to the long, bloody wars that they were
fighting in Angola, Guinee and Mocambique took up
strategic positions in Lisboa, and by the end of the
day had forced the resignation of Prime Minister
Marcelo Caetano. In the next few days the joy of
the thousands of people who filled the streets,
embracing the soldiers and decorating them with red
carnations, seemed unbounded as the new government
immediately started to talk about ending the wars,
restoring democracy and improving the lot of the
common person. Although anti-war feeling ran deep
and the prospect of elections without the
surveillance of the secret police seemed attractive,
it was the promise of better living and working conditions that consolidated support for the 25th April
Revolution.
    Both the first wall slogans and early examples
of direct action showed that better housing was a
major concern and, in the two hectic years that
followed, the struggles to achieve it seemed central
to the very 'spirit of April'. In the next year,
some 5,000 spontaneous occupations of empty houses
took place in Lisboa alone, while shanty town
dwellers formed their own associations to negotiate
with the Lisboa council about improvements in their
areas. Further North, in Porto, the major struggle
was over subleeting and poor facilities and led to a
widespread appreciation of the depth of the city's
housing problems through the circulation of stories
such as this (from the residents of Block 402, Rua

*   Grateful acknowledgement is given to Peter
    Williams for his comments on an earlier version
    of this chapter.

281

de Dom João IV):

> "We are 15 families here: with 20 children, a
> total of 100 people. The building has no
> amenities. There is not even a bathroom, we
> have to go to the Municipal Baths to wash. The
> ceilings are falling in. There is only one
> toilet and no flush. It's wet right through to
> the basement. A pig wouldn't live here. We
> pay rents of 600 to 1,000 escudos for small
> rooms where our families live."[1]

Ordinary people were discovering their voices and the
Revolutionary governments were not deaf to their
messages for they passed rent control laws, created
a framework for local housing action groups and
allocated extra funds to stimulate house building.
Some of these responses are still part of the
housing policy today even though the popular pressure
for reform has almost vanished - despite the fact
that housing shortages and poor housing remain as
problems for millions - so that to understand the
current dynamics of housing provision and policy in
Portugal the events of 1974 are vital.

To explain why housing became such a central
issue in 1974 - and continues to be a source of
problems today - it is necessary to start this chapter with a review of the economic, political and
social context within which housing need and production have developed in recent years. These elements
of political economy provide the framework within
which the housing crisis and state policies can best
be analysed. The nature of the housing crisis is
considered in the second part of the chapter which
shows that housing in Portugal has a number of
features[2] which are common in other Mediterranean
states[2] but it also has certain distinctive characteristics, especially widespread illegal housing and
shanty dwellings. In the third section, the actual
production of housing, in both the public and private
sectors, is examined so as to identify the most
important processes which have contributed to the
persistent housing crisis. State intervention has
tended to be very limited but in the aftermath of the
1974 Revolution there were major changes in the
housing field which are outlined in the final section.

Housing, uneven development and the corporate state
The best starting point for the analysis of recent
housing trends in Portugal is 1926, the date of a

military coup which overthrew the democratically
elected government. The new rulers soon became
dependent on the man they initially installed as
finance minister, Antonio Salazar, and, once he became Prime Minister in 1932, constitutional changes
to create a 'New State' were introduced. The model
for these changes, at least nominally, was the
Italian idea of a corporate state[3] and the result
was a kind of constitutional dictatorship with a
repressive state apparatus that suppressed trade
unions, crushed political opponents and stage-
managed presidential elections. The economic framework of the corporate state was one of private
ownership allied with extensive state controls on
prices and wages, while Salazar's early economic
policies were essentially conservative, with growth
being constrained in order to balance the state
budget and accumulate foreign reserves.[4]

After a period of somewhat ambiguous neutrality
during the Spanish Civil War and Second World War,
this approach was fundamentally modified. Encouraged
by state investment in infrastructure, investment in
modern industries and in tourism stimulated higher
economic growth rates in the 1950s. However, the
state was unable to maintain its role as a major
source of investment, especially after the onset of
the expensive colonial wars in the early 1960s, so
the laws restricting foreign investment were relaxed
and Portugal joined the EFTA in 1960 in order to
encourage overseas trade. With the stimulus provided
by foreign investment, GDP growth rates in excess of
7 per cent per annum were achieved in the 1960s,[5] but
this was not translated into employment growth or
rising living standards for the majority of the
population so that an unprecedented emigration
occurred. It has been estimated that, from an
initial population of eight million, almost one
million persons emigrated during the 1960s, mostly to
Western Europe where the demand for migrant labour
was rising.[6]

Near the end of the decade, Salazar was incapa-
citated by illness and his position was effectively
taken over by Caetano, but without major policy
changes for Caetano also believed in Portugal's right
to maintain its colonies and continued to encourage
foreign investment and large scale industrialisation.
He was, however, more aware of the contradictions
within Portuguese society and of the demands for
political reforms encouraged by the experiences both
of conscripts in the colonial wars and of emigrants
working abroad. A limited attempt was thus made to

liberalise the state but Caetano retreated from this position in the face of right wing opposition.[7]

Caetano's failure to achieve a more equitable distribution of the benefits of economic growth, to allow a gradual reform of the state and, especially, to end the colonial wars led to the military coup of 25th April 1974. From its initially incoherent base in the armed forces the Revolutionary movement first swung sharply to the left but this was halted in late 1975 when an attempted coup by the far left was prevented by loyalists in the military. Thereafter, the balance of political power swung back to the centre and electoral politics became firmly established with an elected assembly taking power in April 1976 and a centre-left President, General Eanes, was elected in the same year. However, no single party had an overall majority in the Assembly and so a period of instability followed, with a succession of coalition governments based around the Portuguese Socialist Party, the largest single party. In December 1979 the balance of political power swung further to the right when a centre-right electoral coalition, the Alianca Democratica, won an overall majority in the Assembly (which it still held, somewhat tenuously, at the start of 1983). So far, 14 governments have held power since April 1974, reflecting the political instability in the country as a whole. Such instability has made it difficult to develop and apply coherent economic policies to cope with a series of problems that have arisen since 1974. Not only were there domestic crises due to disruptions to industrial production following nationalisations in 1975, reductions in agricultural output after land seizures in the Alentejo, and relentless inflation, but also the international economic crisis has hit Portugal particularly hard through oil price rises and recession in its major markets and emigration destinations (reducing both emigration rates and foreign exchange contributed by emigrant remittances). Under these circumstances, economic growth has been less rapid than in the 1960s and heavily dependent on continued foreign investment in industry and tourism, IMF loans and aid from European governments, the EC and EFTA.[8]

There are two points in this description of economic and political change which are important for the analysis of housing in Portugal. First, during the period of the corporate state, the overall control of housing production was placed firmly in the hands of the private sector. Although some attempts were made to regulate the activities of this sector,

particularly through land development controls, these
were of little importance outside of Lisboa, and,
even there, were fairly insignificant after 1945.[9]
There was also a distinctive approach to public
housing which remained under central government control, who administered it in an authoritarian manner
and tied its allocation to special cases (for
example, for state employees or inhabitants of
dwellings in slum clearance schemes), rather than for
the general purpose of rehousing lower income families. However, with the political transformation
after 1974, there were considerable changes in the
approach of the state towards housing, influenced by
the popular struggles over housing standards. This
has led to limited decentralisation and liberalisation of the administration of state housing, policies
to widen owner-occupation and attempts to re-establish control over private sector development.
    The second major feature of these broader polit-
ical and economic changes is the uneven character of
regional development in Portugal. Since 1950 there
has been a marked shift in national employment from
the primary to the secondary and, latterly, to the
tertiary sector but these shifts have had an uneven
spatial impact and contributed to an enlargement of
existing regional inequalities between the littoral
and the interior. As a result, the most developed
part of the littoral, from Setúbal distrito (equivalent to a British county) in the south, to Braga in
the north, accounted for 77.5 per cent of GDP in
1971. (See Figure 10.1 for the locations of the 18
mainland distritos.) There were also differences in
the economic profiles of the interior and littoral;
for example, in 1970 the secondary sector accounted
for 26.4 to 50.9 per cent of total employment in the
distritos of the littoral compared to 8.8 to 27.6
per cent in the distritos of the interior. As a
corollary of this, agricultural employment in 1970
accounted for 50-75 per cent of employment in the
inherently less fertile distritos of the interior.
Superimposed upon this broad regional pattern, there
was also a metropolitan/non-metropolitan dimension
for the Portuguese economy is dominated by the two
major city regions, Lisboa and Porto. This is particularly evident in the service sector (both public
and private) and in 1970 Lisboa and Porto accounted
for 55 per cent of all employment in the tertiary
sector. The processes underlying these patterns of
uneven development have been discussed elsewhere[10]
so here it is sufficient to note that they relate to
the advantages of the littoral in general, and of

Figure 10.1 Boundaries of 'Distritos' in Portugal.

the metropoli in particular, for capital accumulation
at both the national and international scales and
the disastrous effects of outmigration on the economies of the interior. The limited evidence available on trends in the 1970s suggests that recently
these regional inequalities have been intensified,
primarily as a result of further investment, both

foreign and domestic, in the industries of the littoral.[11]

This growing regional imbalance was accompanied by the substantial population changes which are illustrated in Figure 10.2. Again, there were dis-

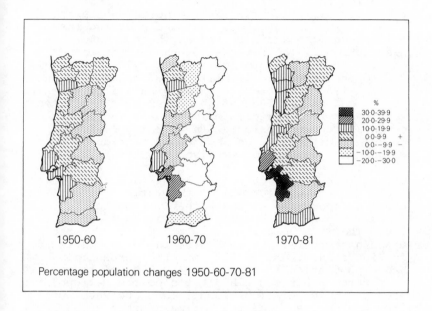

%
30·0-39·9
20·0-29·9
10·0-19·9
0·0-9·9   +
0·0--9·9   −
−10·0--19·9
−20·0--30·0

1950-60   1960-70   1970-81

Percentage population changes 1950-60-70-81

Figure 10.2   Population changes in Portugal, by 'distrito', 1950-1981.

tinctive variations over time, with the largest losses being in the 1960s, but the basic differences between the littoral and the interior remained constant. In the 1950s population losses were apparent at the distrito level for the first time in the twentieth century, occurring in the mountainous central interior and in the south, including Faro (often referred to as the Algarve). The highest growth rates were in Lisboa, Setúbal and Porto. There was a more dramatic pattern in the 1960s for only five distritos - Porto, Aveiro, Braga, Lisboa and Setúbal (all in the littoral) - experienced an increase in population; the rest of the country lost population, at rates that exceeded 20 per cent over the decade in the interior. In the 1970s, the same basic pattern is evident, with the largest increases

being in the littoral (especially in the Lisboa
area) while most of the interior experienced losses
or only small gains.

Emigration and migration to urban areas were
the most important components in these population
changes.[12] In general, there was sustained internal
migration on a massive scale from the interior to
the littoral, reinforced in the north and centre by
high rates of emigration, especially during the
1960s when France and FR Germany became major
destinations. The reversal of the high rates of
decline in the interior during the 1970s is largely
due to the reduced possibilities of emigration and a
combination of the return of emigrants from Northern
Europe and the arrival of well over half a million
retornados from Africa, following the independence
of the Portuguese colonies in 1974 and 1975.[13]

In addition to the regional dimension of demographic change, there was also a distinctive rural-
urban element. The cities of Lisboa and Porto had
populations of 812,385 and 329,104 respectively in
1981, and the populations of the larger metropolitan
areas of these two cities probably amounted to
almost a third of the total population of the country. The limited development of the rest of the
urban hierarchy is evident from the data presented
in Figure 10.3. As in 1981 no other urban concelho[14]
had a population in excess of 150,000 and there were
only three urban concelhos, outside the metropolitan
areas, with populations larger than 100,000. Over
time the dominance of the two main urban areas has
increased and between 1970 and 1980, for example,
the proportion of total population resident in the
distritos of Lisboa, Porto and Setúbal increased
from 41.6 to 43.5 per cent. Even in the interior
there have been rural-urban population shifts so
that urban concelhos such as Évora and Mangualde have
shown substantial population increases in the 1970s
(47.1 and 21.0 per cent respectively) in contrast to
the vast majority of more rural concelhos which have
continued to decline.

This spatially uneven development had a critical
influence on the need for housing. Particularly
after 1960, population growth created a sharp
increase in the need for housing in the littoral,
especially in the metropolitan areas. The housing
shortage that ensued was serious enough to represent
a double thrust to the continuation of the very economic growth that was sucking labour out of the rural
interior. First, there was a threat to the reproduction of the labour force, both in absolute terms and

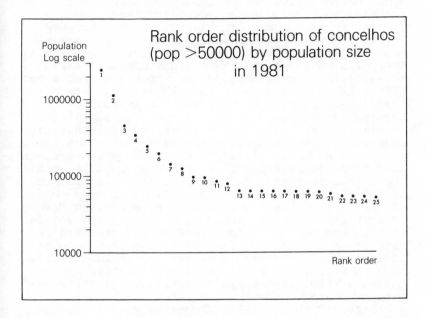

Figure 10.3   Rank-order distribution of 'concelhos'
              by population size in Portugal in 1981
              (only concelhos with populations
              greater than 50,000 included).

in locational terms, that is, whether a labour force
could actually be assembled in areas chosen for
investment.[15] Secondly, the shortage of housing
increased accommodation costs, increasing the pressure for wage rises that would reduce the rate of
profit. Given that industrialisation in Portugal was
heavily dependent upon low-cost, labour intensive
production,[16] this threatened the overall development
strategy for the economy. Under such conditions, the
need for increased state involvement in housing was
considerable but, prior to 1974, the total amount of
public housing remained limited by the ideological
guidelines of the corporate state.

Housing provision and the housing crisis
Portugal is widely recognised as having suffered a
severe housing crisis in the past three decades. It
is as much a theme of reports of the 1950s[17] as of

289

those of the 1970s[18] and is the direct outcome of
construction rates having failed to match the
increase in need, both in aggregate terms and in
particular locations. The result is that housing
shortages have a highly uneven distribution and the
main features of the housing crisis vary from one
type of area to another. This basic shortage is,
moreover, compounded by a number of housing problems
which, if not unique to Portugal, at least are observed here in more acute form than in most other
European countries.
     First, the aggregate shortage of dwellings is a
product of under-supply in the face of the need for
new or improved dwellings. This need does not simply
stem from the demands of an expanding population for
the population has been fairly static until recently
as the result of constant emigration and only
increased from 7,921,913 in 1950 to 8,074,960 in
1970 (although it has since shot up to 9,784,201 in
1981). However, this is not as straightforward as it
first seems for there is evidence that many of the
newer houses in Portugal, especially in rural areas,
have been built by emigrants (who do not figure in
the population totals) in anticipation of their
return home.[19] Furthermore, although the population
has been virtually static, household size fell
sharply from an average of 4.0 in 1950 to 3.6 in 1970
and reached 2.9 by 1981 - an outcome of the ageing of
the population as well as of an increase in the
number of two person households.[20]
     Part of the reason for the housing crisis in
Portugal, then, is the demand for dwellings for new
household formation. However, a more important
reason is the limited supply of new housing. Housing
completions have increased dramatically from under
10,000 per annum in 1950[21] to about 35-41,000 per
annum in the early 1970s. Nevertheless, even at this
higher rate of completion an ILO team estimated that
it would take 43 years to meet the existing housing
deficit and 90 years if the renovation of substandard
housing was to be included![22] Portugal remains at
the bottom of the international league table for
housing development[23] and there is a lower proportion
of Gross Fixed Capital Formation in construction than
in almost any other European country. Even as late
as the period 1971-5 the increase in the housing
stock was lower in Portugal (6.9 per cent) than in
any other European country except Italy, and was less
than a half of the rate achieved in neighbouring
Spain (16.0 per cent).[24] One incidental outcome is
that the housing stock in Portugal is the fourth

oldest in Europe (West and East), with 63 per cent
having been constructed prior to 1946, but the main
result is the twofold dimension of the housing crisis
already referred to - first, acute shortages contributing to 24.8 per cent of the population being
classified officially as 'overcrowded' in 1970;[25]
and, secondly, the lack of adequate facilities in
many dwellings, which partly reflects the age of the
housing stock. The 1970 housing census provided
numerous examples of the lack of facilities, such as
the facts that 35 per cent of dwellings had no
electrical fittings, 67 per cent had no bathrooms
and 43 per cent had no sanitary toilets.
     These aggregate statistics, however, only
present the bare outlines of the housing crisis.[26]
Following on from the spatially uneven development
of the economy, there are also important regional
and urban/rural dimensions of housing problems to be
noted. The regional dimension can itself by subdivided into two elements - the availability of
housing and the standards of basic amenities available - and spatial variations in both are illustrated
in Figure 10.4. The average number of dwellings per
1,000 persons identifies the level of need relative
to the level of provision and shows the expected
distinction between the interior and the littoral.
The greatest pressure on housing is in the littoral
so this is the region with the smallest ratio of
dwellings to population and within it the housing
stock in Lisboa and Porto distritos seems to be under
extreme pressure. If all else is equal, then the
inhabitants of these more congested regions have to
pay more for smaller quantities of housing space; in
other words, the raw edge of the housing shortage is
experienced in these regions.
     The second element of the regional dimension of
the housing crisis is the variation in the level of
amenities. Figure 4 displays the proportion of
dwellings which possess all four of the basic amenities recorded by the 1970 census (piped water,
electricity, bathroom, sanitary installations). The
littoral has far better provision and the levels
exceed 20 per cent in Aveiro, Porto, Setúbal, Lisboa
and Faro, while in most of the interior the level is
less than 10 per cent. These variations reflect the
greater age of the housing stock in the interior for
new housing can be expected to possess these basic
amenities, and the only distritos where more than a
half of the housing stock pre-dates 1920 are Beja,
Braga, Braganca, Evora, Guarda, Portalegre, Viana do
Castelo, Vila Real and Viseu - all but Viana located

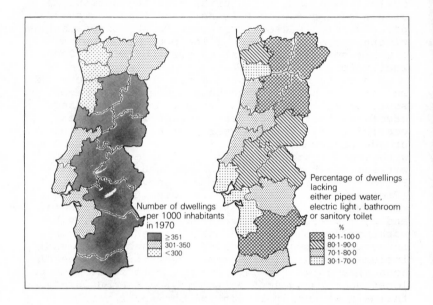

Figure 10.4   Density of occupation and availability
of basic housing amenities in Portugal,
by 'distrito', in 1970.

in the interior.[27]   Therefore, a fairly simple
pattern seems to emerge; more developed areas have
more newer housing and therefore facilities tend to
be better, but the housing shortages are more acute.
In contrast, less developed areas have less pressure
on the housing supply, but the stock tends to be old
and poorly equipped.

These broad regional patterns also suggest an
urban-rural element as an important feature of the
housing crisis.   As the rate of economic development
has been greatest in the metropolitan areas it is
here that the pressures and problems are most severe.
No overall figures are available but a breakdown of
the characteristics of new housing built in 1978
gives a useful indicator.   Certainly costs are
greater in urban areas (populations greater than
10,000) than in the country as a whole, the price
per square meter being 5,800 compared to 4,700
escudos.   In Lisboa and Porto the pressure on
housing has caused even higher costs, exceeding

6,000 escudos per square meter.[28] However, although
dwellings may be more expensive in the metropolitan
areas, they do possess better facilities. Over 99
per cent of new dwellings in Porto and Lisboa have
electricity and running water, but in the country as
a whole some 4-8 per cent of households lack these
facilities.
     This is not to state that much of the housing
in the metropolitan area does not have any important
shortcomings. On the contrary, numerous studies
have highlighted both the problems of older city
centre areas, with decaying physical fabrics in overcrowded, congested zones, and the problems associated
with some of the poor quality nineteenth-century
working class houses.[29] The Ribeira-Barredo area in
Porto (Figure 10.5), the Alfama and Baixo in Lisboa
(Figure 10.6) and the Alto in Coimbra are all well
known historic central areas which are overcrowded
and poorly serviced. Examples of poor quality
working class housing in these nineteenth-century
inner-urban areas also abound, but any list would
include the patios of Lisboa (court-like groups of
houses) and the ilhas of Porto (terraces of houses
located on long narrow plots behind the buildings on
the main streets - Figure 10.7). The ilhas are
notorious and were estimated to contain 13,594
dwellings in 1940 - almost a half of the housing
stock of the city. There is a lack of ventilation
and light in these areas, and piped water and sani-
tation are usually communal.[30] An additional problem
of the ilhas is that in many cases they are built on
adjacent plots and are of a type known in Britain as
'back-to-backs'.
     The details of the housing crisis which have
been outlined so far are not really very different
from those which can be observed in most European
countries. However, in one very distinctive way,
the housing problems of Portugal are characteristically Mediterranean - this is the bairros clandestinos,
illegal housing which may sometimes be of a shanty
town nature (known locally as bairros de lata).[31] In
fact illegal housing has been endemic in contemporary
Portugal and is a more acute problem here than in any
other European country save, perhaps, Greece, and
shanties are relatively more numerous than in any
other country except Turkey.[32]
     Illegal housing, by its very nature, is very
difficult to quantify. The best available data is
from a questionnaire survey[33] of local authorities
(camaras municipais) which was carried out in June
1977 by the Gabinete de Planeamento e Contrôle (GPC)

293

Figure 10.5   Poor quality housing in the Ribeira-
             Barredo, Porto.

of the Ministério da Habitacão e Obras Públicas, although 41 of the 274 camaras did not respond. Even
so, it does provide a valuable source[34] which may
underestimate the real extent of the clandestinos as

Figure 10.6   Eighteenth and nineteenth century
              housing on the edge of the 'baixo', in
              Lisboa.

the GPC study estimated that there were 83,015
illegal houses in Portugal but other estimates have
put the number at 110,000 and even as high as
150,000.[35] The distribution of clandestine dwellings
is, of course, highly uneven, as can be observed in
Figure 10.8. The largest number are to be found in
Lisboa and Setúbal, which had 47,444 and 16,466
respectively. These are followed by Porto (over
7,000), Faro (over 6,000) and Evora (over 2,000).
None of the other distritos had more than 1,000
clandestinos. Without, for the moment, discussing
the underlying causes of such widespread illegal
development, there are three immediate reasons for
this spatial distribution. These are the shortage
of housing in the metropolitan areas (especially at
relatively low purchase prices); the desire for
second homes in attractive environmental areas,
along the coast and in the Algarve in particular;
and the need for housing in the main towns of the
distritos which have been gaining population from
the surrounding rural areas. This last trend

295

Figure 10.7 'Ilhas', viewed from the main street in Porto.

accounts for the importance of clandestine development in the interior distrito of Evora, for although
the distrito has consistently lost population, there
has been substantial growth in the main city and
administrative centre.

The distrito map can only provide a very
generalised picture of the development of clandestine
housing. A more detailed concelho map would indicate
how spatially selective the process has been.36 Such
a map would pick out the concentrations in West
coastal concelhos such as Espinho, Figueira da Foz
or Alcacer do Sal and, outside of the main metropolitan areas, the belt along the Algarve coast. It
would also reveal that it is the larger cities such
as Coimbra, Marinha Grande or Aveiro which have
important nuclei of clandestinos. This more
detailed level of analysis also reveals that the
single most important area is the Metropolitan Area
of Lisboa (disguised in Figure 10.8 within the
distritos of Lisboa and Setúbal). This metropolis
alone accounts for over half of all the illegal development and it has been shown that there is a very

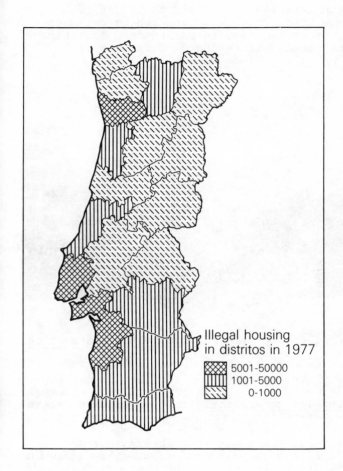

Figure 10.8   Illegal housing in Portugal, by 'distrito', in 1977.

close relationship within this area between the number of <u>clandestinos</u> and population growth rates.[37]
    The importance of clandestine development is not simply that it is illegal but that certain consequences follow from this fact.   For example, a study of non-shanty <u>clandestinos</u> in the Lisboa area[38] revealed that <u>most of the</u> houses are relatively well-built and may, on occasion, be luxurious.   For example, in Lagoa de Albufeira there are a number of illegal second homes which possessed swimming pools or tennis courts.   Typically, however, the

<u>clandestinos</u> represent solidly-constructed, self-built family homes which are occupied by commuters to Lisboa, as is the case in Quinta do Conde (Figure 10.9). The great shortcoming of this type of

Figure 10.9 <u>Illegal housing, in cleared woodland, in Quinta do Conde.</u>

clandestine development is that, being illegal, they lack publicly-supplied services. They tend to lack sewers (this applies to even the most luxurious), do not have piped public water supplies, and may not always have mains electricity; they also tend to lack properly surfaced roads. Furthermore, it becomes very difficult to rectify such problems because it is far more expensive to install such services after the houses have been built.

There are also a number of wider planning problems associated with clandestine development. They tend to lack both social and commercial facilities; for example, in the developments of Morgados I and II in Quinta do Conde there were 418 houses but no commercial facilities at all so long journeys-to-shop, -to-school and -to-health facilities become necessary. Also, being uncontrolled, the

clandestinos often tend to be at very low densities
and absorb relatively large amounts of land. Apart
from the problems of sprawl and the loss of good
agricultural land, this also creates additional costs
in the supply of public services subsequently.
Finally, the widespread extent of illegal housing
has made it especially difficult to follow through a
coherent plan for the Lisboa metropolitan area.
Illegal housing tends to occur on the cheapest land
and this is usually in places zoned as 'green' areas
and reserved for recreation or agriculture. As a
result, actual land use may become the inverse of
planned land use. Therefore, there are serious consequences associated with clandestine development
and many of these immediate difficulties will recur
as more serious and compounded problems at a later
date.
     The most acute problems, however, are to be
found in the shanty towns, although not all of these
are actually illegal. These Bairros de lata are
especially prevalent in the Lisboa area where many
of the shanties are enormous; for example, there
were 12,000 dwellings constructed of wood or tin in
Brandoa de Figueira in the mid 1970s.[39] In addition
to all the problems of the clandestinos, they also
suffer from being poorly constructed and also poorly
located (Figure 10.10). They are usually located on
the least desirable land - adjacent to motorways or
the airport, or on very steep slopes - and may
actually be very dangerous.[40] Numerous attempts
have been made to ameliorate the extent and the
problems of these dwellings but they continue to be
important in and around the city of Lisboa. If the
raw edge of the housing shortages is to be observed
in the metropolitan area of Lisboa, then it is the
shanty towns which are the saddest and most obvious
symbols of this.

The control of housing production
Thus far it has been argued that the process of
uneven regional development has shaped the pattern
of housing need in Portugal and that the failure to
meet this need has led to the types of housing
crises described in the previous section. The
question to be considered here is why the supply of
housing was so inadequate and the answers to it will
be divided into two parts, the first considering the
nature of the private sector, and the second, the
limited role of the state both in the direct provision of housing and in the regulation of the private

Figure 10.10 'Bairro de Lata', located near the
airport in Lisboa.

sector. This takes the discussion back to the
issues, identified earlier, of collective consumption
and the reproduction of labour power.

It is essential to re-emphasise at the outset
the fact that Portugal has had one of the lowest
rates of housing construction in Europe. For
example, during 1971/76 - effectively the last years
of construction under the corporate state - only 4.2
dwellings per 1,000 persons were completed in
Portugal. Only Turkey had a lower construction rate
in Europe and several other South European countries,
including Spain and Greece, had rates twice as high
as this.[41] Table 10.1 shows that, within Portugal,
the highest rates of completions were in the littoral
region, especially between Braga and Setúbal - with
Faro as an important southerly pocket - and within
this zone the highest rates were in the three
distritos which have had the most rapidly growing
population, that is, Setúbal, Lisboa and Porto.
Illegal building would tend to further exaggerate
the differences between these areas and the remainder
of the country.

Table 10.1   Housing Construction in Portugal 1971-6

Distrito	Public and Private Sectors		Public Sector	
	Absolute increase	Percentage increase	Absolute increase	Percentage of all completions in public and private sectors
Aveiro	12,467	8.5	636	5.1
Beja	1,721	2.1	133	7.7
Braga	14,329	9.8	659	4.6
Braganca	2,747	4.3	137	5.0
Coimbra	9,171	9,0	90	2.2
Castelo Branco	4,106	2.9	257	2.8
Évora	2,249	3.2	283	12.6
Faro	13,154	12.5	697	5.3
Guarda	3,830	4.3	161	4.2
Leiria	11,558	8.8	971	8.4
Lisboa	53,469	11.2	7,539	14.1
Porgalegre	1,899	3.1	529	27.9
Porto	29,641	9,0	2,252	7.6
Santarem	10,727	6.8	483	4.5
Setúbal	32,896	20.1	3,586	10.9
Viana do Castel	4,991	6.5	125	2.5
Vila Real	3,503	4.3	224	6.4
Viseu	6,739	4.6	175	2.0

Source: Gabinete de Planeamento e Controlo (M.H.O.P.)
A Oferta Habitacional Recente: A Situacão do
Mercado de Arrendamento

The main role in the development of housing has
always been taken by the private sector. Even with
the increase in housing production during the past
few decades, the private sector continued to be
dominant and accounted for 90 per cent of completions
between 1971 and 1975.[42] Given the lower rates of
public sector completions in earlier years, 97 per
cent of the actual housing stock is in the private
sector. Most of the output of the private sector
between 1971 and 1976 was for owner-occupation (59
per cent) but a sizeable proportion (41 per cent) was
destined for renting. Construction for renting was
most important in the Lisboa metropolitan region and
only in the distritos of Lisboa (59 per cent) and
Setúbal (58 per cent) did it exceed a half of all new
private sector construction. This, in turn, may
partly account for the high rates of illegal construction of owner-occupied dwellings in this metropolitan area.

There are three basic reasons why the housing
supply, dominated as it was by the private sector,
has been unable to keep up with the need for housing.
The first lies in the structure of demand and stems
from the distribution of incomes, for Portugal had
one of the most skewed income distributions in
Europe.[43] Many families were simply unable to afford
either the purchase costs of new houses or the costs
of adequate rented dwellings. Wage levels did rise
in the late 1960s and early 1970s, as conscription
and emigration began to constrain the flow of cheap
labour to industry but rents also increased rapidly
and generally out-stripped the rise in consumer
prices between 1963 and 1973.[44] As a result it was
estimated in the early 1970s that of the half a
million families who required rehousing, only 10 per
cent could afford the market price for 'adequate'
housing.[45] It was in the case of these considerations that so many families decided to build their
own homes, legally or illegally, even if these were
shanty dwellings in some cases.

However, the low rates of construction in the
private sector reflected more than just a lack of
demand for there were also important reasons associated with the structure of the construction industry
itself. The industry was highly polarised between
very large and very small companies (see Table 10.2).
Only 1.7 per cent of companies employed more than 50
workers (but had 37.8 per cent of all employees),
while 87.6 per cent of enterprises employed less than
10 workers (but had only 39.6 per cent of total
employment). Therefore, the industry was numerically
dominated by very small companies, and it was these
companies which specialised in house building, for
the larger companies were heavily involved in public
works. Furthermore, those larger companies which had
some involvement in house building tended to be more
concerned with luxury housing[46] especially in the
Algarve or Lisboa, or in the construction of hotels
and other facilities for the tourist industry[47] - see
Figure 10.11. The larger and more efficient companies
(as indicated by the levels of their equipment (see
Table 10.2) therefore specialised in large commercial
contracts, leaving low and medium cost house building
to the smaller firms who were, quite literally, ill-
equipped to produce sufficient to meet the demand.
Hence the housing crisis can partly be attributed to
the diversion of building capital during the 1960s
into the massive tourist boom of that period and also
into the lucrative and secure fields of public works
such as motorways and industrial infrastructure.[48]

Table 10.2 The Structure of the Construction Industry in 1975

Employment size of enterprise	Number of enterprises	Employment	Production of housing	Production of public works	Acquisition of equipment
1–9	87.6	39.6	46.4	10.0	24.6
10–19	7.2	10.2	12.7	4.8	17.9
20–49	3.5	12.4	14.0	7.9	29.8
≥ 50	1.7	37.8	26.9	77.3	27.6
	100.0	100.0	100.0	100.0	100.0

Source: Ministério da Habitação, Urbanismo e Construção, Plano de Médio Prazo 1977–81: Diagnóstico de Situação e Estratégias de Desenvolvimento do Sector do Urbanismo e Habitação.

Figure 10.11   <u>Tourist development at Praia de Rocha</u>
                <u>(Algarve)</u>.

As many of the larger construction companies were
owned by large finance-capital groupings,[49] the
switch of investment from mass housing to the luxury
sector or to non-residential projects actually
occurred directly.

An additional problem has been the prevalence of
land speculation, especially since 1950. This has
been especially important in the clandestine sector
where the developers are involved in little more than
the clearing of vegetation and the marking out of
residential plots. With such minimal investment,
there is scope for enormous profit-taking. Precise
data on this is, of course, very difficult to obtain
but one speculator in Oeiras (in the Lisboa metropolitan area) in 1962 is reported to have resold
plots of land for housing development at a price
which was 880 per cent of the original purchase
price.[50] This has obviously forced up the price of
housing (especially in the Lisboa area and the
Algarve) and has contributed to the crisis in housing.

In comparison to the private sector, the state
has made little direct contribution to the production

of housing. Public housing was first authorised in
1918, with Decree Law 4,137 allowing for the provision of Bairros Sociais but construction rates have
been consistently very low so that even by the mid-
1970s there were less than 100,000 state-owned
dwellings. Even this figure needs qualifying because
state housing was provided in a socially segmented
manner, being designed for specific needs rather than
for the general purpose of housing low income
families. For example, the Casas Economicas, one of
the more important of the early types of state
housing, were introduced in 1933 to cater for civil
servants and the Casas dos Pescadores were introduced
in 1946 to provide houses for fishermen. Other types
of state housing were also for specific needs - the
Casas Desmontaveis were to rehouse the dwellers of
some of Lisboa's shanty towns, the Casas das Famílias
Pobres were also for slum rehousing purposes and the
Casas das Rendas Limitadas were to provide low rent
housing mainly in Lisboa.[51] Finally, the Plano de
Melhoramento of 1956 made provision for the rehousing of the ilhas dwellers of Porto in schemes
that were both socially segmented and spatially
selective (Figure 10.12). Therefore, although state
housing was very limited in its extent, it did have
a role in the social control mechanisms of the corporate state by encouraging the separation of workers
into small, often industry-based groups. It should
also be added that, apart from Lisboa and Porto, most
of the provision was controlled by central rather
than by local government; latterly, a large measure
of this control over investment was centralised in
the Fundo do Fomento da Habitacão. The actual day-
to-day administration of state housing tended to be
highly authoritarian and those who failed to pay
their rents or broke the strict rules on behaviour
were subject to fines or eviction. There were a
number of protests against the administrative methods
and the levels of rent[52] but they were largely
ineffective.

Two further points need to be made about state
housing. First, there was a distinctive change in
architectural styles in the mid-1950s. Early state
housing was of the single-family type and was often
built to a very high standard, this being especially
true of the Bairros Sociais. After the mid-1950s,
however, there was a switch to modernist architectural styles and the construction of high rise apartment blocks, sometimes on an enormous scale. Schemes
built under the Plano de Melhoramento in Porto and
the Olivais-Norte scheme in Lisboa, in particular,

Figure 10.12   State housing in Porto.

are often taken to be the major landmarks in this
change.[53] This change was associated with the need
to provide low cost housing (these schemes were built
at very high densities) of a minimal standard for
very low income families who were being rehoused from
shanty towns or the ilhas.
      The second feature to note about state housing
is its regional distribution. Table 10.1 shows that
the highest rates of public sector house building
between 1971 and 1976 were in Lisboa, Setúbal, Evora
and Portalegre. The first two can be accounted for
by the severity of the housing crisis in the Lisboa
metropolitan area but the latter two are probably due
to local political considerations. The absolute
figures, however, show a more straightforward
pattern. Out of nearly 19,000 new state-owned
dwellings, over 11,000 were located in Lisboa and
Setúbal, and the addition of Porto takes this number
to over 13,000. Thus, in percentage terms, over 70
per cent of all state housing was in the three more
affluent distritos, again illustrating the spatially
selective nature of public sector housing development.

    The actual ownership and renting of housing is
only one possible form of state intervention in
housing. The state was also involved in rent control
and in attempts to regulate private residential
development. Rent controls were first introduced in
1920 and in this initial phase lasted until 1928.[54]
They were re-imposed in 1948 but covered only Lisboa
and Porto and seem to have been largely ineffective
as, through evasions and legal loopholes, rents continued to increase rapidly. This was a problem
which was to recur when new controls were introduced
immediately after the Revolution of 1974.
    The other major aspect of state intervention
was the attempt to regulate private development
through land-use planning legislation. Until the
late 1940s this had been effective, partly through
the role played by the influential Minister of Public
Works, Duarte Pacheco. Under Pacheco the municipality of Lisboa used compulsory purchase powers to
acquire a third of the land within its boundaries (to
be resold with strict provisions over development)
and land use plans were strictly enforced. However,
after 1940, the acceleration of the process of
uneven development and the death of Pacheco both contributed to a weakening of state control. Planning
controls continued to be enacted, as in Decree Law
38,382 of 1951 which made it obligatory for all new
buildings to be licenced by the local authority or
Decree Law 46,473 of 1965 which allowed the municipalities to supervise the provision of infrastructure
for all private developments. However, such legislation was less and less likely to be enforced, not
least because most municipalities lacked the financial and technical means to prepare and monitor
urban plans.[55]
    During the period of the New State, public
intervention in Portuguese housing was very limited,
despite the obvious signs of the severity of the
housing crisis - overcrowded families in sub-divided
old houses in city centres, insanitary nineteenth
century dwellings, shanty towns and bairros
clandestinos in urban areas, and appallingly low
standards of amenities throughout rural areas. From
time to time these conditions threatened the supply
and the cost of labour power in particular areas and
yet state intervention in this aspect of collective
consumption was minimal. Elsewhere it has been
suggested that a number of considerations help to
explain this.[56] First, industrialisation in the more
developed North West was spatially diffuse and was
based on limited expansion of the existing dense

307

pattern of settlements. Secondly, where new developments were more highly concentrated, as in the Lisboa metropolitan area, the state did not neglect housing problems to the same extent. State investment in housing was concentrated in this region in response to the acute need for dwellings. There was also a conscious neglect of planning controls over the clandestinos, for it was recognised that, given the lack of public resources for planned development, illegal housing was in a sense the only possible response for people seeking jobs in the urban economy. The state, therefore, seems to have turned a blind eye to these illegal dwellings. Finally, the threat of rising accommodation costs leading to increased wages was not as much of a problem for the corporate state as for other capitalist states for there were direct repressive controls over labour. In short, the state turned a blind eye to the major features of the housing crisis, safe in the knowledge that it controlled wages anyway and that the bairros clandestinos provided a cheap safety-valve for the real accommodation shortages which existed in the Lisboa metropolitan area.

Developments in housing since 1974
The Revolution of April 1974 ushered in a short period of intense political instability as competing groups, from all points on the political spectrum, struggled for power. Even the decisive swing to parliamentary democracy and centrist politics in 1976 has not brought political stability. In the face of enormous internal and external economic and social difficulties, there has been a succession of short-lived governments which have seen political power shift progressively from the Socialists to the centre-right Alianca Democratica. Within this shifting framework there have occurred a number of important developments in housing.

However, starting with the overall level of construction (see Figure 10.13), it is clear that this period has been disastrous for house building. Housing completions stood at just over 40,000 per annum in the last two years before the Revolution. The dislocation to political and economic life which followed contributed to completions falling to a low of just under 30,000 in 1976, and although there has been some recovery since, in 1979 completions stood at only 38,000 (3,000 less than in 1973). A series of deflationary budgets have contributed to this slow recovery of house building.

Housing Production 1971-1979

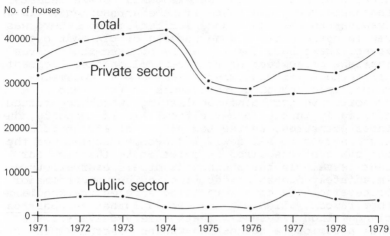

Figure 10.13   Housing production in Portugal, 1971-79.

Figure 10.13 also shows that there were substantial variations in both the public and private sectors, although both shared in the same general trend of a major decline in the mid 1970s. Public sector construction has been particularly volatile and fell by more than 50 per cent from a level of 4,557 in 1973 to less than 2,000 in 1976 (although it must be remembered that there was some shift of resources into housing improvement in this period). Subsequently, there was a sharp rise in construction to reach a new peak of 5,794 in 1977, reflecting a degree of reorientation in housing policy following the urban struggles of 1974-76. However, this was short-lived and construction levels have since fallen back to just under 4,000 per annum, which is a lower level than prevailed in 1973. In terms of the percentage of all new housing, this has meant that the public sector had fallen from 11 per cent in 1973 to a low of 6.4 per cent in 1976, which then became a record high of 17 per cent in the following year, before falling back to 10 per cent by 1979. In terms of aggregate construction statistics, therefore, there seems to have been little sustained change either in overall production levels or in the share accounted for by the public sector since 1974.

Nevertheless, there have been some important changes within both the public and the private sectors.

In the private sector the three most important developments have been the extension of rent control, the expansion of mortgage finance arrangements for owner-occupation, and some limited attempts to regulate the ever-growing numbers of clandestinos. First, there have been a series of attempts to increase the extent of rent control. After 25th April there were a number of residents' movements which protested about the levels of rents and the exploitative system of sub-letting (which occurred especially in the larger cities).[57] In response to these pressures, Decree Law 445/74 of 1974 applied new controls to all newly-let accommodation, whereby the new rent was fixed in relation to the previous rent level. In the absence of other measures, this immediately led to a reduction in the number of properties offered for rent and a deterioration in repair work, which many owners could not afford at a time of high rates of inflation.[58] To alleviate this position, a new decree was proposed in 1979 to bring rents up to date (still within controlled limits) but the Assembly refused to ratify this. Subsequently the present government has contemplated decontrol of rent levels but no definite action has yet been taken.

Probably the most important change in the private sector has been the more active role taken by the state in fostering owner-occupation. This is achieved partly through allowing exemptions from sales and property taxes for all new dwellings but the most important policy has been the subsidies given on interest paid on mortgages. The first subsidies were introduced in 1976 and they have been revised subsequently - especially in 1978 and 1981. Nevertheless, the basic principles have remained constant with mortgage relief worked out in relation to both family income and the unit costs of the dwelling. The subsidy offered is quite considerable and amounts to 20 per cent of the mortgage on average costs. The most valuable data that we have on the scheme comes from a study by the Gabinete de Planeamento e Contrôlo da Habitacão e Urbanismo in 1979[59] which revealed that over two-thirds of all new houses had been purchased with its aid but that, as expected, its benefits were socially and spatially selective. In regional terms, over 80 per cent of all the subsidies were allocated to the Lisboa and Porto metropolitan areas. In social terms, it was shown that 48 per cent of the recipients were office

workers, while 16 per cent were industrial workers
and only 5 per cent were agricultural workers. The
scheme was thus more important in extending home
ownership to the lower-middle and middle classes
than to the working class. Furthermore, it was hoped
that the scheme would help to stimulate the construction industry through increasing demand but, as
approximately a quarter of recipients purchased a
house they had previously rented, its effectiveness
in this respect is questionable. It has led the
current government to discuss policies whereby the
state would give direct subsidies to the construction
industry.

Since 1974 there have also been renewed attempts
to improve and legalise the bairros clandestinos.
This has been particularly important given the
activities of grass-roots movements and the spectacular increase which occurred in illegal house
building immediately following the Revolution. As
many of the areas of clandestine housing are located
astride concelho boundaries, this has meant calls
for joint action by a number of municipalities.
Ideally, such action should be preventative to avoid
the clandestine development occurring in the first
place but, realistically, most such action is directed at ameliorating the infrastructural deficiencies
of existing bairros clandestinos. The overall
guidance for such action in the Lisboa metropolitan
area has been provided by the Comissariado do Governo
para a Região de Lisboa which gives the necessary
technical back-up to the municipalities. Within the
bairros clandestinos they have sought to halt further
building, while legalising existing dwellings, after
having reached agreements with the owners of these
properties.

An example of this approach can be seen in the
case of Vale de Milhacos, where all existing houses
have been legalised but owners of vacant plots have
had to exchange their land for much smaller plots
within a designated settlement nucleus. This re-
organisation frees land for recreational use and
allows for provision of commercial and infrastructural
facilities in future development at lower costs as
these are more nucleated. Additionally, those who
own more than one plot of land will usually only be
offered a single alternative plot within the nucleus.
While such an approach is quite logical in terms of
most planning objectives, it has not always been
popularly received. This has been the case, for
example, in Quinta do Conde where the owners of
vacant plots have been offered only the rights to

apartments and not to separate houses within the
proposed nucleus. There have also been a number of
other problems associated with the legalisation programmes. The act of legalisation required payment
of a fee to the state to partly cover the costs of
providing infrastructure but this has been a special
problem both for the lower income families and those
living in rented illegal dwellings. It can restrict
the access of such families to low cost housing, and
may either lead to new clandestine development elsewhere or to increased pressure on existing, usually
overcrowded, low income residential areas.[60]

Since 1974 some important advances have been
made in the private sector, at least in terms of
statutory legislation. The problem, as always, has
been in the implementation of such laws because,
without complimentary measures to stimulate new
house building, especially in the lower price ranges,
restrictions on their own will lead only to a
decreased supply of dwellings. The subsidies provided on mortgages have had some beneficial effect in
this respect but, as was noted earlier, housing
supply is still lower today than in 1973. Therefore
both central and local government have usually been
cautious in the rigid application both of rent
controls and of restrictions on illegal housing. The
result is that many of the problems of private
sector housing continue to exist, particularly in
the shanty towns, the areas of older urban housing
and the large numbers of poorly-serviced rural
dwellings. Indeed, the most important change in
rural areas has resulted not from legislation but
from the impact of emigration. It has now been well
documented that enormous numbers of new houses have
been built in rural areas (especially in the northern
and central interior), financed by the savings of
emigrants and returned migrants.[61] Usually these are
built to very high standards, sometimes in incon-
gruous North European styles, and located on the
peripheries of existing villages (Figure 10.14). They
have certainly improved the overall standards of
rural housing but, of course, they are not a solution
which assists the occupants of traditional houses
within these villages.

Turning to the direct involvement of the public
sector in housing, there are some more radical
innovations of the post-Revolutionary period to note,
although in the final outcome these appear to have
been no more conclusive than the developments in the
private sector. The changes are not in the level of
production of housing, for it was noted earlier that

Figure 10.14 <u>Returned emigrant's house and business</u>
<u>in Castelo Branco.</u>

this has been rather depressed since 1974, but in the
type of production and especially in the experiments
in the field of urban renovation.

The context for the developments in public sector housing is provided by a number of fairly
dramatic occurrences in 1974 and 1975, when a large
number of residents' movements were born[62] and
bloomed spectacularly for a brief period. The birth
of the residents movements is usually dated to 30
April, just six days after the Revolution, when 100
families from shanty towns in Lisboa occupied a
vacant, newly-completed state housing scheme in the
city; they were expressing both their hopes for the
new political era and their frustrations at a lack of
state activity in the housing field. On the following
day, the residents of a municipal housing estate in
Porto came together and formulated a number of
demands for improved conditions. During the next two
weeks this pattern was repeated on numerous occasions
as residents associations mushroomed all over urban
Portugal, but especially in Lisboa, Setúbal and
Porto. The typical pattern was for a small group to

organise a mass meeting which then established a
formal residents' association, known as commissão dos
moradores. These commissões were usually of two
types. One type, which was prevalent in Porto, was
based on the bairros camarais, the municipal housing
estates, and was usually concerned with a liberalisation of administrative rules, obtaining control of
allocations, and achieving improvements in the state
of repair of dwellings.

The second type, which was prevalent in Setúbal
and Lisboa, was based on the bairros de lata, and
their main objectives were the complete rehousing by
the state of the residents of these bairros. In
order to precipitate suitable government action, they
usually undertook temporary or permanent occupation
of vacant housing. At first, the occupations were
always of state housing but, by the middle of 1975,
they began to be directed at private housing as well.
This usually led to serious conflict with the owners
of these dwellings and various attempts to use the
police or the law courts to evict the 'squatters'.[63]
These two types of commissões were not the only ones,
and other important variations were those in the
ilhas of Porto and also those in older urban areas,
representing tenants who wanted their rents controlled and their properties repaired by their landlords. However, the discussion here will concentrate
on the two main types.

The commissões in Porto had their origins in the
São João de Deus and the Pasteleira municipal housing
estates. The movements spread rapidly, however, so
that soon most of the 50,000 residents of state
housing schemes in Porto were represented by
commissões. They mounted a well organised campaign
to change the rules governing public housing management and allocations, which led to an overall co-
ordinating committee being established to represent
the common interests of the different areas. The
movement culminated in the heady political atmosphere
of May 1975 when the city council, the camara, was
replaced by a Military Activists Committee to run the
city.[64] Within this, representatives of the
commissões of the bairros camarais exercised control
over most of the municipal services.[65] By November
1975, however, with the political swing from the left
to the centre, the revolutionary days were numbered
and in the following year a Socialist Party majority
was elected to run the local council. However, some
concrete achievements did come out of this period and
state housing has subsequently been administered in a
much more egalitarian and liberal manner.

The commissões were also active in the private
sector of housing, demanding both the renovations of
older dwellings and rehousing by the state. In the
long term, the demand for renovation was the more
important as it led to some innovations in state
housing policies. Urban renovation was not a completely new approach in Portugal[66] and the experiments after 1974 have also been influenced by the
experience of other countries in this field in the
1960s. However, the demands of the commissões for
improved houses, infrastructure and community
services did lead to substantial advances being made
and to two important experiments, SAAL and CRUARB.
SAAL, or the Servico Ambulatorio de Apoio Local,
was the more radical of the two experiments. It was
conceived as 'a mobile local support service' whose
aims were "...the rapid resolution of the problems
of the badly housed population through their own
participation and their organised capacity...".[67]
They provided investment and the technical assistance
of small groups of engineers, architects and other
professionals, in order to assist local initiatives
to improve housing. The original initiative, part
of the finance and the bulk of the labour was
supposed to come from within the community itself.
The SAAL brigades were to co-operate in this both
with the commissões dos moradores and with the
camaras who were the channel for finance and had the
powers to expropriate land or houses where
necessary.[68] In practice, there were numerous disputes between the different organisations which
often hampered actual improvement work. Many SAAL
brigades also became as involved in local political
action as in house building and, not surprisingly,
they were effectively closed down after 1976 through
being denied finance.
The operations of SAAL aroused enormous
interest, both inside and outside Portugal, and a
number of useful commentaries have been produced on
their activities.[69] However, even today, it is very
difficult to quantify the contribution of SAAL
because so few accurate statistics were kept of its
work. Furthermore, even those who were involved
most closely with SAAL tend to emphasise its political achievements as much as, if not more than, the
actual improvements in housing.[70] This is not to
decry the importance of the political role, for
after more than 40 years of the Salazarist corporate
state, there was a need to reinvigorate local democracy. With regards to actual housing, one of the
few estimates available[71] suggests that by March

1976 126 operations had been launched with the
intention of constructing 36,340 new houses and
construction had actually begun on 9,435 dwellings.
This was the peak year, however (a fact reflected in
the high level of public sector completions in 1977),
and it is not at all clear what was the final number
of houses which had been built. On the whole, plans
were far more in evidence than houses on the
ground.[72]
     Nevertheless, there were some important achieve-
ments to note in individual schemes. For example, a
small SAAL team was formed in March 1975 to prepare
a scheme for the old area surrounding the cathedral
in Porto and by October 1976 improvements had been
started in 19 of the 615 dwellings.[73] This was
important at least in demonstrating that improvements
could be achieved in these older areas. Another
example of a SAAL scheme can be seen in the Forte
Velho area of Setúbal, where 71 families lived in a
shanty town.[74] They drew attention to their needs
by temporarily occupying a nearby bairro social
during 1974, an act which led to a SAAL brigade
being established and, on expropriated land,
covering 10,376m^2, they planned a scheme of 71 new
terrace dwellings, mostly of two-bedroom size but
with some houses having up to six bedrooms. By 1978
it was reported that 'most' of the houses had been
completed.
     A completely different approach to urban con-
servation was adopted in the case of CRUARB, the
Comissariado para a Renovacão Urbana da Area
Ribeira-Barredo, established as an experiment in
1974. A comissariado is a direct agency of central
government, funded in this case by the Fundo do
Fomento de Habitacao and responsible only to this
body. It was thus an attempt to bypass local government which had been notoriously ineffective in the
field of housing. The Ribeira-Barredo area seems to
have been chosen for the experiment because of its
cultural and historic importance as one of the
oldest parts of the medieval sector of Porto, because
of the undoubted severity of its housing problems and
because of the demands made by its residents through
two well-organised comissões dos moradores.
     The achievements of CRUARB were quite consider-
able and included the provision of better housing
conditions, architectural conservation and cultural
renovation (through the provision of social and
community facilities within the area).[75] The housing
achievement was probably the most notable because of
the difficulties involved. The properties in the

area were purchased by the <u>camara</u>, using compulsory
purchase powers where necessary. Renovation work
involved the complete redesigning and rebuilding of
the interiors of these dwellings, while maintaining
their facades (Figure 10.15). Self-contained, well-

Figure 10.15 <u>Renovated houses in the Ribeira-
Barredo, Porto.</u>

serviced apartments were thus produced in place of
the original multiple-occupied houses in poor
physical condition and with shared facilities.
Lettings were limited to the previous inhabitants of
the area and were at controlled 'social' rents, so
that the traditional community was maintained. Although extremely expensive, the improvements produced
by CRUARB have been impressive and the operation
could be a model for renovation plans now being
prepared for other historic cities such as Évora and
Coimbra.
    Therefore, since the popular pressure for hous-
ing improvement in 1974, a number of innovations have
been tried. The most important were in the public
sector, especially with regards to renovation and the
rehousing of shanty town dwellers while, in the

private sector, mortgage subsidies have probably been the major change. However, despite these advances, a number of the housing problems are still unresolved, the most significant being the 'rump' of poor rural housing (Figures 10.16 and 10.17) and the still-expanding clandestine sector.

Figure 10.16   A farm in Braga.

Conclusions

In retrospect it is clear that the long-standing housing crisis in Portugal was essentially a product both of new needs created by the uneven regional development of the economy and the failures of both the private and public sectors to meet them adequately. Massive rural-urban migration has exacerbated the existing housing problems of overcrowding and degradation within the cities, while adding the extra dimension of the problems of the shanties and the clandestinos. The latter were inevitable in a country where the central state had little need to invest in housing to guarantee the reproduction of labour power, and the local state lacked the means to control private development. Both clandestinos and

Figure 10.17   Rural dwellings in Guarda.

shanties have reduced the immediate crisis caused by the absolute lack of dwellings but at the same time have stored up future problems in that they were both deficient, in very different ways, in terms of acceptable housing standards.

The direct role of the state should not be forgotten. The bulk of state housing was provided in the areas of greatest immediate need, some demolitions of shanty towns and ilhas occurred and a few show-piece housing schemes were developed (such as Santo André, the new town for the Sines growth centre project and at Almada near Lisboa - Figure 10.18).

Figure 10.18 State housing at Almada, near Lisboa.

However, such schemes were generally inadequate in relation to total needs. Since 25th April there has been a far greater awareness of the extent of housing problems and a number of innovative schemes were introduced to renovate historic urban areas, to provide cheaper mortgages, to legalise existing, and prevent further, clandestinos, and to rehouse the dwellers of shanty towns. Advances have been made even in the face of national and international economic crises, political instability and the prob-

lems of assimilating more than half a million
retornados (many of whom returned to Portugal without homes and without money). Such schemes have,
indeed, achieved modest success in urban areas but
have done little to eradicate the continuing deficiencies of rural housing.

Looking to the immediate future, the prospects
do not seem to suggest that there will be any substantial improvements in housing provision or
standards. Fundamentally, the conditions which
foster uneven regional development have not been
altered and inequalities are actually being exacerbated both by recent investments in the littoral and
the prospect of EC membership.[76] The position of
lower income families is also unlikely to be
improved in the face of high unemployment rates,
deflationary state policies and low real wages.
Furthermore, there is no real evidence of any major
reorganisation of the construction industry, such as
would result in its great efficiency, while the
recent revival of tourism will continue to divert
investment from housing. Rural areas, in particular,
will continue to remain neglected, although the
recent devolution of limited financial autonomy to
local authorities may help in some areas.[77] In the
longer term the future of housing in Portugal is
more difficult to predict for it depends as much on
the country's changing role in the international
division of labour and the regional pattern of new
investments as it does on changes in government
policies on housing provision or in the construction
industry. However, at present it seems unlikely
that the thousands who marched through the streets
in 1974 chanting 'Casas, sim: Barracas, Não' (Yes to
Houses: No to Shanties) would agree that their
wishes had been granted.

NOTES AND REFERENCES

1. P. Mailer, Portugal: The Impossible Revolution (Solidarity, London, 1977) p.209.
2. J. Gaspar, Urban Growth in Mediterranean
Countries in the 1980s: Portugal. Unpublished paper
Lisbon, 1980. J. Gaspar, Urban Growth in OECD Mediterranean Countries in the 1980s: Synthesis Report.
Unpublished paper, Lisbon, 1981.
3. A. de Figueiredo, Portugal: Fifty Years of
Dictatorship (Penguin, Harmondsworth, 1975).
4. E.N. Baklanoff, The Economic Transformation
of Spain and Portugal (Praeger, New York, 1978).
5. Ibid.

6. N. Anido and R. Freire, L'Émigration Portugaise: Présent et Avenir (Presses Universitaires de France, Paris, 1978).

7. R. Harvey, Portugal: Birth of a Democracy (Macmillan, London, 1978).

8. O.E.C.D., Portugal (O.E.C.D., Paris, 1981).

9. F. Goncalves, 'A Mitologia da Habitacão Social: o Caso Português', Cidade Campo, Vol. 1 (1978), pp.21-83.

10. J.R. Lewis and A.M. Williams, 'Regional Uneven Development on the European Periphery: The Case of Portugal, 1950-1978', Tijdschrift voor Economische en Sociale Geografie, Vol. LXXII (1981), pp.81-98.

11. J.R. Lewis and A.M. Williams, 'O impacto regional de adessão a CEE', Desenvolvimento Regional, 13, 1983 (English translation forthcoming).

12. J.M. Nazareth, O Envelhecimento da Populacão (Editorial Presenca, Lisbon, 1975) and E.S. Ferreira, Origens e Formas da Emigracão (Iniciativas Editorias, Lisbon, 1976).

13. For a discussion of retornados see Lewis, J.R. and A.M. Williams, 'The Regional Consequences of International Migration in Portugal', forthcoming.

14. The use of concelhos (administratively equivalent to British districts but much smaller in size) tends to exaggerate the actual urban populations.

15. The basic ideas about the role of housing in the reproduction of labour power are outlined in M. Castells, The Urban Question (Edward Arnold, London, 1977) and the critique is summarised in K. Bassett and J. Short, Housing and Residential Structure: Alternative Approaches (Routledge and Kegan Paul, London, 1980). If carefully qualified, this kind of analysis does provide useful insights; see A.M. Williams, 'Housing in Salazar's Portugal: Crisis in the Corporate State', unpublished paper presented to the Social Geography Study Group of the I.B.G. Annual Conference, Leicester, January 6th, 1981.

16. B. Balassa, The Newly Industrialising Countries in the World Economy (Pergamon, New York, 1981, pp.255-280).

17. J.F. Dewhurst, J.O. Coppock and P.L. Yates, Europe's Needs and Resources: Trends and Prospects in Eighteen Countries (Twentieth Century Fund, New York, 1961).

18. Ministério da Habitacão, Urbanismo e Construcão, Plano de Medio Prazo 1977-80: Diagnóstico de Situacão e Estratégias de Desenvolvimento do Sector do Urbanismo e Habitacão (Imprensa Nacional,

Lisbon, 1977).

19. See the case studies reported in collections such as Trinidade, M.B.R. (Ed.) Estudos sobre Emigracão Portuguesa, Cadernos da Revista de Historia Economica e Social 1-2, 1981, or Porto, M. (Ed.) Emigracão e Retorno na Região Centro, CCRC, Coimbra, 1983.

20. Gaspar, Urban Growth - Portugal and own calculation for 1981.

21. C. Topalov, 'La Politique du Logement dans le Processus Revolutionnaire Portugais', Espaces et Societes, 17/18 (1976), pp.109-36.

22. International Labour Office (ILO), Employment and Basic Needs in Portugal (ILO, Geneva, 1979).

23. Ministério da Habitacão, Urbanismo e Construcão, Plano de Médio Prazo.

24. Gabinete de Planeamento e Controlo (M.H.O.P.), A Oferta Habitacional Recente: a Situacão do Mercado de Arrendamento (Estudos de Base 2/78, M.H.O.P., Lisbon, 1978).

25. Although this is considered to be an overestimate by Gaspar, Urban Growth - Portugal.

26. Ministério do Plano e Coordenacão Economica, Plano de Médio Prazo 1977-80: Relatório de Política Regional (Imprensa Nacional, Lisbon, 1978).

27. Gabinete de Planeamento e Controlo (M.H.O.C.), Evolucao Recente dos Sectores de Construcão e Habitacão: Perspectivas para 1978 (Estudos de Conjuntura 1/78, Ministério da Habitacão, Urbanismo e Construcão, Lisbon, 1978).

28. Gaspar, Urban Growth - Portugal.

29. A.A. Costa, A. Siza, C. Guimarães, E.S. Moura and M.C. Fernandes, 'SAAL/Norte', Cidade Campo, 2 (1979), pp.16-60. Goncalves, Habitacão Social.

30. Poder Local, 'O Concelho do Porto', Poder Local, 2 (1977), pp.38-51.

31. L. de Almeida and J. Carvalho, 'Os Loteamentos e a Construcão Clandestina: Accões a Desenvolver', Poder Local, 2 (1977), pp.29-32.

32. Gaspar, Urban Growth - Synthesis.

33. Gabinete de Planeamento e Controlo (M.H.O.P.), O Sistema Informal de Construcão de Habitacões: Situacão da Construcão Clandestina (Estudos Diversos 3/78, Ministério da Habitacão e Obras Públicas, Lisbon, 1978).

34. Data provided by the Comissariado do Governo para a Região de Lisboa.

35. Gaspar, Urban Growth - Synthesis.

36. Gabinete de Planeamento e Controlo, O Sistema Informal.

37. A.M. Williams, 'Bairros Clandestinos: Illegal Housing in Portugal', Geografisch Tijdschrift, Vol. XV (1981), pp.24-34.
38. Ibid.
39. M. de Carvalho, 'Brandoa Falaguieira: Area Critica', Poder Local, 6 (1978), pp.50-54.
40. T.B. Salgueiro, 'Bairros Clandestinos no Periferia de Lisboa', Finisterra, Vol. XII, No. 23 (1977), pp.28-55.
41. Gabinete de Planeamento e Controlo, A Oferta Habitacional.
42. Ibid.
43. ILO, Employment and Basic Needs.
44. United Nations Economic Commission for Europe, Annual Bulletin of Housing and Building Statistics for Europe, Vol. XVIII (1974).
45. Reported in B. Stilwell, 'S.A.A.L.: Slum Rehabilitation Policy in Post-Coup Portugal', unpublished B.Arch. dissertation, Liverpool University, 1980.
46. Topalov, La Politique du Logement.
47. C. Duarte, '1961/74 L'Ouverture Neo-Capitaliste', L'Architecture d'Aujourd'hui, 185 (1976), pp.22-23.
48. L.J.B. Soares, 'Sobre o Desenvolvimento Urbano de Lisboa', Poder Local, 6 (1978), pp.40-5.
49. M.B. Martins, Sociedades e Grupos em Portugal (Editorial Estampa, Lisbon, 1975).
50. Quoted in Salgueiro, Bairros Clandestinos.
51. Goncalves, Habitacão Social.
52. R. da Costa, O Desenvolvimento do Capitalismo em Portugal (Assiro e Alvim, Lisbon, 1975).
53. Goncalves, Habitacão Social.
54. Ibid.
55. Laboratório Nacional de Engenharia Civil, Comentários Sobre A Prática Urbanística Sueca em Confronto com a Experiência Portugeusa (Ministério das Obras Públicas, Laboratório Nacional de Engenharia Civil, Lisbon, 1977).
56. Williams, Housing in Salazar's Portugal.
57. C. Downs, 'Comissões de Moradores and Urban Struggles in Revolutionary Portugal', International Journal of Urban and Regional Research, Vol. 4 (1980), pp.267-94.
58. Gaspar, Urban Crowth - Synthesis.
59. Gabinete de Planeamento e Controlo da Habitacão e Urbanismo, O Crédito Bonificado á Aquisicão de Casa Própria em 1978, (Estudos Diversos 2/79, Ministério da Habitacão e Obras Públicas, Lisbon, 1979).

60.   Gaspar, Urban Growth - Synthesis;
Williams, Bairros Clandestinos.
61.   A recent survey of emigrants who have
returned from North Europe showed that 76.9 per cent
of them had invested part of their savings in
housing; see I.M. Boura, R. Jacinto, J.R. Lewis and
A.M. Williams, 'O impacto economico do retorno:
Dados de Leiria, Mangualde e Sabúgal' in Porto,
Emigracao e Retorno.
62.   Although there had been organised
residents in Porto in 1973 to attempt to prevent
evictions.
63.   Downs, Comissões de Moradores.
64.   A. Botelho and M. Pinheiro, O Conselho
Municipal do Porto: Balanco de Uma Experiencia
(COPSA, Porto, 1977).
65.   Costa et al., SAAL/Norte.
66.   Fundo de Fomento da Habitacão, Relatório
Sobre Renovacão Urbana, I and II (Ministério da
Habitacão e Obras Públicas, Lisbon, 1976 and 1978).
67.   Ibid. II, p.3.
68.   Stilwell, S.A.A.L.
69.   See the entire issue of Cidade Campo 2
(1979). Also, Stilwell, S.A.A.L.; and P. Oliveira
and F. Marconi, Política y Proyecto (Editorial
Gustavo Gili, Barcelona, 1978).
70.   Da Costa, SAAL/Norte.
71.   Oliveira and Marconi, Política y Proyecto.
72.   For example, see the entire issue of
L'Architecture d'Aujourd'hui, 185 (1976).
73.   Conselho Nacional do SAAL, Livro Branco do
SAAL 1974-6 (Lisbon, 1976).
74.   J.P. Bessa, 'O SAAL Valeu a Pena. A
Operacão Forte Velho/Setúbal', Cidade Campo, 1
(1978), pp.127-133.
75.   A.M. Williams, 'Conservation Planning in
Oporto: An Integrated Approach in the Ribeira-
Barredo', Town Planning Review, Vol. 51 (1980),
pp.177-194.
76.   Lewis and Williams, 'O impacto economico'.
77.   F. Marchand, 'Autarquias e Habitacão', in
Poder Local (Ed.), Habitacão, Administracão
Urbanística e Política de Solos (Edicões Avante,
Lisbon, 1981).